NO TRESPASSING!

NO TRESPASSING!

Explorations in Human Territoriality

Cornelis B. Bakker

and

Marianne K. Bakker-Rabdau

Chandler & Sharp Publishers, Inc.
San Francisco

Bakker, Cornelis B
   No trespassing!

   Bibliography: p.
   1.   Interpersonal relations.   I.   Bakker-Rabdau,
Marianne K., joint author.   II.   Title.   [DNLM: 1.   Spa-
tial behavior.   2.   Territoriality.   BF469 B168n   1973]
HM132.B3   158'.2   73-7326
ISBN 0-88316-500-7

COPYRIGHT © 1973 BY CHANDLER & SHARP PUBLISHERS, INC.
INTERNATIONAL STANDARD BOOK NUMBER 0-88316-528-7
LIBRARY OF CONGRESS CATALOG CARD NO. 73-7326
PRINTED IN THE UNITED STATES OF AMERICA

SECOND PRINTING, 1977
THIRD PRINTING, 1978
FOURTH PRINTING, 1981

Book Designed by Joseph M. Roter
Composition by Dharma Press, Emeryville, California

ACKNOWLEDGMENTS

Previously published and copyrighted materials are reprinted with the kind permission of authors, publishers, or copyright owners as listed below:

From THE FIRE NEXT TIME, by James Baldwin. Copyright © 1962, 1963 by James Baldwin. Reprinted by permission of The Dial Press, Inc., N.Y., and Michael Joseph Ltd., London.

From GAMES PEOPLE PLAY, by Eric Berne. Copyright © 1964 by Eric Berne. Reprinted by permission of Grove Press, Inc., N.Y., and Andre Deutsch Limited, London.

From "The Innate Grammar of Baby Talk," by Edmund Blair Bolles, in SATURDAY REVIEW (March 18, 1972). Reprinted by permission of Saturday Review Industries, Inc.

From HUMAN BEHAVIOR IN THE CONCENTRATION CAMP, by Elie A. Cohen. Copyright © 1953 by W. W. Norton & Company, Inc., and reprinted by their permission.

From THE DUTCH PUZZLE, by Duke de Baena. Published by L. J. C. Boucher—Publisher, The Hague. Reprinted by permission of the author.

From EHRENGARD, by Isak Dinesen. Copyright © 1963 by Rungstedlundfondon; copyright © 1962 by The Curtis Publishing Company. Reprinted by permission of Random House, Inc.

From THE MAGUS, by John Fowles. Copyright © 1965 by John Fowles. Reprinted by permission of Little, Brown and Company, Boston, and Anthony Sheil Associates Limited, London.

Reprinted by permission of Coward, McCann & Geoghegan, Inc. and Faber & Faber Ltd. from LORD OF THE FLIES, by William Golding. Copyright © 1954 by William Golding.

From I NEVER PROMISED YOU A ROSE GARDEN, by Joanne Greenberg. Copyright © 1964 by Hannah Green (Joanne Greenberg). Reprinted by permission of Holt, Rinehart and Winston, Inc., and the William Morris Agency, N.Y.

Reprinted by permission of Hawthorn Books, Inc., from EVA BRAUN: HITLER'S MISTRESS by Nerin E. Gun. Copyright © 1968 by Nerin E. Gun & Bild Verlag S. Kappe KG Velbert and Kettwig.

From CATCH-22, by Joseph Heller. Copyright © 1955, 1961 by Joseph Heller. Reprinted by permission of Simon and Schuster, Inc., N.Y., and Jonathan Cape Ltd., London.

From ELIZABETH THE GREAT, by Elizabeth Jenkins. Copyright © 1958 by Elizabeth Jenkins. Reprinted with the permission of the Berkley Publishing Corporation, N.Y.

From THE CORSICAN: A DIARY OF NAPOLEON'S LIFE IN HIS OWN WORDS, by R. M. Johnston. Copyright 1910 by R. M. Johnston. Reprinted by permission of Houghton Mifflin Company, Boston.

(Acknowledgements continued on the following page)

To Paul, Jim, and Gabrielle

CONTENTS

PREFACE

Idealism is back, center stage, and amplified. Peace symbols flash and smiley buttons grin. The word *love* is scrawled on bathroom walls, sex is doggedly casual, and brotherhood comes in "glad bags." Mysticism mushrooms, bumper stickers revive the name of Jesus, encounter groups offer instant intimacy, and communes experiment with conglomerate togetherness. Studiously disheveled and patched middle-class adolescents, earnestly practicing affluent poverty, sneer at their parents' material possessions, disclaiming an interest in either property or wealth. The older, two-car, split-level generation, feeling somewhat guilty over its own good fortune, looks on with mixed feelings of dismay and hope; dismay because the old picture of Utopia—freedom from want—while promising happiness and contentment, is being disfigured by war, crime, and family dissolution; hope because the new generation proclaims the dawning of an age of equality, altruism, and freedom from competition.

What does this resurgence of idealism mean? Is man about to set aside his territorial propensities? Will he at last succeed in eliminating this basic force which has cemented the organizational structure of society as far back as his ancestry can be traced? Is he truly going to kick his centuries-old habit and advance to a life of simplicity where property will play no role? Man has tried to do so many times before. Communal life is not new. It is endemic in times of change, helpful in times of stress, and vital in times of extreme threat, but up until now communal experimentation has proved to be only a short-term success. Even the highly publicized kibbutzim of Israel have undergone reorganization to accommodate the demand for personal privacy and possession. Will the new impetus toward a lessening of the importance of personal property fare better than such attempts in the past?

There can be no quarrel with the fact that society is undergoing rapid change and that man has to find new ways of structuring his community if he is to survive and maintain the opportunity for a rewarding existence. Those who seek to solve society's problems by resisting new ideas and extolling the virtues of the past will surely not provide an entry into the future, but neither will the idealists who speak of the brotherhood of man, if they ignore the forces which form the foundations upon which the social organization of man rests. Western culture has accumulated much painful experience with attempts to deny basic human tendencies. In the nineteenth century the Victorian discontent with the nature of man sought to remove sexual pleasure from the human scene. It took a whole new branch of psychiatry to counter the disastrous results. Now, as the last effects of that excursion into folly are being eliminated, will man head into another black comedy of errors? If the new idealism again stems from a puritan dissatisfaction with man's most deeply ingrained tendencies, and we consider human territoriality to be such, and if the new direction of social organization is chosen in spite of this basic inclination, we predict another humiliating failure and a waste of much precious time. Change in the social structure is unavoidable. The disintegration of the family unit, the disappearance of church dominance, and the impending environmental crisis, combined with the rapidity of information accumulation and distribution, demand new forms of adaptation. Successful change, however, requires knowledge of what is, exploration of what can be, and avoidance of zealous proclamations of how man *should* be.

Our observations on human interaction have convinced us of the pervasive importance of human territoriality for the life of the individual as well as the group, and they have also shown us that an assertive realization of this inclination is an essential part of individual self-actualization. This book seeks to place this neglected dimension in the central position it deserves in the study of human behavior. Obviously we cannot assert that territoriality is equally important in all societies. Our own experiences are limited to parts of Western Europe and the United States. As a consequence we feel the greatest confidence in the validity of our observations and especially in the effectiveness of our approach to conflict resolution when applied in those cultural contexts.

Our recognition of the importance of human territoriality evolved gradually in the course of teaching a class on interpersonal relations at the

Adult Development Program of the Department of Psychiatry at the University of Washington. As we applied these insights to the analysis of conflict situations, we became increasingly impressed with the practical utility of this approach for the resolution of interpersonal problems. The positive feedback of co-workers, students, and clients helped us decide to commit our observations to paper. We have written this book in a style which we believe will make it most readable and useful to any individual interested in understanding human behavior. Where we thought it useful we have given references to articles and books which can give the reader access to more detailed information concerning any particular point.

Although it was not our primary intent to write a contribution to science, we have attempted to present an internally consistent, plausible model which provides for a cohesive approach to the understanding of many significant aspects of man's social behavior. We have done this from the vantage point of what the late George Kelly has called constructive alternativism. With this formidable term he called attention to the fact that each theory has limited uses only. Einstein's theory of relativity, for example, has great importance for the prediction of astronomical events, but it is totally useless as a basis for playing the stock market or as a blueprint for the nation's foreign policy. Each theory throws some light on a small segment of the human reality. The usefulness of this light is ultimately determined by the improved mastery with which it provides the human race. Territoriality is a model which focuses in on interpersonal behavior and has its greatest utility therefore for the development of effective social behavior and the resolution of interpersonal conflict. Within that social context, we have concentrated our attention primarily on those areas in which we personally have the most experience, that is, the interaction between individuals in marriage, work, and leisure. On occasion we have made brief excursions and have considered larger groups and even nations to indicate that the territoriality model may yield interesting insights into broader fields also.

Our philosophical position is rooted in existentialism, but our approach has been entirely pragmatic. We have refrained from moralistic judgments, but at the same time, we have maintained one clear purpose which is the same for this book as it was for the course out of which it emerged: To increase the individual's freedom and autonomy, to enhance his mastery of life within a society. As our objective is practical rather than theoretical, this book will have to be judged by its usefulness and applicability in everyday affairs. Some of our colleagues in the behavioral sciences will perhaps take exception to the fact that we have included hypotheses in our theoretical framework, even though they have not been proved beyond a shadow of a doubt. However, theories and concepts serve a purpose beyond the establishment of the truth. They provide an instrument which allows the careful observer to see reality from a different perspective. If a new perspective highlights realities which have never caught his eye before, or if it generates ideas for ways in which he can deal with that reality in a new, constructive way, it has established its value regardless of its current ranking on the scale of the ultimate truth. Some of our mental health colleagues may find fault with many of our clinical examples, because of the straightforward and simplistic ways in which they deal with important problems. We may even be accused of being naive and lacking in appreciation for the depth and the complexity of the human mind. To such criticism we can be direct in our answer. Our formulations are indeed simple, and our suggestions based on the obvious, for profundity and sophistication have not impressed us with their efficacy in solving the problems of daily life. Being able to see the obvious is a most difficult skill to learn and its mastery is scarcely abetted by a search for the obscure. However, the changes that people make in their lives when they recognize obvious aspects of their territorial situations and take simple steps toward specific alterations in their behavior have often impressed us as profound and far-reaching.

Before proceeding we want to thank those individuals who have played a major role in the completion of this book. First of all we are grateful to Benjamin S. Asia, who read the first manuscript with the practiced eye of a lawyer. His suggestions sent us back to do an extensive rewriting of the material, which has resulted in the present text. Dr. Brenda D. Townes gave a major impetus to our persistence with her active interest in our ideas and her utilization of them in her teaching at the University of Washington. Gerald B. Bartley was of invaluable help with his patient and careful scrutiny of the text and his contributions to the glossary and index. Ruth E. DeLand, with the assistance of her typewriter, formed the vital link between our notes and thoughts and the final transcript. Finally, we wish to express our appreciation to the staff and students of the Adult Development Program, for it was their interest and involvement in our projects which ultimately sustained our decision to write this book.

NO TRESPASSING!

CHAPTER 1

INTRODUCTION

"IT"

A wee little worm in a hickory-nut
Sang, happy as he could be,—
"O I live in the heart of the whole round world,
And it all belongs to me!"

*James Whitcomb Riley**

It is a warm spring afternoon. We are stretched out on comfortable chairs in the garden behind the house, enjoying the sun. Our two dogs, shiny black Labrador retrievers, lie in the grass as lazy as their masters. In the back of the yard a visitor arrives—a small poodle from the neighbors', cautiously peering from between the bushes, then entering the grassy area. In a moment the peace of the afternoon has come to an abrupt end as both our dogs jump to their feet and dash, growling, toward the surprised little intruder, who hurriedly withdraws next door with a frightened squeal. Satisfied, their tails up, the victors lumber back to their previous position, their territory intact, the invader successfully driven off.

On another morning we are wading through a swift stream in the Cascades, trying to outwit the trout which are supposed to abound in it. Thus far our luck has not been impressive, but as we round a bend where the left bank rises up as a sheer cliff, we come upon a promising hole. We are sure to find trout in it, for the area is remote and the geography just right. The water is deep here; we will have to throw our lines in from the shore. Luckily the right bank is level, and the trees are set far enough back to provide us with room to maneuver. We wade ashore and are suddenly stopped in our tracks. On a weathered board nailed to one of the trees

*From *The Complete Works of James Whitcomb Riley* (E. H. Eitel, Ed.). Indianapolis: Bobbs-Merrill Company, 1882, 1913, p. 244.

1

we read: NO TRESPASSING—PRIVATE PROPERTY. We look around. Further back between the trees stands a dilapidated cabin; not a sign of anyone there. This is ridiculous! Here we are, deep in the mountains, not a human being in sight, and this little square board with a few letters on it robs us of a beautiful fishing spot. We decide to fish anyway, but with the warning beside us we feel vaguely guilty and soon move on.

A great many animal species, including the human race, display a propensity toward defending against intruders an area of land which they consider their own. This inclination is usually characterized by the term *territoriality*. Territoriality has been extensively observed and described by students of animal behavior for a good many years. Recently it has been brought to the attention of a much wider public by the writings of Robert Ardrey (*African Genesis*, 1967; *The Territorial Imperative*, 1966; and *The Social Contract*, 1970). Whether or not one agrees with Mr. Ardrey's theories concerning animal territoriality, one must at least admire his flair for language which makes the border scrimmages of the Madagascar lemur as exciting as the battle scenes in Tolstoy's *War and Peace*.

Animal territoriality is a fascinating and colorful topic.[1] The vicissitudes of ownership lend excitement to the interaction of animals as well as man. Territoriality is most apparent and concrete when the animal claims a well-defined area as his own. The size of the area may vary from a square foot to several square miles, depending on the species and the individual, but ownership is clearly indicated by various, often ingenious means to forewarn potential competitors. The songs of many birds primarily serve to proclaim property rights rather than romantic intent. Other animals outline the limits of the land they own by chemical means, as does the dog who deposits small amounts of urine around the periphery of his realm.

Ownership, even for animals, includes considerably more than control over a specific stretch of ground. Some species of subhuman primates display a group organization in which one dominant male controls the troop and has the exclusive privilege of mounting the females. This dominant monkey "owns" these sexual prerogatives, and he is as willing to defend this right as he is to guard his physical territory.

The intricacies of territoriality in various animal species, however fas-

---

[1]See Carpenter, 1958, and Hediger, 1961, for reviews of territorial behaviors of animals. A careful definition of terms and concepts related to animal territories is provided by Jerram L. Brown and Gordon H. Orians in an article, "Spacing Patterns in Mobile Animals," published in the *Annual Review of Ecology and Systematics*, Vol. 1, 1970, pp. 239-262.

cinating they may be, will not preoccupy us here except to underscore how widespread the sense of territoriality is among living beings.

The essence of territoriality is ownership. Although the importance of regarding something as one's own property is particularly apparent where it concerns a specific stretch of ground, the same basic processes are operating whether the ownership concerns land, objects, privileges, or rights. The term territoriality was introduced when the tendency towards ownership among animals was first observed relative to a specific space. It is the tendency toward ownership, however, rather than the particular object of this tendency, that constitutes the essence of territoriality. As a consequence the term *territoriality*—as used in this book—will indicate *the inclination toward ownership*, whereas the word *territory* will refer to *the object of the ownership*, be it a stretch of land, a particular object, an idea, or anything else that holds an individual's fancy to such degree that he seeks to own it.

It is impossible actually to observe the tendencies or inclinations that motivate human behavior. The observer, therefore, must base his inferences concerning such tendencies on actions he can directly perceive. Thus, it is possible to deduce the existence of territoriality by noting a person's territorial behaviors. Similarly, one cannot decide whether any area—concrete or abstract—is, indeed, claimed as a territory until an individual demonstrates territorial behavior relative to it. The key, then, to an understanding of territoriality lies in territorial behavior, of which there are four main types:[2]

1. Marking of an area to indicate ownership.
2. Warning displays to let intruders know they are trespassing.
3. Defense, by whatever means, of the area claimed.
4. Active attempts to acquire new areas or expand old ones.

The importance of territoriality in the life of Homo sapiens is no less impressive than it is in the animal kingdom, although it has not received more than passing attention until recently.[3] Perhaps it is the very ubiquity

---

[2]We are in agreement here with C. R. Carpenter (1958), who, in discussing the definitions of territoriality, made the following observation: "It is clear that those who have studied territoriality have attempted to conceptualize the behavior mainly in two ways: as a spatial or geographic phenomenon and as a behavioral phenomenon. It would seem advantageous to view territoriality primarily as a *behavioral system* which is expressed in a spatial temporal frame of reference." [Emphasis added.]

[3]Exceptions are the excellent studies by Robert J. Paluck and Aristide H. Esser (1971), and by A. H. Esser, A. S. Chamberlain, E. D. Chapple, and N. S. Kline (1965).

of the phenomenon which has led to its being ignored, for frequently it is the obvious that is overlooked. Another reason for this oversight, however, is man's diversity and ingenuity: his territory encompasses far more than simply a segment of physical space; it includes the total realm in which he lives his life.[4] In the following chapter, the term *territory* will be defined in greater detail, but for the present it can be described as *that area of an individual's life which he experiences as his own, in which he exerts control, takes initiative, has expertise, or accepts responsibility.* It is the realm in which a person has a sense of independence and feels free to act on his own initiative.

Mr. Bridges, a partner in an engineering firm, is an expert in bridge construction. Bridge building constitutes his territory in the company. One afternoon another partner, Mr. Rhodes, discusses the merits of a certain material in the construction of a highway while Mr. Bridges listens with interest. Mr. Rhodes, however, wanders off the subject of highways and starts to extol the advantages of the same material in building bridges. Very shortly he finds himself put in his place by a few well-chosen remarks by Mr. Bridges, who, because of his superior knowledge of bridge building, has no difficulty defending his territory. Human beings not only have a strong sense of territory, but are also ready to defend it—a readiness which may be signaled to others by tone of voice, change in posture, or by the simple sign "NO TRESPASSING."

In a crowded world territoriality implies competition, and observing human behavior from a territorial perspective means recognizing that life is an ever-continuing struggle to maintain, or to expand, the territory under control. From the day he is born until the hour of his death, a substantial part of man's energy is expended in the service of this never-ending contest. An individual leaves home early in the morning to compete for a better social situation, a more influential job, a bigger share of the limelight. He saves his money to buy a bigger home, a fancier sports car, or a pair of suede pants and a fringed jacket. His son goes off to the army to defend his country and its wealth against foreign powers. At home, he may have a dog to keep out unwanted intruders. Children extort an ever-expanding number of privileges from their parents, while outside

---

[4]Erving Goffman, in his book *Relations in Public* (1972, p. 29), devotes a chapter to what he calls the territories of the self and discriminates between eight different types of territory. ". . . to facilitate the study of co-mingling—at least in American society—it is useful to extend the notion of territoriality into claims that function like territories but are not spatial and it is useful to focus on situational and egocentric territoriality."

the home they must work hard to hold their own among their peers. The young person grows long hair, smokes pot, and talks about revolution, while the adult goes to cocktail parties where he seeks to monopolize the attention of the guests with his knowledge and wit. Indeed, man's territorial struggles are all-pervasive, and he who tires of defending his ground will soon have nothing left.

Territorial defense is an extremely serious matter which may at times result in the death of the invader, although it is usually carried out on a much more subtle level. A few real life situations will illustrate.

In Phoenix, Arizona, a 43-year-old man lives alone in a mobile home. Unfortunately he has lost his job and has been unable to keep up the mortgage payments. The bank decides to repossess the trailer, but the owner refuses to surrender it to the representatives of the bank. Two policemen are sent, and only minutes after their arrival both lie dead, shot by a man determined to keep his property.

In our program at the University of Washington we recently needed some new duplicating equipment. We explored the characteristics as well as the cost of different types of copying machines and eventually found one which was reasonably priced and suited our needs. However, when we sent a requisition through the regular channels of the University, we found that matters weren't quite that simple. Naively we had assumed that choosing the equipment was our prerogative, but we soon found how mistaken we were. The University had assigned the job of coordinating the purchasing of all duplicating equipment to one man; in other words, the buying of duplicating equipment was his territory. He defended his territory well, and it became clear that the only way in which we could obtain the necessary equipment was to respect his authority over the area and leave the decision about what to buy up to him.

Once one recognizes the role of territoriality in everyday life, it seems surprising that it has escaped intensive scrutiny. Many volumes have been written of course about man's territorial struggles on a larger scale—the history of man is, to a considerable extent, the history of nations which have clashed for the control of land, trade, recognition, or power. On a visit to the library one can find many books on the art of waging war, the strategies which have held favor with armies and navies, and the intricacies of international negotiations. There is also ample information available concerning the resolution of conflict in courts of law. Little, if anything, however, will be found if one looks for a book which discusses the strictly private wars or which analyzes the strategies employed in the common disputes encountered by every individual in his daily life.

DETERMINANTS OF HUMAN TERRITORIAL BEHAVIOR

What are the roots of the territorial behavior which plays such an important role in the society of man? Robert Ardrey (1966) builds a case in support of the thesis that territoriality is primarily a genetically determined behavior pattern, an automatic response to specific situations; in other words, an instinct. Aggression, which is a major component of territoriality and of focal concern to man's conflict-torn community, is similarly explained as an instinctual drive. This position is essentially identical to that of Sigmund Freud, who believed that inborn in every man there exists a destructive drive seeking its expression in behavior.

In 1939 Dollard and his co-workers published a monograph, *Frustration and Aggression,* in which they took the position that aggression, rather than being an ever-present drive seeking its way into action, is always a consequence of frustration. This hypothesis gained much favor among social scientists and led to a vast amount of research, which in turn prepared the ground for further modification of the theory. Subsequently experimental data have been gathered which suggest that aggression is a learned response rather than an inborn drive or an automatic result of frustration.

In recent years a series of ingenious experiments has been carried out in which frustrating and tension-provoking situations were created in order to study whether such tension was reduced by an aggressive response (Hokanson, 1970). The findings indicated that human subjects rapidly learned to respond in a manner effective in removing the frustration. The response that works is the one the subject chooses to apply. If the frustration can be eliminated by an aggressive response, the subject soon learns to use aggressive behavior. If frustration is more effectively resolved with a friendly or submissive response, the individual soon learns to be friendly or submissive. Early learning has been demonstrated to be of enormous importance in the development of competitive and fighting behavior in animals. It is possible, for instance, to succeed in teaching cats, dogs, birds, and rats to live together in peace if one properly manipulates the conditions in which they are raised (Zing, 1960). Such findings do not disprove that territoriality itself is an inborn tendency. They do demonstrate, however, that in man, as well as animals, the behavior patterns related to territoriality—of which aggressive behaviors are particularly important

—are to a remarkable degree based on individual experiences and are modifiable by means of new learning.

The question of whether territorial tendencies themselves are inborn or learned is not resolved. However, we wish to avoid constructs such as drives or instincts for explanatory purposes. These constructs are deceptive, for they have an impressive scientific sound but fail to explain anything for practical purposes. A brief example of such deceptive use of the concept of instinct may clarify this position and is taken from Ardrey's book *The Social Contract.* In it he tells of the experiments of David Hopcraft in Kenya with the Thompson gazelle. Hopcraft attempted to domesticate this friendly little antelope, and to do so he netted about half a dozen of them and placed them inside a 90-acre enclosure. A surprise was in store for him. Within ten minutes one male killed two females, and shortly thereafter all the animals were dead. As it turned out, Hopcraft had made the mistake of using animals from two different herds. We mention Hopcraft's interesting experience only because of the interpretation that Ardrey applied to these facts. He concluded that the Thompson gazelle must possess by nature a violent drive which is kept in control by territorial factors, for he says, "Territory is perhaps the supreme peacemaker" but "latent violence is there" (Ardrey, 1970, p. 261). Superficially this sounds plausible, but the absurdity of such a statement becomes apparent when it is turned around, which would make it read something like this: The Thompson gazelle has a latent "peacefulness drive" which is kept suppressed under circumstances of territorial disruption. Clearly such statements about drives add nothing but a pseudo-scientific aura to the observation that under some circumstances the Thompson gazelle behaves peacefully while under other circumstances it does not. Therefore, if Thompson gazelles are to be domesticated, one of two conditions will have to be met: either one has to start with animals from the same herd or teach the individual gazelles to share available territory. That the latter can be done was also shown by Hopcraft.

We have belabored the above point because we would like to avoid such common but untenable statements as "man is basically violent," or the recently less popular, "man is basically good." Statements about man's *basic nature* are more indicative of the speaker's personal bias than of human nature in general. Instead, we take the position that an individual will handle his territorial inclinations in accordance with the following three principles.

LEARNING

Observations of animals as well as human beings who have grown up under circumstances that deprive them of social learning from adults or peers have shown the failure of these deprived ones to acquire the skills needed to hold their own within their society. Experiments with primates reared in total isolation, as well as observations of children who have suffered extreme parental neglect, corroborate this statement (Harlow and Harlow, 1962; Caldwell, 1971). Harlow's monkeys, which grew up without a mother and without peers, were later placed in a group of normally reared monkeys. The deprived animals would huddle in a corner, frightened and unable to interact effectively with the other monkeys. Observations in more natural settings have shown that dominant monkeys usually had dominant parents, again indicating the importance of learning for the acquisition of behavior patterns relevant to territoriality (Bartholomew, 1967). In the human situation a similar importance of learning can be exemplified by the many individuals who, having been reared in a rural situation, experience difficulties in finding a place for themselves in the crowded conditions of the inner city. Oscar Handlin's book *The Uprooted* (1951), which movingly describes the great migration from rural Europe to the large cities of the American East Coast, provides a dramatic example.

The reverse situation, the slum dweller who suddenly finds himself in the country, has a parallel impact. We have been told many anecdotes illustrating this fact by a former superintendent of a Civilian Conservation Corps (CCC) camp located in Northern Idaho during the depression years of the 1930's. He observed numerous cases of overwhelming anxiety and fright among these young men when they had to live and work in the wilderness, a setting entirely foreign to their previous learning. They were well trained to hold their own among neighborhood toughs, but were unprepared to deal with this new threat: nature.

INTERPRETATION OF THE SITUATION

An individual will respond to a situation in a manner consistent with the personal interpretation he gives to it. He will do so no matter how inappropriate such a response may seem to others who may view the same thing quite differently. Nearly everyone has had the experience as a child of being alone in the dark, hearing strange sounds, and having terror grip him as objects assumed the shapes of frightening figures. Fleeing to the safety of his mother, the child behaved in a manner consistent with his perception of the situation. In the folk tale "The Three Sillies," a young man enters a village late in the evening and sees by the light of the full moon that the villagers are frantically raking in the water of a small pond. He watches for a while and then asks one of them what it is they are trying to do. The villagers tell him that the moon has fallen into the pond and that they are trying to get it out. This story conveys very well that a person's interpretation of an event can be pretty far out, but that his behavior is nevertheless determined by it. Thus, if Mr. Jones suspects Mr. Smith of territorial infringement, even though no infringement has actually occurred, Mr. Jones will behave in a manner appropriate to that suspicion. On the other hand, if Mr. Smith is able to convince Mr. Jones that he is not invading his territory, even though he is actually in the process of appropriating an important segment of it, he will get away with this take-over without a fight.

AVAILABLE RESOURCES

A person will use the resources he has available to him to handle his territory. In the story of David and Goliath, David used his superior manner of fighting to obtain the desired results. A man with a clever tongue may never have to flex his arm muscles to keep his domain intact. At times brute force is the only resource available to a person, and he will use it accordingly.

Depending on his learning, his resources, and his interpretation of the situation, an individual may choose many different courses of action in dealing with territorial problems. He has the tools and often the training to act violently and destructively when he believes it necessary or advantageous to do so. Man's physical characteristics show that he is well equipped for exploration of new territory. He walks upright, his eyes constantly scan the space ahead of him, and his brain is automatically alerted and prodded into high interpretive activity whenever he spots anything new or unexpected. But though he is well endowed for exploration, he can choose, as it were, to put on a blindfold, plug his ears, and place himself in isolation to contemplate the past instead of the future. Regardless of the source of his territoriality, man has the possibility of determining for himself in which way he will handle this vital part of his existence. He has a supreme capacity to learn from experience and act on the basis of knowledge. The control of human territorial behavior, therefore, cannot depend on the naive notion of eradicating the sense of territoriality itself, but rather, must begin with the exploration of the vicissitudes of the territorial impulse.

CHAPTER 2

BASIC CHARACTERISTICS OF HUMAN TERRITORIALITY

SOLITUDE

I have a house where I go
When there's too many people,
I have a house where I go
Where no one can be;
I have a house where I go
Where nobody ever says "No";
Where no one says anything—so
There is no one but me.

A. A. Milne*

An individual's territory consists of those areas in which he has special expertise, shows initiative, and takes responsibility—in other words, where he has control. The plural *areas* is used because man's sense of territory is not limited to physical space alone, but extends to many other aspects of his social and intellectual life. Daily he is confronted with many territorial conflicts, some trifling, some serious, some simple, some of great complexity, and in order to handle these effectively he needs first to identify precisely which area is under dispute. To facilitate this process we will begin by making some distinctions between different types of territories.

PRIVATE DOMAIN

Private domain is the area which an individual stakes out in order to insure his privacy and security. This space may vary from vast stretches of land to

*From Now We Are Six. New York: E. P. Dutton & Co., Inc., 1955, p. 3.

the confines of the human body itself. Privacy and security are so important to man that he will spend enormous amounts of time and energy
establishing a claim on privacy and defending it against intruders. This
intense desire for a place he can call his own is already observed in small
children. The toddler chortles over a game of peek-a-boo, turns away from
the gaze of a stranger, or hides behind his parents when unfamiliar guests
arrive. He may crawl behind a curtain, under a table, or simply crouch in
the corner of the room with a blanket over his head, contented in his own
little den. Later, around the age of five, he begins to search for a secret
place at home or in the garden where he can be alone, by himself, away
from the surveillance of adults. A camp behind a cluster of bushes, a
corner in the attic, or a tree house becomes the child's first privacy retreat.

PRIVACY RETREAT

Melford E. Spiro, in his book *Kibbutz* (1963, pp. 30-31), describes how,
at one time, the wish for a privacy retreat was considered a menace to the
community among members of the Kibbutz Kiryat Yedidim. The desire
to be alone was interpreted as disloyalty to the group, for the complete
sharing of everything at all times formed the very foundation of the
kibbutz. Spiro writes,

> The emphasis on the moral value of the group means, finally, that group
> living and group experiences are valued more highly than their individual
> counterparts. Indeed, so important is the value of group experience that those
> cheverim who seek a great degree of privacy are viewed as "queer." The kibbutz
> is interested in creating a *chevra* ... The term, chevra, literally, denotes a
> society; but its connotation ... is a group which is characterized by intimacy of
> interaction, and by mutual concern, if not by love .... It is apparent, therefore,
> that the individualist, the person who cherishes his own privacy more than a
> group experience, constitutes a threat to the group ....

This insistence on group interaction and complete subordination of the
individual to the community, so essential for the success of the kibbutz
during its very difficult beginnings, was the cause of considerable resentment and contention when eventually more and more members sought
increasing amounts of privacy. Spiro wrote his book in 1955, but had
occasion to revisit the kibbutz in 1963, and following this he wrote (1963,
pp. xii-xiii) in his "Preface to the New Edition":

Early kibbutz collectivism comprised three distinct but . . . related values. These were: group ownership of all economic goods, the primacy of group over individual interests, and group experience as intrinsically valuable . . . . In 1951, an important source of tension in Kiryat Yedidim was to be found in the conflict between this mystique of group experience, derived from the romantic currents which had fed into and been expressed in its Youth Movement traditions, and the strong desire for privacy created by the reality of kibbutz living. Today Kiryat Yedidim appears to be much more inclined to view collective living within the context of its present social reality, rather than from nostalgic distortions of its youth movement past; and the demand for privacy seems to have been recognized as legitimate.

These experiences in the kibbutz underscore the strength of man's wishes for privacy, even if this urge goes against the ethic of the group.

Patients in a state mental institution will pay a high price for free space, described by Erving Goffman (1961) as an area where they are on their own, away from the medical supervision which presses on them everywhere else. Free space may be a poorly lit tunnel used to pass from one building to another, or even such an unattractive area as the bathroom. In spite of the unpleasant odors, patients would spend hours in this rather repulsive atmosphere, sitting on the toilet, enjoying the sense of relaxation derived from being alone.

Victims of concentration camps in World War II have commented on the demoralizing experience of having absolutely no area where they could escape the attention of others. A survivor of three years in the extermination camp Auschwitz, describing what the different camps had in common, wrote (Cohen, 1953, p. 130),

The last factor that obtained in each type of camp, which must be discussed here, is that the prisoner was *never alone,* not even when occupied in his normal vegetative functions; there was nowhere for him to settle down for a single moment; he had not a shred of private existence left. To live continuously in the company of others became agony. As Dostoievsky, who spent ten years . . . in the penal camp at Ostrogg in Siberia, has put it: "Besides the loss of liberty, besides the forced labor, one more torture in the convict's life . . . which is almost harder to bear than any other: this is the *forced community of life.*"

The social psychologist Philip G. Zimbardo conducted an experiment at Stanford University which simulated life in prison. A very realistic model of a prison cell was built in the basement of a campus building, and students were hired to function either as inmates or as guards during the two weeks of the experiment. Several students had to be "paroled" after a few days because they could not tolerate the situation. One of them reported:[1] "I thought this would be a piece of cake, but it got to me—the whole thing—*the total loss of privacy*—the humiliation of being slaves to the guards, *being in a small, small cell with two other guys 24 hours a day* and the complete loss of freedom." [Emphasis added.]

These examples dramatize what everyone knows from his own daily life experiences. An individual needs a place where he can escape the attention of his fellow man, a privacy retreat where he finds the quiet to relax and replenish his energies and ready himself for the stresses of renewed interaction with other people. Much of the irritability and fatigue of the young mother, for instance, could well be attributed to the fact that her privacy is almost continuously invaded by her offspring.

PERSONAL SPACE

Aside from the specific privacy retreat which an individual claims as his own, he also has a number of definite perceptions and feelings about the area which immediately surrounds him. This area is usually called his personal space.[2] Edward Hall devotes his book *The Hidden Dimension* (1969) to the exploration of this type of spatiality. He observes that man has a very keen sense of distance. Each person maintains a certain distance between himself and others, depending on the type of relationship and the situation. The "hidden dimension" refers to an invisible barrier surrounding each individual, the penetration of which he responds to with a vague sense of discomfort and an automatic attempt to reestablish the previous distance. The preferred distance is greatly influenced by the character of the relationship. Hall distinguishes between four distances, which lie as concentric circles around the individual: The intimate (0-1½ ft.), the personal (1½-4 ft.), the social (4-12 ft.), and the public (12 ft. and more). Public distance can be exemplified by a speaker who stands in front of his audience; at the speaker's stand, he will prefer a greater separation

---

[1] The quotation that follows was taken from a newspaper report (UPI) on Zimbardo's research at Stanford University. A more detailed description of the study can be found in Zimbardo, 1971.

[2] An extensive discussion of the impact of personal space on human interaction and the consequences of this for architectural design has been given by Robert Sommer in his book *Personal Space* (1969).

from others than he would, for instance, while standing around with a group of friends, enjoying a casual conversation (personal distance). Direct physical contact, on the other hand, is reserved for relationships where intimate distance is appropriate.

Most individuals have a keen sense of the specific distance appropriate to a relationship and will adjust the space between themselves and others automatically in any given situation (Little, 1965). If one enters a crowded elevator one must accept direct physical contact. However, if the elevator contains only a single occupant and one moves to within a foot of that person, the other will immediately move away until the space in the elevator is divided into roughly equal parts. The comfortable distance is also affected by characteristics of the physical setting. A person tolerates greater frontal proximity, for instance, when there is ample space to either side of him (Daves and Swaffer, 1971).

Human spatiality is analogous to the so-called flight distance of animals. Most animals will move away if approached nearer than a certain distance, which varies from one species to another. The distance is primarily determined by the necessity for the animal to maintain sufficient room to allow himself to escape in case of attack. This analogy, carried over to the human situation, would mean that an individual's personal space is primarily determined by the degree to which he trusts those around him. This notion is supported by studies with prisoners, which have shown that in order to feel comfortable, paranoid individuals with a history of violent behavior need a larger distance between themselves and others than their colleagues who are not so characterized (Kinzel, 1970; Hildreth et al., 1971). Schizophrenic patients also require a greater distance for comfort than nonschizophrenics (Horowitz, 1968). It is important to remember that approaching an animal closer than the flight distance often results in an attack if no opportunity exists for that animal to retreat. The same response occurs with human beings who feel extremely threatened and see no way out. In approaching this type of individual, therefore, it is crucial to leave him ample room to move away. Awareness of these spatial aspects of man's territoriality is of practical value to the person who deals with psychiatric patients. Considerable trouble can be avoided by carefully assessing the degree of closeness which each patient can comfortably tolerate, always leaving him an avenue of escape.

Awareness of personal space is also vital for ordinary interpersonal encounters. Most everyone has experienced irritation when another individual disregards his spatial requirements by standing too close during a conversation or by putting an arm around his shoulders when the relationship does not warrant such intimacy. The sense of distance varies from one culture to another. In the Arab countries, for instance, one requires less interpersonal distance than in the United States. Thus, moving to a different culture can create considerable interpersonal confusion until the new standards have been learned. In this context it is interesting that Japanese monkeys observed in their natural surroundings also show variations from troop to troop in the personal space requirements of their members. In one troop, for instance, where the tolerance was highest, there was often no room left between individuals at the feeding ground. In another troop each animal remained separated from the others by approximately five feet while feeding (Kawamura, 1967).

Crowding has a profound impact on the behavior, and it has been suggested that many of man's problems may well have their basis in overcrowding (Morris, 1970). There have been numerous observations that animals under conditions of overcrowding are subject to a large increase in mortality and especially in heavy die-off of the young even when there is an adequate supply of food. Such crowding, with its reduction in inter-individual space, is extremely stressful to several types of animals. Autopsies on deer that died during a period of overpopulation on an island showed that they had a significant enlargement of their adrenals when compared with animals living under less crowded conditions (Hall, 1969). The probable explanation for this observation is that under crowded conditions the animal's flight distance is more frequently violated. As the adrenals are the central organs which prepare the body for flight or fight, they are more frequently activated under crowded circumstances and an increase in size is the result. Rats reared under abnormally crowded conditions show that under such circumstances a wide variety of unusual and often destructive behavior patterns occurs in addition to the rise in mortality already mentioned (Calhoun, 1962).

A simple transfer of observations made on animals to the life of human beings is perhaps unwarranted, especially as the latter have many more possibilities for obtaining a personal territory than the former. It is not far-fetched, however, to speculate that in a crowded world the need for personal space, security, and privacy is particularly compelling.

Privacy is obtained by establishing a territory to which one can retreat from the influence and scrutiny of others. Personal space regulates interpersonal physical closeness, thus maintaining a degree of privacy in a social setting. The ultimate reaches of privacy, however, are the thoughts and fantasies of the individual—the most personal enclaves of his existence. Invasion into the privacy of a person's thoughts is, therefore, least tolerable of all. An individual experiences such invasion to a mild degree when he becomes irritated at another person who reads over his shoulder. This reaction is understandable, for by reading along, the invader can penetrate the thoughts evoked by the reading material. The aggravation is more intense when a person finds that someone has read his personal mail or his diary without permission. A similar response occurs when one is asked very personal questions by an individual to whom one does not feel close.

Personal ideas must be shared voluntarily if one is to preserve a sense of integrity. Interestingly, the most severe psychiatric disorder, schizophrenia, has as its most ominous symptom the patient's feeling that he has lost all privacy. He complains that his thoughts are controlled by others and that his every idea is immediately read by those around him. He feels like an open book, not by choice but because powerful forces have penetrated his innermost being.

The private domain is the realm to which man retreats to refresh his spirit, to order his thoughts, and to plan his future. Eventually, however, he returns to the excitement of the public arena.

THE PUBLIC ARENA

Without privacy man cannot regain the energy he needs to meet the challenges of the public arena, but it is in the latter realm that the vicissitudes of territoriality attain their most interesting visibility. In the public arena we distinguish two types of territories which are the most frequent objects of competition: psychological space and action territory.

PSYCHOLOGICAL SPACE

A large audience is held spellbound by the daring antics of two acrobats who perform at a circus. Children squeal with delight at a chimpanzee who rides a tricycle. A silent crowd stares in horror as a young woman threatens to jump from the top floor of a tall building. Four young men abruptly stop their discussion and turn around to watch a well-endowed young woman who has just passed by. There are many ways of catching attention, a need felt in varying intensities by most every member of the human race. Thus, attempts to occupy the limelight or capture the thoughts of others for extended periods of time provide a major arena of human competition. In order to bring out the territorial aspects of this process we will look more closely at a common situation.

A group of students has gathered around a table in the lunch room. The conversation is largely dominated by one person. He speaks with emphasis and somewhat louder than the rest, occasionally gesturing with his hands to underscore a particularly important point. While he is talking the others listen, or so it seems. Occasionally another member of the group makes a comment, but no one is able to hold the floor for very long against the pressure of the dominant speaker. Closer observation shows, however, that one individual is preoccupied. He is busy thinking of a different topic of conversation, one on which he can speak with greater self-assurance. Now he is more alert, waiting to take the first opportunity to move in. When the speaker pauses briefly to catch his breath, this quiet plotter makes his move, "Say, did you guys see that CBS Special last night?—That was really fascinating!" He has raised his voice sufficiently to overpower his opponent's attempt to regain control, and now he is on his way. All turn to him and for the time being he has conquered the group's psychological space.

The term *psychological space* indicates a characteristic feature of man's behavior in a group. Whenever a group forms, each member takes or receives a certain amount of the attention and interest of the other individuals present. We selected the term *psychological space* to indicate the *sum total of attention of a group* or, what amounts to the same, *the total amount of influence which each person exerts over the thoughts and feelings of all the individuals present.* In looking at a group engaged in discussion, such as the one portrayed above, it becomes apparent that the distribution of psychological space is continually changing. In our example, the dominant speaker controlled, for a time, nearly all of the psychological space available. Then one person withdrew his attention and took control of his own thoughts while planning his attack. In doing so, he effectively defended himself against the speaker's attempt to hold his psychological space. Finally, he went into the offensive and took a substantial part of the available attention for himself. Thus, the two major areas of competition in the realm of psychological space are the acquisition of the attention of others, and the control over the amount of attention given to another. To the extent that one seeks to influence, capture, or in any way affect the thoughts and feelings of another, to that extent one is trying to take possession of his psychological space. Control over another's psychological space is not an all-or-none affair. It may range from a near-100 per cent level in the case of a gifted story teller who keeps his audience completely spellbound as he approaches the climax of his tale, to near zero for the shy, unobtrusive person who goes almost unnoticed in his attempts to capture a slice of attention.

Psychological space is acquired in two different ways: the first depends on the immediate drawing and holding of attention in the situation at hand, whereas the second results from the remote (in time as well as space) impact on the thoughts and feelings of others. The latter is perhaps best exemplified by the world's religious leaders, such as Jesus, Mohammed, or Buddha, who, centuries after their deaths, still keep the thoughts and feelings of millions of people in their grip.

In order to play a role in relation to his fellow man and to maintain a position in the social order of any culture, the individual must have some capability of capturing and defending his control over the psychological space of others. Field studies on primate behavior have revealed that the dominance of one or several males in a group of primates principally depends on their ability to hold the almost constant attention of the other group members (Chance, 1967). A fascinating example of this phenomenon among chimpanzees was described by Jane van Lawick-Goodall (1965, pp. 802-831):[3]

> Many chimps displayed with our belongings, but only Mike used them in a way that effected a drastic change in his own social standing.
>
> The year before we set up New Camp, Goliath, J.B., and Leakey were the top-ranking males. Mike, though just as big, ranked low in status. We didn't know why, but he was constantly attacked or threatened by nearly all other males. When we left the reserve at year's end, Mike was cowed and nervous, flinching at every movement or sound.
>
> On our return we found a different Mike: He was feared by every individual in the community. We shall never be sure, but it seems likely that by leaving empty kerosene cans lying about, we ourselves had helped his rise to power. He had learned to throw and drag these cans along the ground, and they made a tremendous noise.

[3]For a more detailed account of Mike's rise to dominance, see Chapter 10, pp. 122-139, in Dr. van Lawick-Goodall's book *In the Shadow of Man* (1971).

Mike often walked to the tent while a group of chimps was resting peacefully nearby, selected a can from the veranda, and carried it outside. Suddenly he would begin to rock slightly from side to side, uttering low hoots. As soon as the hooting rose to a crescendo, he was off, hurling his can in front of him. He could keep as many as three cans in play, one after the other.

Chimpanzees as a rule hate loud noise—except for their own screams—and so Mike, with his strange display, frightened the others. We ourselves grew to dislike his behavior and hid all cans. But by that time, if artificial props had indeed raised Mike's rank, he had no more need of them. The other chimps, at his approach, would pant nervously and bow to the ground, acknowledging his dominance.

The need to hold the attention of others reveals the purpose of such traditions as the wearing of a jewel-studded crown by a king or a glittering miter by a prince of the church. Wigs worn by judges in England, as well as the brooch or necklace decorating the bosom of a woman, all seem to have the same objective: to capture attention and thus to establish control over the existing psychological space.

The ability to acquire psychological space is dependent on a number of different factors, and the skills and methods which are effective in holding immediate attention differ from those which acquire remote psychological space. To draw immediate attention one needs the proper expectations in the audience. In other words, reputation is of considerable importance. If a person often offers valuable ideas, others are more prone to listen to him than to someone who has the reputation of being a crank, even if the crank may at times say something worthwhile. The form in which an individual casts his communications also has an important bearing on his ability to hold attention. The tone of his voice, the rhythm of his speech, and his personal way of emphasizing words are as important as the content of the message itself. If he lowers the pitch of his voice at the end of each sentence, for instance, he will lose the attention of his audience in a very few minutes. Gestures and body postures play an equally important role in the acquisition of psychological space. More crucial, however, than any other single factor is the face, which is dominated by the eyes. When eyes meet, a relationship is established which is confirmed and continued as long as both parties maintain eye contact. The relationship is negated or suspended when one person turns away. Eye contact also provides an opportunity for one individual to exert control over another. A lecturer who seeks to hold the attention of an audience can increase his effectiveness by slowly shifting his gaze from person to person, looking each of them briefly in the eyes, while continuing to speak. A waiter who lets his eye be caught by a customer is placed under an obligation to respond (Argyle and Dean, 1965).

The person who takes up much psychological space fills, as it were, the minds of the others with himself. His ideas prevail, his persuasion wins out, his problems are made the other's problems. This is not to say that the taking of psychological space is always accompanied with great force or insistence. A quiet, soft-spoken individual may hold more psychological space than an unusually loud person, provided the latter has less status in the group than the former. Psychological space can be gained by rather paradoxical means. A display of helplessness or dependent tears can be just as effective as a straightforward demand in absorbing the attention of all persons gathered. Any behavior that is unusual or unexpected can serve this purpose. Lady Godiva, stark naked, riding on a horse through the streets of eleventh-century London, captured the psychological space of a large number of people. However, if the same lady were to ride in the raw through a modern nudist colony, the horse would no doubt garner more attention than the lady herself.

The competition for psychological space is not limited to large groups. It takes place between two individuals as well. When a couple sits down at night over a cup of coffee to share the experiences of the day there has to be a division of the time each has the floor, and the division must be acceptable to both. If the husband routinely dominates this situation, he may soon find himself engaged in a monologue while his wife pursues her own thoughts, uttering an occasional grunt or nod of her head to fake attention. In the broader family circle one commonly encounters the scene around the dinner table when the children want to tell their parents about the movie they saw that afternoon. The competition is fierce: "Now it's my turn!" . . . "Let me tell that part where he . . .!"

Each individual is in a position to relinquish his own psychological space to another member of the group by giving his attention to the other, and he will do so if he finds the returns rewarding. If the story being told is interesting or humorous, if the speaker's opinion seems valuable, or if the speaker has obtained the rights to the attention of the audience by virtue of being a teacher or a minister, the listener will give his psychological space to him. However, if his attention is taken against his will or by means of unexpected behavior from a source which he does not consider legitimate, then the result is irritation and an attempt to close the other out. In the example of the couple, the wife withheld her psychological space from her husband by focusing on other things. His continued efforts to get her attention would only lead to her being irritated. Similarly, irritation results when one's total immersion in a fascinating stage play is disturbed by the fellow in the next chair who whispers his critical commentary in his girl friend's ear.

The degree to which a person considers the attention of others as his own property once he has acquired it is revealed in the irritation he experiences when he is interrupted in mid-sentence. A far more vehement response is likely to stir him, however, if he is impertinently or in-appropriately "sh'ed" by another individual. The "sh'er" thus directly denies him the right to psychological space. Irritation and anger directed to the intruder are the logical result of such an unauthorized invasion. (Feldman, 1959).

Psychological space, as discussed above, occurs only in a group of two or more and is extremely temporary in nature. In each new encounter a person must acquire the share of the psychological space that he desires. The remote method of occupying psychological space is an entirely different process. Propaganda and reputation-building, for instance, serve to establish the hold which any one person may have over the many. The clever use of existing media has often catapulted the struggling young politician into the public view and thereby vastly increased his chances of succeeding in the capture of political office. One example was the rise of Adolf Hitler to political power in the late 1920's and early 1930's. In his book *Eva Braun: Hitler's Mistress* (1969, p. 39), Nerin E. Gun describes how Hitler's friend and confidant, Heinrich Hoffman, was instrumental in Hitler's success.

> The role that he played in Hitler's fabulous rise to power can be considered fundamental. It was he who succeeded in introducing photography as the prime asset in a German political campaign. Thanks to him, Hitler, who had been unknown in 1923, became a hero, a father, a husband, and perhaps even a God to every man and woman in Germany. Hoffman was one of the chief fabricators of this image of the Führer. The methods he used were known to some extent in America and certainly in Fascist Italy but were completely new in the Reich. For instance, even today in Eastern and Western Germany, and also in Swit-zerland, the most reputable daily papers rarely publish photographs, and hardly ever on the front page. Hoffman changed this during the Nazi era.

In the last two decades television has emerged as a potent political weapon. The Kennedy-Nixon debates in the presidential campaign of

1960 resulted, in many people's estimation, in a coup for John F. Kennedy for the simple reason that, although both candidates were on view, Mr. Kennedy was able to use the television medium to his best advantage, whereas Mr. Nixon was naive about makeup and camera placement, thus losing out in this game of psychological spacemanship.

The struggle for psychological space takes place in the public arena. Its reward is the attention of others. In this respect it stands in direct contrast to the realm of private domain, which, as we saw, seeks to exclude others and establish a haven of privacy.

ACTION TERRITORY

Another major dimension of human territoriality, closely related to psychological space, but having its own unique features, is action territory. We define *action territory* as *the area in which a person considers it his prerogative to act, exert control, make decisions, exercise his expertise, and take responsibility, in other words an area of action which a person claims as his own.*[4] Action territory always refers to a specific activity which an individual considers his right to perform, and it can, therefore, best be described by an action word or verb. Each individual has many diverse action territories which he claims. A few examples will further clarify the concept.

It is Sally's second birthday and her mother has called the family together for a little party. The cake arrives with its two burning candles and Sally, after much encouragement, finally manages to blow out the candles while the family members laugh and clap their approval. Sally is obviously pleased with her performance and has learned that blowing out candles on a cake is something she is expected to do, something she is able to do, and something that is, therefore, her action territory. Two weeks later Sally attends the birthday party of a neighbor boy, Billy, who has just

---

[4]G. J. Sawrer-Foner of McGill University has drawn attention to the territorial nature of activity areas in an article entitled "Human Territoriality and Its Cathexis" (1970, pp. 82-87). As he puts it in the rather obscure language of psychoanalysis, "The author's data show that man cathects not only literal geographic space, but also symbolized personal space 'or territory,' including man's intrapsychic visualizations of his intellectual interests, activities and social sign posts of positioning in relationship to his fellows with what appears to be much the same instinctive energies and drives as the lower-than-man animal cathects his survival territory."

turned four. When the cake is brought in Sally leans forward and tries to blow out the candles and is rewarded by a bop on the head from Billy, who immediately defends his candle-snuffing prerogative. Sally cries and withdraws, but she has been shown that her action territory does not extend to blowing out candles on Billy's cake. Later, through more experience, she learns that her specific action territory is confined to blowing out the candles on her own cake.

Cynthia, hired as a receptionist at a dental office, has an action territory which includes answering the telephone, receiving patients, making appointments, keeping books, sending out the bills, watering the plants, and cleaning the reception area. Not included in her duties is caring for the several tanks of tropical fish; this task is an action territory claimed and reserved by the dentist. Cynthia, a very competent and responsible person who likes to keep herself busy, soon starts to assume care of the aquaria when the dentist is too busy to care for the fish properly. As she does an excellent job, she is given more and more responsibility until she has the total care of the fish under her control. Thus she has added a new specific activity—caring for fish—to the general action territory she already possesses.

In the working world a person's action territory is ordinarily defined by his job description, which specifies the activities he is expected to carry out. Role definitions accomplish the same for many other social situations. In the past, the role definition of the husband, for instance, outlined his action territory relative to the family, which included such activities as providing the money, paying the bills, making repairs in the home, and disciplining the children. This portrayal of action territory is rather straightforward, but the practical interpretation of role definitions is far more complicated. Action territory, as we have defined it, refers to the area of functioning which the individual *considers* to be his own. Ideally, a job or role description coincides with what a person considers as his own action territory; in reality, such coincidence rarely occurs.

The discrepancy between expected and assumed responsibility is hilariously described in Joseph Heller's epic of territorial confusion, *Catch-22* (1970, p. 27). In one incident:

The U.S.O. troupes were sent by General P. P. Peckem, who had moved his headquarters up to Rome and had nothing better to do while he schemed against General Dreedle. General Peckem was a general with whom neatness definitely counted. He was a spry, suave and very precise general who knew the circumference of the equator and always wrote "enhanced" when he meant "increased." He was a prick, and no one knew this better than General Dreedle, who was incensed by General Peckem's recent directive requiring all tents in the Mediterranean theater of operations to be pitched along parallel lines with entrances facing back proudly toward the Washington Monument. To General Dreedle, who ran a fighting outfit, it seemed a lot of crap. Furthermore, it was none of General Peckem's goddam business how the tents in General Dreedle's wing were pitched. There then followed a hectic jurisdictional dispute between these overlords that was decided in General Dreedle's favor by ex-P.F.C. Wintergreen, mail clerk at Twenty-seventh Air Force Headquarters. Wintergreen determined the outcome by throwing all communications from General Peckem into the wastebasket. He found them too prolix. General Dreedle's views, expressed in less pretentious literary style, pleased ex-P.F.C. Wintergreen and were sped along by him in zealous observance of regulations. General Dreedle was victorious by default.

Ex-P.F.C. Wintergreen, who sorted the mail, also counted as his action territory the settling of disputes between his superiors, engaging in literary criticism, and directing Air Force policy by his judicious censoring of any mail he did not agree with.

The receptionist in a dental office may be officially designated as the person who answers all phone calls, but perhaps there is another secretary in the office who has been there much longer and has acquired the habit of picking up the phone first. If the receptionist does not resist the temptation of letting the secretary answer the phone, the new employee will, in the end, lose this part of her action territory. Conversely, a person who is hired as a business manager for a firm may find himself, as a result of the president's incompetence or lethargy, saddled with the major responsibilities for decision-making in the company. As he assumes this expanding responsibility, his action territory becomes far more extensive than his job description would lead one to believe.

In order to maintain action territory, one has to continue to carry out the functions that provide its substance. A university president has included in his action territory the passing of judgment on all major decisions pertaining to the university, planning for the future, setting priorities, and the like. To maintain this action territory, he needs to exercise these functions at all times. The moment he ceases to do so and allows these activities to be carried out independently by others, he loses the specific action territory, even though he will retain, at least for a while, the title of president. A person can justify holding on to a certain action territory in many ways: by job description, role definition, "having always done it," or expertise. However, it is his exercise of the prerogative to act in the given territory which actually maintains that territory for him. This description of action territory clearly shows that it lies very much in the realm of competition; that like psychological space, it lacks concrete attributes to give it continuity and that it therefore requires an ongoing effort for its maintenance.

To have a genuine sense of ownership over an action territory, a person must have the feeling that the relevant activities are under his own voluntary control. It makes considerable difference whether one carries out certain functions by choice or through coercion. If a father tells a son to take care of carrying out the garbage for the family, and if the young man is given no choice in the matter, he will experience a reduction in territory rather than an increase. A segment of his own time has been taken from him by his father, while at the same time he does not experience a true sense of autonomy over the job of carrying out the garbage. *To the extent that a person feels coerced to take care of a certain territory, he does not experience it as his own.* One's sense of ownership varies with the degree of autonomy, control, responsibility, or competence he possesses in the area. In a hierarchical association this sense of ownership also varies with the status of interacting persons relative to one's own position in the hierarchy. The personnel officer in a company has final control over hiring and firing all employees. When he talks about such matters with other company officers he does so with a sense of authority which stems from his feeling that he is clearly within the limits of his own action territory. When, however, he discusses the same issues with the company president, he shows by his deference and his less self-assured tone of voice that in relation to his boss he temporarily yields his action territory and allows his superior the prerogative to overrule his decisions if he so chooses.

Action territory plays an important role in the social life of every human being. A substantial part of a person's effort is related to the acquisition and defense of it. In it lies a major source of his sense of self-directedness. If the individual wishes to take stock of his territorial status, he can map out this area in detail by describing which activities in every sector of his life he considers his personal prerogative. His action territory becomes quite clear from answers to questions such as: Who really decides how we spend the evenings at home? Who disciplines the children? Who spends the most money? Who chooses a vacation spot? Relative to the work situation, a person may ask himself whether the activities over which he has control coincide with the actual job description. By means of this type of scrutiny a person acquires a precise knowledge of which action territories he actually owns. This knowledge affords him the opportunity to decide whether he would like to change his holdings and helps him recognize his probable competitors.

The separation of man's total area of possession into four different realms—privacy retreat, personal space, psychological space, and action territory—is intended to serve one purpose only: to aid the individual in recognizing which area is involved in a territorial conflict. An individual, after taking an inventory of his holdings and analyzing each specific situation carefully, can then proceed to assess his methods for handling each segment of his area by keeping in mind three different territorial functions: management, defense, and acquisition.

MANAGEMENT

Ownership is not an undivided blessing, for with it comes the pressure to manage the territory which one has laid claim to. The effectiveness and efficiency with which one handles it have many important consequences and deserve close attention. Knowing that the financial affairs of a given family are part of the wife's territory does not necessarily imply knowledge about the way in which she handles these affairs. How does she manage the expenses, the bookkeeping, the borrowing, or the paying of bills? How effectively does she control the spending of the other members of the family?

Questions of this type lead to an assessment of the individual's management capabilities in an area. Each specific territory makes its own demands on the time, abilities, and energies of the owner. If he lacks certain essential skills or if he simply has too many areas to take care of, the management of his total territory suffers. In such a situation he becomes overextended and cannot avoid the painful discomfort of trying to meet all the obligations without being able to do so. Such situations often occur after a rapid territorial expansion. A young woman who gives birth to several children in the first years of her marriage is likely to attest to this fact.

In order to cope with such harassing situations the individual has available three avenues for change: (a) Reduction of the overall territory, either by elimination of some areas or by limitation of the size of each or several of them: Thus, the young overworked mother can drop some of her social obligations or delay her career ambitions for a time. (b) Acquisition of additional managerial skills: The woman in the example can learn, for instance, how to organize the household work more efficiently, streamline meal preparation, and simplify childcare by using newly learned aids. The wife who has problems with the budget can learn how to plan a month's spending in advance, write down her expenditures, and pay the bills at regular times. (c) Obtaining of assistance from others: Help can be acquired by enlisting the services of friends or relatives or by hiring an assistant to do a specific job. The harassed young wife can call on her mother to help out or ask her husband to take over certain chores.

The problem of overextension is common in today's demanding society. It is easily recognized by its symptoms: The individual is tense, unable to see an end to his chores, and deeply dissatisfied with his own work. As the load increases he becomes more tense, and more frantic in his attempts to cope and consequently less and less successful. In spite of the presence of these obvious symptoms, they may not be recognized as being the result of management overload, especially if the territories involved appear relatively small. To resolve such problems one needs to recognize the overload by its symptoms and proceed to rectify the situation by means of the courses of action outlined above.

DEFENSE

If an individual values the territory which he considers rightfully his, he will ordinarily resist any attempt of others to take it away from him. The key to this defensive action is not whether he is lawfully entitled to this territory but, rather, that he believes it to be his own.

Hediger (1963, pp. 34-67), who has observed the territorial behavior of various animals in the Zurich Zoo for many years, describes the behavior of a ring-tailed lemur who had a well-defined territory in which only a specific zoo keeper was tolerated. However, on one occasion "he was accompanied by a volunteer who wanted to help him with the cleaning. She was immediately bitten in the leg so severely that one of the larger arteries was opened, necessitating protracted hospitalization." To this Hediger adds the general observation, "When territorial defense is at stake, even small and apparently harmless animals and birds may become dangerous to man." The same clearly holds true for the interaction between humans.

As is often the case, the area which an individual considers of value is also attractive to others, who may therefore seek to lay claim to it. Adequate defensive skills are consequently vital to the maintenance of territorial integrity. For the sake of clarity, the ability to defend one's territory should be separated from the ability to manage it, which was discussed above. However, poor management can weaken one's defensive position. If, as in an earlier example, the wife manages the finances for the family but does it poorly, leading to repeated problems, she will find herself in a rather indefensible position when her husband moves in to take over. Territorial defense requires a separate set of skills. Like all skills, they need to be acquired through learning. If this process has been insufficient, the individual will not be effective in repulsing incursions into his area and is bound to experience defeat. A great many practical problems of daily life stem from inadequate defensive efforts when a person's territory is under attack. Effective living implies the ability to hold one's own.

To remedy problems of defense it is important to know the three factors that bear on adequacy of defense: (a) The specific defensive skills which one has at his disposal. These capabilities depend on past learning. (b) The prediction of the outcome of the conflict. When this prediction includes ultimate defeat, a person is not likely to make a maximal effort. Only when he believes in a possible victory does he give it every last ounce of effort. Prediction is always closely linked to past experience. An individual who has experienced a number of defeats acquires the idea that his defensive skills are insufficient for the task and will, therefore, anticipate additional defeats. In turn, such thinking is likely to lead to loss because the individual will not put in the full effort necessary to succeed, a typical example of a self-fulfilling prophecy. (c) The importance which the individual attaches to the area under dispute.

These three factors interact in any given situation. To assist the inadequate fighter in becoming more effective, each of these three contingencies should be reviewed. A person lacking skills needs a coach and a place to practice. A pessimist must test his abilities in actual competition and learn to make more appropriate predictions. When the essential factor is lack of interest in a specific area, the absence of defensive action is understandable and no remedy is needed.

ACQUISITION

The continual border struggles of daily life keep each person on his toes, but life's excitement does not derive solely from defending oneself against attacks. More importantly, it stems from the joy of adventure, the investigation of new areas, and the mastery of new realms.[5] This territorial extension may take place in two ways: by displacement or by expansion.

Displacement involves the aggressive pursuit of that which already belongs to or is claimed by someone else. The novice politician runs against the incumbent in an effort to displace him in his seat of power. If he does so successfully he may continue this endeavor, taking on a new opponent in a contest for a more important office.

Expansion into new territory can occur by venturing into no-man's land without displacing anyone else, as a scientist does when he advances into a new area of research. Man's exploration of the moon and the planets symbolizes the collective acquisition of territory which belonged to no one before. Expansion is, indeed, one of the most exciting aspects of human life—there is no limit to the number of new frontiers which allow man to expand his territory without trespassing on that of others. Of course, no sooner has one gained such a new area that it begins to look attractive to someone else and the competition is on. If the new research of a scientist pays off, his colleagues will rapidly move in and try to get a piece of the action.

An individual is likely to seek expansion when the territory he presently manages no longer provides any challenge to him or when new possibilities exert a great attraction, for the search for newness and excitement motivates much of human behavior. It has been shown that the same holds true for some of the higher animals. A monkey, for instance, will perform tedious tasks if, as a reward, he is allowed to spend some time in front of a window where he can see the interesting events going on outside (Butler, 1953). Even rats prefer circumstances which offer greater diversity over those which have relevance to security and feeding only (Nissen, 1930).

As was the case with territorial management and defense, the degree to which an individual is inclined toward territorial acquisition depends on several interacting factors: (a) Skill. The ability to take over someone else's territory depends on aggressiveness and specific skills in overcoming the

[5]Robert White (1959), in a review of the relevant literature, demonstrated convincingly that animal and human behavior is profoundly affected by the deep-seated desire to expand the realm of effective interaction with the environment.

other's defenses. To seek expansion into no-man's land requires imagination and relevant skills. To be a scientist or an artist demands creativity as well as competence to deal with scientific data or to handle the artistic craft. (b) Attractiveness of other territories. In order to expand or to displace, one must first recognize something as worth the effort of acquisition. To perceive something as attractive, one needs experience that has demonstrated the positive aspect of the desired acquisition. Inasmuch as the value of territory depends on a person's position in society relative to others, it is not possible for him to perceive many things to be of value unless he is truly a part of that community. Consequently, an individual may not be attracted to things which seem highly desirable to his fellow man. (c) Hope of acquisition. If one has absolutely no hope of gaining the object he desires, he is bound to abstain from expending any effort toward the goal.

A common judgment about a person who exerts little or no effort toward extension of his territory, in spite of the fact that his domain is very limited, is that he is lazy or that he lacks motivation. It is more likely, however, that, rather than lacking some hypothetical innate drive, the "unmotivated" person does not see the same territories as desirable or does not recognize them as accessible to himself. A person is called lazy because he fails to do what others want him to do or what they believe he should be capable of. That the absence of expansive action is not due to lack of energy becomes apparent when the same individual invests enormous amounts of time and energy in an endeavor that appears both possible and desirable to him. A teenager, for instance, may spend countless hours taking apart the engine of a car and rebuilding it over and over again while neglecting his school work.

If one wishes to spur a person on to territorial acquisition, three basic avenues are open to him: (a) Teach the person the skills necessary to attain the goals. (b) Convince the individual of the desirability of certain new areas by providing some taste for them. (c) Show the accessibility of these new areas by clearly outlining the precise steps the person needs to take to arrive at the desired place. It is vital to make these steps small enough so that he clearly sees how he can move from one level to the next. Man gets joy out of the exhilaration of territorial acquisition. Once the obstacles are removed and the individual sees an avenue open, he will not fail to move into the path of exploration.

The relative importance of each of the three major territorial functions, defense, management, and acquisition, varies for each of the major types of territory. Privacy retreat and personal space depend for their existence primarily on the individual's capability to defend them. Action territory is dependent on the management of the area; in fact, it is the person's expertise and the ongoing exercise of the function itself that keeps the territory in existence. The moment the owner ceases to manage the specific functional area he loses it. Psychological space needs to be continually conquered, for it is instantly relinquished when one relaxes the efforts necessary to seize the attention of others. Acquisition skills are crucial, therefore, to the person seeking to maintain control over that elusive segment of the public arena.

Territoriality, no matter its source or the restrictions or blessings a society places on its manifestations, allows man to measure his personal assets against the norms of his reference group. His identity, security, and freedom are intimately tied to his territorial holdings, for—to paraphrase an old saying—territory makes the man.

CHAPTER 3

IDENTITY, SECURITY, AND FREEDOM

That man who is forced each day to snatch his manhood, his identity, out of the fire of human cruelty that rages to destroy it knows, if he survives his effort, and even if he does not survive it, something about himself and human life that no school on earth —and, indeed, no church—can teach. He achieves his own authority, and that is unshakable.

James Baldwin*

Man's territorial sense pervades every aspect of his existence. He constantly divides all things into categories of possession: mine and yours, his and hers, ours and theirs. This territorial index helps him measure himself in relation to others and serves as a map to refer to in case of conflict. A man wakes up in *his* bed, or at least on *his side* of the bed. Being concerned about *his* physical shape, he does *his* daily exercises before sitting down to breakfast. A glance at *his* watch reminds him that it is time to go, and soon he is driving *his* car through *his* town to *his* job. At a morning conference he presents *his* plan for a new sales promotion, and at lunch he argues with *his* colleagues in defense of *his* political views. From early morning when he rises until late at night when, tired from a hard day's work, he pulls the covers over his shoulders, he differentiates between what is *his* and what belongs to others. Although man's whole life is permeated by his territoriality, there are three aspects of his existence which it influences in such a fundamental way that we have singled them out for more detailed discussion: identity, security, and freedom.

*Baldwin, James. *The Fire Next Time*. New York: The Dial Press, 1962-1963, pp. 112-113.

IDENTITY

In order to clarify the impact of territoriality on man's identity, we first need to describe in some detail what we mean by this commonly used but extremely complex concept. The term *identity* does not indicate a separate entity; rather, it denotes a category. In this respect it is similar to the term *university*. The latter is made up of the students, the faculty, the buildings, the books, and so on, and the process of interaction among them. The word *university* does not indicate something which is separate from or in addition to all these factors. On the contrary, the term is used to refer to a totality. The word *identity* has a similar function; it indicates *the sum total of an individual's past history and his expectations for the future, combined in the process of his present social interaction.* All of these elements together constitute a person's identity, which in its uniqueness distinguishes him from all other people.

To clarify further the nature of the identity concept requires a close look at the several events subsumed under it, just as it would be necessary to consider separately students, faculty, facilities, and other factors in order to know more about the university.

Past experiences build the basic matrices of each individual's identity. In a sense, his identity *is* the history he evolves. It has, therefore, an indestructible quality of continuity. This continuity goes even beyond his personal life span, for incorporated in it is his heritage as a member of a family, a culture, and ultimately of the species.

The future influences the individual's identity in an important way by the objectives he chooses and the goals he pursues. A young man, studying to become a nuclear physicist, creates an entirely different identity than his peer who studies the violin with dreams of one day becoming a Menuhin, a Heifetz, or an Oistrakh.

The present furnishes the truly creative moment in which the matrices of the identity provided by the past experiences and the hopes for future gains are transformed into a new actuality. Each new day adds a page to the story of a person's life. Perhaps it is a better analogy to compare it with a painting rather than a book. Each day one adds new colors and shapes to the canvas, and with each additional stroke of the brush a subtle transformation occurs which somehow profoundly affects the whole composition. In this fashion one experiences his identity as a continuity; and yet with each act, each choice, and each new experience, he becomes a new individual.

For many years Mr. Day was the town drunk. His behavior was well known to everyone for miles around. He lived with his wife and two sons in a dilapidated old house on the edge of a small town. His wife worked as a postal clerk and assumed all the responsibilities for the family. Mr. Day worked occasionally at odd jobs when he was sober; during his drinking sprees, however, he usually became belligerent, disorderly, and destructive, often beating his wife and children. This behavior pattern suddenly changed. Mr. Day turned to religion and decided that he would never drink again, and while he had made such promises before, this time he stuck by them. Before long he got a steady job and eventually became a respected member of the community. This example not only shows how a new act, such as Mr. Day's conversion, completely changes a person's identity, but also that, however radical this change may be, it does not destroy the individual's sense of continuity.

The stability of a person's identity is of great practical importance for his social interaction. It provides others with a set of expectations concerning his behavior under a variety of circumstances, which make it possible for them to play a role relative to him. By the same token, the individual himself derives from his overall identity the possibility of predicting his own behavior. Without a stable sense of who one is, it is difficult for a person to cope with the vicissitudes of daily living; for without a routine response pattern, each event requires a totally new effort of decision-making.

For the convenience of social interaction, an individual's identity is usually characterized by a relatively small number of labels and definitions which indicate certain sets of expectations. He may be labeled as honest, pushy, reliable, shy, rebellious, and so on. The person himself, as well as those around him, finds out what his identity is through the process of his interaction with the environment. In other words, *through his actions the individual creates his identity, learns about it, and makes it known to others, all at the same time.* He finds the limits of his physical strength and endurance when he fells a tree with an axe, climbs a mountain, or armwrestles with an opponent who matches his strength. A grown-up man does not learn about his own strength by wrestling with a six-year-old. He perceives whether he is courageous or cowardly when he is confronted with a dangerous situation.

An interesting consequence of the establishment of a new aspect of one's identity is that it enhances the probability of the recurrence of similar behavior in the future. An extremely attractive opportunity presents itself to a person, and he takes advantage of it in spite of the fact that he knows his action to be harmful to someone else. Through this act he recognizes himself to be an opportunist. Others who have noticed this sequence of events characterize him in the same manner. These recognitions in turn have consequences for the future, because they lead to the anticipation that under similar circumstances he will act in the same way. The expectation itself increases the probability that he will, indeed, behave in this manner, and if he does, it will confirm his identity as an opportunist.[1] *With each decision to deviate from his usual pattern of action, a person creates a new aspect of his identity which henceforth will be a determinant of his behavior.*

After this brief discussion of identity and its importance in social interaction, we will now examine the impact that territoriality has on it, considering separately each of the aspects described in Chapter 2:

Privacy retreat. This part of an individual's territory reflects his identity in a thousand different ways. In the private realm of his secret fantasies and in moments of candid reflection, man learns about the aspects of his identity, which outsiders can only guess, but which no less profoundly affect the course of his life. More concretely, the house in which he lives and the part of his personal history which it presents to him provides an important building block of his identity. He is reminded of that history by the squeaky door, the paint job he did last year that did not come out too well, or the cabinet he built in the kitchen that looks just right. Every detail that makes the house *his* house reflects his history, his special interests, his strengths, and his weaknesses—in short, his identity. Fritz Perls contended that it does not matter where one starts, if one looks carefully enough one will find the essence of the individual mirrored in any part of his world (Perls et al., 1951). There is a considerable degree of truth in this statement; for although all of a man's identity is never revealed at one time, each part of his territory reflects an aspect of himself.

Personal space. Aside from the cultural differences in personal space, readily observable individual variations exist. One person enjoys close physical contact, whereas·another prefers to maintain a safe distance. Such characteristic qualities contribute to the individual's identity and

[1]The impact of expectations and their tendency to become self-fulfilling prophecies have been extensively studied by R. Rosenthal and L. Jacobson (1968). Their work in grade schools, which showed that children will become better students if their teachers are made to anticipate that they are unusually talented, provided an impressive documentation of this fact.

reveal this identity to himself as well as to others in the spectrum of different interpersonal relationships.

Psychological space. This is the most public and the most temporary of man's domains. In the process of maintaining the attention of others and establishing his relative dominance, a person creates as well as learns about this part of his identity. For example, the knowledge that he can hold his own in social gatherings and command the respect of his colleagues earns him the label *self-confident.*

Action territory. Man also learns who he is from the many roles he plays in the context of society. However, his identity is not sufficiently revealed by enumerating his roles, such as boss to his workers, consultant to a firm, father and husband at home, or son to his parents. It is the precise area of functioning he occupies in each of these roles which reveals his identity. To be a father may mean as little as providing 50 per cent of the child's genes, or as much as being the sole carrier of the responsibility for every detail of the child's development into an adult. The individual's identity as a father is reflected in the specific territory he controls relative to his child.

Management. The style in which a person manages his territory, the effectiveness of his management, the degree to which he depends on others for it, the competence with which he handles it, and the willingness with which he shares it all reflect and determine his identity. In the realm of psychological space, for instance, one can attract attention by wearing an unusual hippy garb or by donning an expensive dress from the latest collection of a French couturier. *The purpose as well as the result are very similar for both actions, but the identity established with each is obviously different.*

Defense. Another cornerstone of an individual's identity is provided by the way in which he defends his territory. A person experiences himself as defenseless when he observes that he fails to protect his interests effectively. The strategies and weapons which he uses in his protective struggles also have an impact on his identity. A person who uses flattery and seduction as primary ways of maintaining control is likely to be characterized as coy, sweet, or perhaps as interested in other people. An individual who accomplishes the same objectives by means of a direct, forceful, and outspoken approach is likely to be identified as aggressive or even domineering. *From a territorial perspective the result of each of these actions is the same, but the identity created is greatly affected by the weaponry used.*

Acquisition. A person who finds himself in the process of extending his territory either by the exploration of new realms or the displacement of others creates an identity which earns him such labels as adventuresome, ingenious, creative or ambitious, ruthless, and driven. Again, the manner in which he seeks extension, as well as the direction in which he moves, determines the specific trait that is likely to be assigned to his character.

Psychiatrists and psychologists have long recognized an individual's needs for a strong, well-integrated identity for the effective conduct of his life. However, the tradition of Western thinking has emphasized that the personality and character traits of the individual are intrinsic qualities which dominate his identity. This emphasis has led to the rather pessimistic stance that it is extremely difficult to change human beings. Most psychiatric attempts to do so have used the avenue of psychotherapy: By means of intensive review of his past experiences, the person is led to a new perspective of himself and his environment. Once the importance of territory for identity formation is recognized, it comes as no surprise that such therapeutic intervention reaps but limited benefits, for *as long as the individual's territorial conditions do not change, his identity also remains the same.*

From our point of view, the idea that individual characteristics are primarily intrinsic, part of the individual rather than of his situation, is fallacious. Mounting evidence indicates that a person's behavior changes drastically if his situation changes (Milgram, 1965; Latané and Darley, 1969). For instance, personality characteristics are a far less reliable basis for predicting human behavior than knowledge of the situation in which the behavior takes place. Zimbardo's simulated prison experiment mentioned earlier is a good case in point. All subjects used in the study were chosen because they were judged to be mature, well-adjusted individuals. Their personality profiles gave no indication that their behavior subsequent to becoming either a prisoner or guard would be at all pathological. The fact that, within a couple of days, many of the guards developed cruel behavior while the prisoners became passive, fearful, and anxious provides a dramatic demonstration of the enormous impact of environmental and situational factors on behavior.

It is not our intent to belabor this theoretical dispute, but we do want to underscore a point of practical relevance: *If a person wants to change his identity, he can do so by altering any aspect of his total territory.*

Moving to a new city or a new home makes an impact and so does a drastic change of furnishings in the old house. Changing one's job or one's style of clothing has important consequences, as does the decision to pursue a new goal. A shy person can alter his identity if he seeks training in dealing with a variety of social settings, whereas an extrovert may become a new person by learning and applying the technique of meditation. These possibilities are just as important for child-rearing. A youngster who cannot hold his own with his peers, who avoids fights, and who has become the common target of others' merciless teasing is obviously in the process of building an identity which will include defenselessness and vulnerability. This history is characteristic of many of the withdrawn, severely disturbed individuals who come to psychiatric institutions at a later age. From our discussion it follows that a practical approach to building a more effective identity would be to teach the young person techniques by means of which he can hold his own, including such concrete skills as the art of self-defense.

Once we recognize that by means of an educational approach it is possible to teach an individual the skills needed to manage, defend, and extend his territory, the avenues towards change become clear: *The individual can change his identity in the direction that he chooses by acquiring relevant skills and making appropriate changes in his territory.* This realization puts him in a position to examine the labels which he has accepted for himself and decide which of them he would like to change and how to go about it. However, the myth of intrinsic qualities has great strength, readily illustrated by a commonly held belief that some people are by nature excellent joke-tellers while others are not. This conclusion overlooks the fact that some people are good at telling jokes because they have done it a lot (and continue to do it because they are good at it), whereas others practically never give it a try and consequently don't do it well. This myth must be set aside before an individual who wishes to change will alter his territory and thereby his identity.

SECURITY

Security implies a state of relative invulnerability. It is dependent on a person's capacity to respond adequately to the specific social, environmental, or psychological challenges encountered. Security varies, therefore, with the level of mastery an individual has (or feels he has) in every situation he meets in the course of his lifetime.

The person who feels secure in a situation will enjoy a concurrent sense of well-being, comfort, and relaxation, whereas the man who feels threatened will experience anxiety in proportion to his interpretation of the degree of his vulnerability. Anxiety in its milder forms, together with pleasurable anticipation, may provide a positive feeling of excitement, but in its more severe form it is an extremely unpleasant experience, causing a marked decrease in one's capacity to cope and at its peak leading to panic. *Anxiety occurs when an individual finds himself in a situation in which he wants or needs to act, anticipates unpleasant consequences if he does not, but has insufficient experience, information, or knowledge to behave in a way that will give him control.*

A businessman riding in an airplane thinks he hears a suspect sound in the engines. What is going on? He feels the urge to do something, for if anything goes wrong at 30,000 feet the consequences tend to be rather unpleasant. However, he is totally without information about the situation, and besides, he lacks the skills to deal with it. He has no control, no mastery. He feels his mouth become dry and is aware of the rapid pounding of his heart. He tries to read but cannot concentrate. He glances around with increasing agitation. At this moment he hears the captain's voice over the intercom calmly pointing out that in just a moment the passengers will be able to catch a glimpse of beautiful Mt. Rainier through the windows on the right side of the plane. The anxious passenger sinks back in his seat; comfort is restored, everything is obviously in order.

Anxiety is likely to occur when a person has to undergo an important examination, especially if he is poorly prepared, or when he has to give his first public speech. The young wife who suffers a fallen soufflé at an important dinner party may have her moments of panic, as may the most sophisticated hostess when she discovers that her miniature schnauzers have just vanquished her guest's chinchilla cape.

Mastery over the situation provides the single most potent antidote to anxiety, but mastery itself depends on a variety of factors. The skills acquired through past experiences are of great importance for effective handling of a situation. If one has encountered a specific set of circumstances before—preferably many times—one is likely to have acquired the skills to cope with it with relative ease. The first public lecture might be anxiety-provoking for the speaker; by the time he has a hundred of them behind him, however, he is likely to be quite relaxed. Of equal importance is one's skill in predicting the outcome of events, for mastery ultimately depends on the ability to act in such a way that the outcome becomes predictable as well as favorable. Information and knowledge are essential to foresight and mastery. The more a person knows about the situation the greater the likelihood that he can handle it adequately. If anxiety derives from lack of mastery due to inadequate skills, insufficient information, or inability to predict, then it follows that comfort, the counterpole of anxiety, derives from the security of being in a situation which one knows well, has the skill to handle, and for which one can foresee the outcome with accuracy.

The establishment of territorial boundaries is one way in which both man and animal seek to improve their overall security. The little field mouse knows every inch of the area which he occupies and can quickly hide when threatened. For the human species home ground also provides safety; what is familiar terrain to the defender is likely to be strange geography to the aggressor. The better an individual knows his territory, the greater his managerial skills; and the more adequate his defenses, the more profound will be the security he derives from his territory.

That an individual is more effective in defending himself on his home ground than in a foreign area is apparent in situations as diverse as the Vietnam War or a homecoming football game. The degree to which this tendency holds becomes impressively apparent from a study of the social behavior of psychiatric patients in a state hospital (Esser, 1970). These patients, when engaged in interpersonal conflicts, won on the average of 87.5 per cent of the time if they were on their own territory. Outside of their own area this percentage dropped to 55 per cent.

The importance of territoriality for human security is impressively documented in a comparative study of the crime rates occurring in housing projects whose design either fostered or discouraged territorial definition (Newman, 1972). Even though the areas compared were identical in density and social characteristics of the residents, the study showed crime rates in the housing which lacked adequate territorial marking to be three times as high as those in the housing which provided clear territorial definition. Newman points out that while territorial definition is most easily acquired in single dwellings, it is nevertheless possible, when high density housing is unavoidable, to design structures so as to maximize territorial definition. In doing so a major item is to subdivide the high-density project in such a way that outsiders as well as occupants can readily perceive various portions of the terrain as being under the sphere of influence of a particular group of occupants. It is interesting that such boundaries are not only created by real barriers, but also by symbolic ones. Open gateways, lighting, a short run of steps, planting, changes in texture of the walking surface—all of these can serve as territorial markers. They "serve a common purpose: to inform that one is passing from a space which is public, where one's presence is not questioned, through a barrier to a space which is private and where one's presence requires justification." (p. 63).

A small, well-managed, and easily defended area provides greater security than a vast territory which one has under poor control. A person who feels threatened, therefore, will often respond by limiting the size of his domain. In extreme cases he might literally withdraw himself from all human contact, locking himself in his room, even refusing to come out for meals. Conversely, on the other side of the coin we find that venturing outside one's territory creates anxiety. A history professor who has lectured for years on the Middle Ages goes into the classroom relaxed, for he knows his field thoroughly. One day he is asked to give a lecture on the French Revolution for a colleague who is out of town. This is a different matter altogether. Now he has ventured outside his own territory, not being as familiar with this segment of history. On unfamiliar grounds he experiences a disturbing sense of discomfort as he faces the class.

One's home ground provides security even if the territory is boring or unattractive for other reasons. An attorney who knows everything about copyright law may have lost all interest in this field. Often he thinks about moving on to a new area, criminal law, but he hesitates for he feels comfortable when he deals with the subject he has mastered, even though he dislikes it. *The security an individual feels as long as he stays on his own territory provides a strong force against change.* On the other hand, the boredom and perhaps the dissatisfaction with the area he knows well may spur him on to make a move in spite of the anticipated anxiety, for an individual is seldom satisfied with security alone, but likes his cup of contentment laced with novelty and adventure. He will often brave anxiety, uncertainty, and retaliation for the exhilarating experience of exploring new realms and discovering new worlds, even though such exploration may mean invading the territory of his neighbor.

Man is forever suspended between these two pursuits: the security and comfort of the familiar and the anxiety and the excitement of the new, each exacting a price and each offering a reward.

FREEDOM

The careful exploration of the territorial aspects of one's life yields its ultimate benefit if it results in greater personal freedom. To this end, it is necessary to analyze the relation between territoriality and freedom. *Freedom,* as we use the word, does not mean freedom from the burdens of life; neither does it represent the illogical notion of a man who, unaffected by the laws of the universe, can attain all his whims and wishes. *On the contrary, freedom to us means that man engages in his actions by his own choice, on his own initiative, in the pursuit of his own goals, and with a sense of personal responsibility.* A person who is free in this sense experiences himself as the initiator of his actions, rather than as a victim of forces beyond his control.[2] Most unfree, on the other hand, is a person who experiences himself under the control of some peculiar conspiracy, a condition often encountered in patients of psychiatric hospitals.

A man was admitted for observation at a psychiatric hospital after his wife had petitioned to commit him because of his bizarre behavior. He claimed to be the victim of a strange scientific experiment. Some time ago he had been knocked unconscious, he said, and before he came to, a small electronic gadget was placed in his head, and through this device he was being controlled by a mysterious group of people. The gadget allowed them to read all his thoughts and completely control his behavior. At the height of his psychosis the patient was overwhelmed by fear, for he was sure that he would be killed. Every last remnant of freedom had disappeared for him, as he had no control left, not even over his own private thoughts.

Territoriality plays an important role in creating a sense of freedom. This observation is already implied in the earlier definition of territory as the area in which one exercises initiative and control. Freedom is intimately tied up with the ability to maintain relative control over a territory, to employ the skills to manage it and, perhaps most of all, to defend it. The psychiatric patient who thought he was controlled via the implanted gadget in his brain felt utterly devoid of freedom because he had no defense left. The "enemy" had penetrated into the center of his very thoughts.

The territory which he controls, his home ground, provides the realm in which a person experiences the liberating feeling of freedom, a state readily observable in his behavior, for with freedom comes a very different set of expressions than with the sense of being vulnerable. At home alone

[2]We do not address ourselves to the metaphysical—and rather academic—question whether man's action is ultimately free or caused by sequences of events beyond his control. In the actuality of life such questions are far less important than the immediate sense which each individual has of acting as his own agent or being a victim of outside forces.

in the shower a person may sing at the top of his voice, while in church, where he is expected to sing, he is barely audible. When a man feels that he is on his own territory he speaks with authority, moves with ease, and looks others firmly in the eye. One can easily recognize when a man is outside what he considers his territory by his hesitant gait, the slight quaver in his voice, and his searching eye.

If one wishes to undermine a person's confidence, one can deliberately lure him away from his own territory: meeting in one's own office or home rather than in that of the opponent, leading the conversation to topics with which the opponent is barely acquainted, or playing unusual music and asking the other for his opinion about it. One can serve exotic food that has to be eaten in an unusual way, as with chopsticks or with the fingers. However one goes about it, another's confidence and poise can be effectively whittled away by leading him step by step away from the territory where he feels in control. This technique is frequently used with great effectiveness in court by attorneys who wish to undermine the credibility of an expert witness. Perhaps the expert is a psychiatrist who has given his opinion about the condition of a claimant in a liability case. The attorney proceeds to explore the limits of the area where the psychiatrist is comfortable. Perhaps he will say, "Doctor, as you know, Johnson and Johnson, in their book on head injuries, have said . . . . Do you agree with this?" If the expert witness is unfamiliar with the book, the attorney can readily recognize the uncertainty from the change in the witness's voice, posture, and self-confidence. If the expert makes the mistake of responding as if he is familiar with the book when in fact he is not, he has been lured outside his territory. With subsequent questions the attorney will lead him farther and farther afield in order to gradually undermine his authority. As a result the jury will tend to discredit his testimony, for it, too, will recognize by the behavior of the witness that he has gone beyond the boundaries of his expertise.

Man's final bastion of autonomy and ultimately the most private section of his personal space is his body. His clothing does not only serve to keep him warm, it also protects his physical privacy and, importantly, it helps him conceal his emotional states, which otherwise could be so easily interpreted by his fellow men, for the body readily reveals sexual arousal, embarrassment or fear to the observing eye.

The most radical expression of our freedom can be found in our ability to commit suicide, which constitutes the final control of every man over his existence. Our body itself is the basis of this freedom. When this crucial function of the body as the core territory is breached, the results are most devastating. For instance, rape usurps that ultimate freedom, and understandably is most severely punished by society. A form of rape which is far more common, but left unpunished and even unnoticed under its cover of humanity, frequently happens in hospitals. The Russian Nobel-prize winner, Alexander Solzhenitsyn, in his book *Cancer Ward* (1969, p. 74) vividly describes this kind of rape. A patient, Kostoglotov, an ex-inmate of a concentration camp, has been admitted to the hospital, where the diagnosis of cancer is made. After an initial phase of treatment he feels somewhat better and seeks to be released from the hospital. He is arguing his case with Dontsova, his doctor:

> "What was I trying to do?" He spoke without heat, but emphatically, as Dontsova had. He sat up, his back firm against the back of the chair. "I simply wanted to remind you of my right to dispose of my own life. A man can dispose of his own life, can't he? You agree I have that right?"
>
> Dontsova looked down at his colorless, winding scar and was silent. Kostoglotov developed his point:
>
> "You see, you start from a completely false position. No sooner does a patient come to you than you begin to do all his thinking for him. After that, the thinking's done by your standing orders, your five-minute conferences, your program, your plan and the honor of your medical department. And once again I become a grain of sand, just as I was in the camp. Once again nothing *depends* on me."

To lose the autonomy over one's own body is perhaps the ultimate blow to one's sense of self and one's experience of freedom. This agonizing experience can be alleviated only by complete confidence and trust in the individual to whom one gives his body. This trust is as vital to the sexual relationship between a man and a woman as in the delicate relationship between the doctor and his patient. If this trust does not exist, the defenseless individual has no other recourse than to relinquish his control over the body to the other by taking a detached view of the body as a mechanical thing, an object which is not the real self. Unfortunately, however, it is difficult for a person to regain the true sense of autonomy over his physical existence if he has to give up this territory repeatedly to an invader. Such loss may occur when the body is used as a unit of exchange, as in prostitution, or when a person's most basic physical functions are taken over, as happened in the case of a child whose extremely possessive mother insisted on giving him enemas three times a day.

One of the major health problems of an affluent society is obesity. In many individuals the problem of overeating can be traced to an insufficient development of personal autonomy in respect to the mouth. While growing up the person has learned that his mouth belongs to everyone but himself. It is as if all others, with the parents and relatives leading the way, have staked out the prerogative of filling the "fatty's" stomach. Such an obese individual will never succeed in reducing his weight until he has firmly established control over his oral cavity and is truly able to close his mouth against all alimentary invaders.

Some of the examples given above are extreme cases of loss of autonomy. That a person resents even slight reductions in the control over his own territory is shown in the following rather trivial occurrence. We were standing in line at a newly opened fish-and-chip restaurant. A special promotional sale was in progress: With every order placed a second one was given free, provided one said the magic words, "malt vinegar." The man ahead of us in line had just placed two orders, anticipating that he would get two additional orders at no cost. The salesgirl somewhat teasingly looked at him and said, "Can you say the magic word?" The question obviously made the customer extremely uncomfortable, for he hesitated, turned red, and looked away. After a moment of inner struggle he mumbled the magic word, not knowing what to do with his resentment.

The individual jealously guards his autonomy. Even small, seemingly unimportant incursions into one's territory are deeply resented, if they imply a basic, albeit brief, loss of personal freedom. Inversely, the ability to protect territory and to expand it in new directions constitutes an ultimate source of freedom. Freedom also depends on the accessibility of new terrain, the availability of new avenues, leading in new directions. It thrives on the ability to venture into the unknown in pursuit of the possible. Indeed, this exploration of new territory with the potential of settling down in a new area is as vital a part of man's freedom as the autonomy over the territory he presently calls his own. This fact is most impressively exemplified by those rare moments in life when new vistas suddenly open up. Such moments may occur when the young adult moves away from home to go to college. As his plane takes off he leaves behind all the bonds of the past, and ahead of him lies a totally new realm to be discovered and conquered. Similarly the emigrant to a new country feels overpowered with exhilaration over his freedom, mixed with pangs of anxiety. To a lesser extent such sudden exhilarations may happen at any moment in life. The child who enters a neighborhood park alone senses the adventure which his daily interaction with friends can bring. The tourist on vacation derives much of his enjoyment from the fact that for a brief period of time he plays at leading a new life. The fact that it is play reduces the anxiety and leaves only the excitement of adventure.

Freedom is dependent on the status of man's territorial affairs. To experience freedom an individual must own an adequate amount of territory which is firmly under his control, which he can manage and defend, and which he will share only if he so chooses. He also needs to know that he can seek and find new areas if he wants to move on. To this end his confidence in his abilities to explore new territories is essential. When one sees freedom in this light it becomes self-evident that a clear awareness of the many aspects of human territoriality can only help to enhance one's autonomy. Scrutinizing his territorial management, his system of defense, and especially the desirability of his own territory, can greatly intensify man's autonomy. Knowledge of the weapons used in territorial struggle, the consequences of invading the territories of others, and the availability of new terrain cannot fail but increase his freedom to pursue new possibilities and perhaps reach different, if not greener pastures.

CHAPTER 4

AGGRESSION

The life of wild animals is a struggle for existence.
*Charles Darwin**

Every person needs a territory, a place to live, a field of action, a stage on which to act out the story of his life. Just how much of a territory he needs is an individual matter, depending largely on his own expectations, but certainly no one can do without. Each day scores of new citizens enter the world, born without anything to their name. The major effort of growing up, therefore, centers around the acquisition of a territory and the skills to maintain and defend it. Even the adult with an established territory usually continues a gradual expansion of the area over which he has control. At work he seeks to move up the hierarchical ladder and extend his influence by increasing his skill and expertise. As he earns more money new avenues are opened up that give him greater access to the resources of the community. As he gains more respect he becomes a dominant member of society. In these and many other ways a person's territory continues to grow throughout much of his life.

Competition is inevitable when mature, long-lived individuals continue their territorial expansion, while newborns in unparalleled numbers muscle in to demand a piece of the action. Consequently, it is a fact of the daily practice of life that each man's borders are disputed in one way or another. Even to maintain his territory as it is means he has to exert a steady outward pressure. Human territorial interaction can be viewed as a dynamic balance of forces. If a person reduces the pressure on his borders, his neighbors will automatically expand their area and vice versa. When a vacuum is created in the otherwise tightly organized interpersonal space,

*From "The Origin of Species," *The Darwin Reader.* (Marston Bates and Philip S. Humphrey, Eds.). New York: Charles Scribner's Sons, 1956, p. 107.

someone moves in to fill the gap. If, for instance, the president of a company reduces his direct involvement in the management of the business affairs, the vice-presidents will automatically expand their control. If a new and vigorous person takes over the presidency, he will enlarge his grasp over management, and the area now held by the vice-presidents will simultaneously shrink. *The reality of the human condition shows that throughout the course of man's life territorial competition is inescapably a major, if not dominant aspect of his existence.*

Many people dislike fighting, especially when they equate the word *fighting* with physical violence. Numerous pacifists have accepted great personal discomfort in order to avoid the distasteful duty of having to kill their fellow men. Many more have refused to fight on foreign soil in wars which they could not recognize as defensive. The Christian doctrine of turn the other cheek has provided an idealistic model to millions upon millions; yet the fact remains that no one can avoid the struggle of which physical fighting is only a very small part. Whoever would truly succeed in avoiding all defense of his own territory would end up without any, and in all probability he could be found as an anonymous patient without any remnant of autonomy, without any freedom, mute and noncommunicative in the back wards of a state mental hospital. The territorial struggle is a fact of life, and the better one is prepared for it the more effectively he will be able to hold his own. One can lament about this fact, one can even refuse to accept it and commit suicide, but one cannot live and avoid it. Even Jesus, whose theme was brotherly love, could not do so. He drove the moneychangers out of the temple, which he considered his Father's domain, and he ended on the cross because he seriously threatened the community's rulers. Does this mean that love and brotherhood do not exist? Does it imply that this world is nothing but a scene of dog eat dog, where the strongest and most vicious win? Not at all; it simply means that one cannot live without recognition of this reality of human existence, and that brotherhood and love, compassion and concern have a real chance only if one takes the territorial aspects of life into consideration.

In human affairs the territorial boundaries are continually under stress; borders can move outward or inward, and the pressure on each side can be increased or decreased. For the purposes of this book we label as *aggression any attempt at moving the boundaries outward,* and conversely, *the act of moving the borders inward,* as *regression.* (When conceptualizing an aspect of reality in a different way, one has the choice between inventing a new word with which to label the new concept or using a standard term which comes closest to it and then carefully delineating the precise way in which the term is used. Both choices have disadvantages. New use of old terms often leads to confusion when readers fail to absorb the specific definition; but newly invented terms ordinarily have such an aesthetic as well as communicative drawback that in this case we prefer the risk of sticking with familiar words.)

In a language the meanings of different words are often imprecise and overlapping. In English the terms *aggression* and *hostility* are a good example. Much of the time these two words are used as if they meant basically the same thing. Commonly one labels behavior as aggressive if it involves the use of force and violence, or if it is accompanied by a loud and angry voice. Hostility is equally recognizable by the presence of destructiveness and violence, and probably for this reason both terms are often used interchangeably. This imprecision leads to a double confusion: not distinguishing between hostility and aggression, and being unable to recognize either one unless it appears in an obvious and violent form.

The specific way in which a language labels an event is not just an innocent accident of fate; on the contrary, it largely determines how the individual experiences and judges that event. Confusing aggression with hostility results in the rejection of both as equally undesirable. There is, however, an *aspect of the word* aggression *which indicates active pursuit and exploration rather than destruction. It is this distinction between aggression and hostility which we will emphasize in our own use of these words.* As both terms play an important role in territorial competition, we will define each separately.

In the context of territoriality, *aggression* means *any act which results in the extension of the territory that a person holds.* This extension may be of long duration or just momentary. The latter may be the case, for instance, when the extension involves the invasion of the territory of a good defender who immediately asserts his ownership and retakes the lost ground. In other words, *any behavior* that leads to enlargement—no matter how temporary—of a person's territory can be labeled *aggressive.*[1] In no way does it imply destructiveness, an attribute of hostility which we will discuss later. Defined in this way, aggression is a phenomenon which lies

[1]This definition of aggression comes close to the view George Kelly (1969, pp. 281-288) has expressed: "We can, if we wish, employ a psychology which casts its explanations in terms of what the person himself is doing, not what others do to him or what they think he has done to them. Aggression, in such a psychological system, is more akin to initiative. It is an expression of the audacity of man."

at the root of life itself. Life is dynamic, it moves, it grows and expands beyond narrow boundaries. Aggression does not refer to anything that is either good or bad in itself; it simply is an integral part of the living community of man.

We will use the term *regression to indicate a decrease in the size of a person's territory,* and similarly *any behavior* which actively reduces territorial size we will call *regressive.* This definition should be carefully distinguished from the customary psychiatric use of the term *regressive,* meaning a return to more infantile levels of operating, or less precisely, a reduction in the effectiveness of social functioning. Obviously, there is considerable overlap between the psychiatric usages of the word *regression* and the territorial meaning of it. A reduction in social functioning and a return to childlike behavior usually results in a loss of territory, but this sequence does not always hold. In many instances a person uses childlike behavior to gain territory. Sometimes such behavior functions as a weapon; and although it may seem regressive in the psychiatric sense of the word, in territorial terms it turns out to be aggressive. In other words, *in order to determine whether behavior is aggressive or regressive in a territorial context, one needs to observe who gains and who loses territory and to disregard other apparent qualities of the behavior.* A practical advantage of this approach is that it readily reveals the aggressive purpose of childlike behavior so that it can be distinguished from similar behavior which results from regression, the loss of territory. In any society certain behavior patterns are considered childlike and tend to elicit protective responses. In our culture, weeping, covering the face with the hands, sitting huddled up with face averted, or raising the arms with palms upward are actions which indicate a need for succor or assistance. Tears can indicate the personal loss of someone or something held dear, but tears can also effectively disarm an adversary. Sitting dejectedly, shoulders rounded and head down, may suggest depression or loss of hope, but it may also be a powerful weapon for gaining desired concessions. Extended arms may invite tenderness and compassion, but the stance may be merely a preparation for the barter of one piece of territory for another.

VARIANTS OF AGGRESSION

As we discussed earlier, not all expansion of territory involves invasion of occupied areas. Aggression is an important aspect of being adventuresome, of moving into new areas, experiencing new things; it has to do with the willingness to take risks, to do that which has never been done before. Aggression is going over Niagara Falls in a barrel, sailing from Africa to South America in a papyrus boat, unlocking the molecular structure of DNA, hybridizing a new rose, or writing a song. Aggressiveness, in this sense, gives life its vitality. It is the essence of growth, creativity, and innovation. Looking at aggression from this perspective, one can readily discern the tyranny of the social demand that a woman should not be aggressive. In fact, this seeks to deny to a woman the right to extend her territory beyond the narrow confines of the areas allocated to her by society: the home, childcare, and other such functions. This confinement keeps her from entering the broader public arena of open competition. The linkage of the word *aggression* with hostility, anger, and fighting has helped much in convincing women that behavior which hints of aggression is unfeminine and therefore most unbecoming.

The above is a typical example of a common practice which we call *shouldmanship*. Shouldmanship is the art of decorating all methods of keeping others in their place with moral crepe paper and artificial virtue flowers. Thus statements like "women should not be aggressive," "children should be seen and not heard," and "men should be self-reliant" become ethical directives alluding to an outside higher authority; instead, they actually are the justification one person uses to control the behavior of another. If the victim can be convinced that he is confronted with a legitimate standard of right and wrong, he has lost his ground without a chance for a fair battle, a battle he would have had a chance to fight if he had been faced with the same exhortations expressed in a straightforward manner. In such a case, "women should not be aggressive" may become "I don't want you to express your own opinion about the stock market and politics, or have a better job than I do"; "children should be seen and not heard" might turn into a laconic "Shut up!"; and "men should be self-reliant" could be translated as "Don't come borrowing any money from me, buddy."

Although techniques such as shouldmanship can effectively block certain avenues of change, it is nearly impossible to keep human beings from growth. Women barred from many of the opportunities available to men have exacted a heavy price in the form of special privileges, conquered with highly effective weapons of great subtlety and minimum open forcefulness.

If an individual loses part of his territory or has come upon an insurmountable obstacle that brakes his expansion, he is likely to seek compensatory extension elsewhere. A certain degree of balance between the different types of territory which a person occupies is desirable but not necessary. The actress who holds the attention of millions has a great amount of psychological space, but may need little privacy. A hermit has just the opposite kind of an arrangement. A man who is in the center of action, whether he is a crusader for consumer protection, a radical activist, or a religious leader, may have little interest in personal property. Many a politician has given up material possessions for the power of public office. His obverse is the collector or the miser who seeks property which he can own and control, but who abstains from action in the public arena. No matter which type of territory an individual has as his major ground, if he loses it he will move into new directions. Man is eminently versatile, and if no opportunities are left in the community of man he will create his own in the realm of make-believe. A prisoner in solitary confinement or a chronically ill, bedridden individual may only have his imagination left to him to create a place where he can live. A person who declines to escape into the imaginary has only suicide left as a final way out.

The person who has enough space to live in and enough potential free area to grow into is not likely to invade the territory of others. If, however, an essential part of his territory has fallen away, his territorial balance is upset and one should anticipate that he will seek compensation for the loss elsewhere. In a real sense, a person who has lost some of his territory is a potential menace to the holdings of others, unless, of course, he is in the position of having new, unclaimed frontiers available.

In a family a young teen-age daughter is stricken by a chronic illness which confines her to her bed. She is a sweet, nondemanding person who responds to any offer of assistance with a characteristic, "Oh, you shouldn't do that for me." To get a picture of the impact this girl's illness leaves on the family we will observe more carefully what takes place in the home. We notice, among other things, that the moment any person enters the house he lowers his voice in order not to disturb the girl and aggravate her headache. The meals are all especially planned around her wishes, which are never openly expressed, but are sensed by the mother from the responses of the daughter to the various dishes suggested to her. A major share of the finances of the family is absorbed by the expenses for her medical care. This financial burden has resulted in considerable hardship, and the other children have had to give up their favorite sport, skiing, in order to economize. In the past all of them used to go out on weekend camping trips, but now part of the family stays home in order not to leave the daughter alone. Looking at this situation in a pragmatic way reveals, unavoidably, that the girl, in spite of her sweetness, occupies a tremendous territory and that *all members of the family have lost areas which were previously theirs.* The expansion of the girl's psychological space is in turn the result of her own tremendous loss of action territory due to the illness. In other words, her initial regression was followed by aggression in new directions.

This brief discussion does not imply a moral judgment of what happened. Whether or not the girl is a good or a bad person is an entirely separate question which does not depend on her territorial aggression and which does not concern us here. What should be clear, however, is that she expanded her territory at the expense of those around her, and that she did so with a sweet and helpless smile as weapons, against which the others found themselves defenseless. One of the reasons the family members were defenseless was that the absence of violence and of an obvious fight failed to alert them to the fact that they were losing ground. Of equal importance, their obligation to feel sorry for their unfortunate sister and daughter made it difficult to recognize clearly that each of them had lost some precious territory as a result of her illness. This observation exemplifies once more the principle which it is essential to understand if one wants to throw light on a territorial conflict. *Whether or not territorial aggression has taken place is not determined by the loudness of the battle noise, the obviousness of the weaponry, the content of the words that are exchanged, or the type of territory under dispute. The ultimate criterion for territorial aggression is whether one person's territory has expanded while someone else's has been reduced.*

RECOGNIZING AGGRESSION

The recognition of changes in territorial boundaries is not a mere intellectual game. On the contrary, it has practical consequences which become easily apparent in specific interpersonal situations. A common occurrence in American middle-class families provides an illustration. An eight-year-old boy has been given a trumpet by his parents and is provided with a teacher. This boon came as a special gift after the child had repeatedly pleaded for the opportunity. At first everything goes well, but after half a year of lessons the boy becomes less conscientious about his practicing. Now the parents move in, suggesting with ever-greater insistence that he work harder at it. As this form of encouragement has opposite effects if any, they eventually demand that he practice his lessons every day at a specific time. In spite of this new strategy, the situation continues to deteriorate, and at the end of the second year they reluctantly give their boy permission to stop playing the trumpet altogether. This situation is common, and can be analyzed in a variety of ways. From a territorial perspective, however, the interaction between parents and child appears as follows:

Act I: Aggression by the child. The boy sought to expand his territory by learning to play the trumpet, undoubtedly having fantasies about the area which would open up to him as he became a good musician. This aggressive move did not encroach on anyone else's territory as it entailed a free area. Thus he acquired the privilege of playing the trumpet, but obviously needed training to gain the skills to handle this new area effectively. The parents did not interfere with this process as long as their son was making steady progress. They were, however, looking on from the sidelines, for no sooner did the boy show signs of failing to handle this part of his life than they moved in to take over.

Act II: Aggression by the parents. The first intrusion into the child's territory took the form of letting him know that he was not totally autonomous in the area of trumpet playing: he was free to play and practice, but not free not to practice. After all, the parents were paying the bill. Herein lies the conflict. The child thought that the trumpet was his territory for it was given to him, while the parents felt that they had the right to control his practicing as long as they paid for it. One could easily make a case for either position, but taking sides does not alter the fact that the child experienced a loss of territory. *Justifications for one's actions are only of secondary importance in the arena of human conflict.* If we understand these territorial implications, we should not be surprised that the boy's motivation to work disappeared completely, for the territory was no longer his and working it must have felt about as attractive as carrying out the garbage from his mother's kitchen.

Act III: Response to the territorial invasion. Whenever an individual experiences a loss of territory, a response of some kind must be anticipated. In our example this response took the form of protracted conflict in which the parents eventually lost out. The son succeeded in being allowed to drop his trumpet lessons, thus regaining control over the time which otherwise he had to spend on forced practicing. Unfortunately, in the process he lost access to the whole area of trumpet playing. Not infrequently the losses increase for both parties when the conflict escalates into moves and countermoves that take in more and more different areas. Starting with the assumption that initially both parents and child had the same objective—for the son to learn to play the trumpet—one must ask whether the territorial analysis of the situation leads to suggestions of how this goal could have been reached. There are indeed a number of ways in which the young man could have been encouraged to play the trumpet, but taking over his territory certainly was not one of them; children respond to such take-over no more positively than do adults.

Several alternate strategies for dealing with this type of situation suggest themselves. The first and most obvious recommendation which follows from our discussion is that the parents stay out of the child's territory *once they have given it to him.*

A more promising approach to the problem would be to enhance the value and importance of the territory to the child, which could be done by showing an interest in trumpet music, providing a model through playing an instrument oneself, extending the function of the son's playing by facilitating participation in a group, and so on. An intriguing method of teaching, which is consistent with our observations, has been developed by Shinichi Suzuki (1969, p. 107). To stimulate a child's talent in playing the violin he begins with a very clever way of making the instrument important and desirable to the child. He starts with the parents rather than the child:

> Although we accept infants, at first we do not have them play the violin. First we teach the mother to play one piece so that she will be a good teacher at home. Children are really educated in the home, so in order that the child will have good posture and practice properly at home, it is necessary for the parent to have firsthand experience. . . . Until the parent can play one piece, the child does not play at all. This principle is very important indeed, because although the parent may want him to do so, a three- or four-year-old child has no desire to learn the violin. The idea is to get the child to say, "I want to play too"; . . . The mother, moreover, both at home and in the classroom, plays on a small violin more suited to the child. The child will naturally before long take the violin away from his mother, thinking, "I want to play too." He knows the tune already. The other children are having fun; he wants to join in the fun. We have caused him to acquire this desire.

Simultaneously, the family is encouraged to play frequently and to show interest in good music. It is clear that this method raises the value of the territory to a maximum level. In all probability similar conditions prevailed in the homes of great musicians, for many of them had parents who were musicians also.

It is not our intent to exhaust the subject of how children can be encouraged to learn. However, the example hopefully suffices to underscore that analysis of the territorial situation can generate ideas for dealing with practical problems.

To summarize the discussion of this chapter, we would like to emphasize that aggression—that is, a behavior directed at territorial expansion—is an unavoidable part of human interaction. In situations of conflict or interpersonal difficulties of any sort, the question must be asked whether any territory has changed hands. Such analyzing will help one recognize aggression even if it takes place without any apparent violence and will alert one to the probability of a counterthrust from the loser, who will seek ways to reestablish his territorial equilibrium.

CHAPTER 5

RESPONSES TO AGGRESSION: ASSERTIVENESS AND HOSTILITY

When firmness is sufficient, rashness is unnecessary.

*Napoleon**

Aggression unavoidably leads to a reaction on the part of the individual whose territory has been invaded. Although a wide variety of specific responses is possible, they can be grouped into two easily recognizable categories: assertiveness and hostility.

ASSERTIVENESS

We consider a response to be assertive when it is direct, and specific to the area under attack. The purpose of the response must be to retain or regain control over a disputed area and effectively to rebuff the aggressor. The forms which the assertive reaction take vary widely, depending on the situation and the defender's preferred style. A small girl stands at the edge of her lawn and tells a neighbor boy to go home and never come back. In a crowded bus a man with a pained expression on his face tips his hat to a lady standing next to him and politely asks her to get off his foot. A student ceases whispering to his classmate when he catches a stern glance from his teacher. A crotchety old man threatens some youngsters with a gun when they cut across his garden. A toddler bites his sister when she tries to take his teddy bear. No matter what specific form it takes, the assertive re-

*From *Forty Thousand Quotations* (Compiled by Charles Noel Douglas). New York: Halcyon House, 1917, p. 732 A.

sponse makes it clear to the aggressor that he has invaded occupied territory, and it also tells him unequivocally to remove himself forthwith from the premises.

As aggression can take a myriad of subtle forms, each individual's ability to be assertive is tested in many different ways. During a visit to an exhibition of the paintings of a well-known and respected artist, Mr. Surrey comes to a large canvas which is supposed to be the most outstanding work in the collection. He studies the painting carefully for some time, but after due consideration he finds that it does not really move him. As he is about to go on to the next item in the room, his companion takes him by the arm and, directing his attention to the same painting, says, "This is supposed to be one of the finest examples of the artist's later period. I really do like it. I think it's one of the truly great works of art, don't you?" This statement-question brings direct pressure to bear on Mr. Surrey's independence of judgment. The force of public opinion, combined with his friend's support of it, can lead to his giving up his own views and bowing to those of others. If he acts in an assertive fashion, he may carefully look at the painting again to determine whether he might have missed something, but if he still doesn't like it, he may say, "I know that this is supposed to be a great work of art, but personally I don't care much for it." If he would fail to assert himself fully he might respond with a half-hearted, "I guess you are probably right," or "Well, I don't know much about art." Perhaps he would react with total surrender, yielding to the pressure with, "Yes, I think you are right; it's a beautiful painting."

A zoology professor, lecturing on the social interactions of a certain species of birds, found herself confronted with a restless group of students. It was only the second session of the academic year, and neither teacher nor students knew each other as yet. A couple of students in the back of the room paid no attention to her at all and kept up a steady, quite audible conversation. Several others repeatedly interrupted the continuity of the discourse by rudely asking irrelevant questions. At this point the teacher stopped her lecture, looked with a steady gaze at the culprits, and told them to hold their questions until after she had finished, and advised the talkers in the back row either to pay attention or continue their conversation elsewhere. The area under dispute was the psychological space of the classroom, which is traditionally the territory of the teacher. Students are uncannily adept at recognizing a teacher's ability to maintain control over this space. In the above instance, the students realized that the teacher had every intention of holding her ground and therefore order was reestablished.

The assertive stance is an act of independence whereby the person maintains control over all parts of his territory, whether it be the right to judge a painting, the attention of a class he is lecturing to, the privacy of his thoughts, or his prerogatives at work.

Assertiveness does not imply that a major confrontation has to result from each territorial invasion, no matter how minor. In fact, it has been observed among animals that an assertive stance prevents actual fighting. In dogs, for instance, standing firm instead of running or submission has a 65 percent chance to stop or avoid an aggressive attack (Zing, 1960). The situation is similar for human beings. Ordinarily the assertive person gives a warning when his territory is invaded. This first warning is usually a gentle one. It does not by itself threaten friendly, comfortable social relations. Frequently one resorts to humor to give a gentle warning. "Oh, oh, that's a no-no," said with a smile, can be sufficient; or, "You must be kidding"; or, "My goodness, she's doing it again"; or, "Yah, boss!" said to a person who, inappropriately, has assumed a superior attitude.

The essence of the gentle warning is that it assumes that the other's invasion was without ill intent, that it happened more or less by accident. This gives the aggressor an opportunity to retreat graciously without losing face. If this warning is not recognized, or heeded, the assertive individual will follow it up with a firm warning, which addresses itself directly to the issue without the pleasantness of humor and, for the moment at least, interrupts the smoothness of the social relationship. In essence it says, "You're on my territory; I would appreciate your leaving without delay," to which the other is supposed to respond with, "Excuse me, I did not realize that I had crossed your boundaries. I will withdraw immediately. No offense." Such a response clears the air and the situation finds a new balance. However, if the aggressor does not give up his position and the defender does not wish to give ground, the battle can no longer be avoided and is bound to be waged with whichever arms the opponents prefer.

A person who has the reputation of being assertive usually finds it sufficient to give a gentle warning. Only rarely does he have to give a firm response and this usually only with those who do not know him.[1] After all, the others anticipate that a tough battle will follow if they press the issue. *The paradoxical result is that assertive individuals enjoy longer periods of*

---

[1] A. H. Esser and his colleagues observed that "recently admitted patients tend to fight more frequently than the older inhabitants of the ward." This supports the idea that actual fighting is prevented when individuals know what to expect from one another (Esser et al., 1965, pp. 37-44).

peace in their lifetime than the people who are less effective in their territorial defense.

Assertiveness must not be confused with defensiveness. The assertive person does not live in constant expectation of attack, but rather answers a specific aggression with a specific defense. He does not overdefend his territory, and he relies primarily on his warnings to keep out potential intruders. Assertiveness is based on a feeling of adequacy and strength. The defensive person, on the other hand, operates from a position of weakness. He is unsure of his borders, or of his ability to defend them. As a consequence, he cannot convey self-assurance to others. His sense of inadequacy causes him to respond to even the smallest incursion with a massive counterattack. To the defensive person, any attack is life-threatening and therefore it must be repulsed at all costs. Defensiveness is particularly prone to occur when one doubts the legitimacy of his own claims to a territory.

Many examples of this principle are found in the entertainment business. To be a star entails the ability to hold an inordinate amount of psychological space. Because of its nature, psychological space is the most difficult territory to maintain. Entertainers, therefore, are often very defensive and given to dramatic displays seemingly far in excess of provocations suffered. Such overdefensiveness also holds true for other occupations in which the holding of psychological space is very important. Politicians and teachers need a lion's share of the available attention if they are to be successful. Here, too, however, an overreaction to aggression conveys a lack of self-assurance and implies uncertainty about one's own claims to the area in dispute. Thus, the teacher who overreacts to interruptions or infractions of the rules will appear defensive instead of assertive to the students, inviting repeated skirmishes over the territory in question.

The response to aggression is not always immediate. A delayed reaction is common, especially when the aggressor has made a sudden and unexpected move. A woman who has a reputation of civic-mindedness is told by an acquaintance, "I have volunteered you for membership in a citizen's committee for the Community Mental Health Center. I just knew you would be glad to do it, and you are absolutely just the right person for it. I am sure you will accept the position, won't you?" The first response to this unexpected foray, especially camouflaged as it is by flattery, might be a hesitant, "Oh, sure, certainly I am willing to do it." Later in the day, however, the lady becomes aware of a minor degree of irritation, and suddenly it dawns on her that by volunteering her services her acquaintance took away some of her autonomy, her personal control over her own life and over her own time. After a brief consideration an assertive countermove is planned and carried out. She calls up the acquaintance who was so generous with her time, and a conversation ensues in which is incorporated the following key sentence: "I'm sorry, I do appreciate your nominating me, but after careful review of my time commitments I realize that I won't be able to assume this new obligation."

The longer the delay between the aggression and the response, the less effective and, by the same token, the less assertive it turns out to be. Al, a trumpet player, told the story how one evening he was playing in a band when he noticed that George, the saxophone player, was a bit off-key. Before the next number started, he suggested to George that he tune his sax up a quarter tone. George did not say anything at the time, but after the performance he quit the band. About two years later Al was playing for a dance in a private club when he was approached by George, who told him with considerable malice that he was off key and suggested to him that he tune his trumpet up a quarter tone. Obviously, this response is hardly an example of assertiveness; in fact, it comes very close to the response which we will discuss next, hostility.

HOSTILITY

The term *hostility*, as it is used in the present context, can be defined as *behavior which seeks to destroy or injure an individual or his territory.* Defined in this manner, hostility is clearly separated from aggression, for the latter seeks the conquest of new territory and not destruction for its own sake. By the use of the word *seeks* we do not mean to imply that it is the actor's intentions which ultimately determine the distinction between hostility and aggression; as we have emphasized in discussing territorial concepts, we are concerned with what actually happens and not with suppositions about intention. If a distinction is to be made on the basis of what people say about their intentions, one is in real trouble, for human beings are masters of deceiving themselves as well as others. We want to reemphasize our position, therefore, that the *judgment as to whether any behavior seeks to destroy, on the one hand, or acquire new territory, on the other, must be made on the basis of the observed behavior and its consequences.* Using this measuring rod, it is rather easy to recognize whether one is confronted with hostility or aggression in any specific situation. It is vital to make this differentiation in order to deal effectively with such behavior.

A further clarification of the term *hostility* can be made by comparing it with assertiveness. In our observations on interactions between individuals, it became apparent that there is a mutually exclusive quality in hostility and assertiveness. We can formulate the following hypothesis: When an individual fails to react to territorial loss with an assertive response, he will resort to hostility.[2] A warning is implied—*beware of the individual who does not stand his ground.* On the other hand, *if a person does not leave his opponent any avenue of defense, he should expect destructiveness in return.*

The question arises as to whether there are no other possible responses to aggression besides assertiveness or hostility. There are, indeed, alternatives, but all of them are, in essence, subtle or disguised means of regaining or substituting for the lost area. Our thesis is that if a person loses territory which he wishes to keep and if he uses no avenue of effective defense, hostility is all but unavoidable.[3] There is plenty of anecdotal support for this hypothesis, and also our experience has upheld the practical value of it. A brief example may clarify the point.

John, a student in one of our courses, told of his strong antipathy for his neighbor, Joe. This dislike stemmed from the fact that this neighbor had a habit of taking his garden clippings and depositing them on a corner of our student's back yard. Even though John resented this intrusion, he never countered the invasion directly. We wondered, therefore, whether he

[2]This hypothesis finds support in Maslow's studies (1968, p. 158) of successful or, as he puts it, "self-actualized people." One of the characteristics of this group of individuals is "the decrease of hostility, cruelty and destructiveness (although decisiveness, justified anger and indignation, self-affirmation, etc., may very well increase)."

[3]Vance Packard draws an interesting parallel to loss of territory when he describes loss of social position in his book *The Status Seekers* (1959, p. 295): "The person standing still in a culture that glorifies upward progress often suffers hurts. The greater menace to society, however, is the person moving downward. Any society that has a good deal of upward circulation is bound to have some downward circulation, too. We can't all stay at the high level our elders or we ourselves achieve. The person being declassed is, as previously indicated, almost invariably in an ugly mood. He is seething with humiliation and apprehension. If society has not developed a mechanism for quickly and gently helping him find a new, more humble niche, then he becomes a bigot, a searcher for scapegoats, and an eager recruit for almost any demagogue who promises to set up a completely new social order."

launched any counterattacks to compensate for this obvious loss of territory, and it turned out that he had, on several occasions. When the opportunity presented itself during neighborhood parties, John attacked Joe, who was absent, by making some sharp, denigrating remarks about him to Joe's bridge partners. Gossip often serves the purpose of an indirect, hostile counterattack, our student's behavior being a good example. As is always the case with hostility, John's behavior was directed at causing the opponent harm, not at regaining the coveted territory. We discussed this fact with our student, and once he recognized the impracticality of his attacks, he resolved to design a more effective defense. A week later he returned with a story of the results. One late afternoon he had observed his neighbor working in his back yard and anticipated that soon the clippings would arrive. He decided to wait it out and, indeed, not too much later Joe approached with a wheelbarrow full of grass, ready to deposit it on the usual spot. This time, before his neighbor had an opportunity to dump the contents of his wheelbarrow, John told him that he would appreciate it if he would dispose of the material somewhere else. Joe responded with surprise, claiming that it was his understanding that this particular corner, which wasn't well marked, was his property. A more extensive discussion followed, which resulted in a clear delineation of the boundary and an apology from the neighbor. Both parted amicably.

To his surprise, John also observed a peculiar kind of "fallout" from this satisfactory solution to the problem. He no longer felt hatred or resentment toward his neighbor, and when a suitable occasion offered itself he also had no urge to tear him down by means of vicious gossip. This result is consistent with the notion that assertive behavior is a direct antidote to a hostile attitude. The overriding principle is that hostility derives from a position of weakness, not of strength. Rather than being a form of aggression, it is quite the opposite of it. *Hostility is retaliatory in nature.*

Consider for a moment a football game which has gained extraordinary importance for some of the players because their personal career potential is tied up with its outcome. At the point where the game seems almost certainly lost one should anticipate a possible change in the conduct of those members of the losing team who have the most at stake. These players may shift from fighting hard to win to attempting to injure the opponents. One can observe a rapid increase of penalties called by the referee for illegal actions that endanger the safety of the players. The participants themselves may recognize a shift from the usual joy of playing to a bitter resentment toward their adversaries.

A more striking example of hostility engendered by a position of complete helplessness is seen in Lagerkvist's novel *The Dwarf* (1945, pp. 43-46). The dwarf, who serves as a jester at an Italian Court during the time of the Renaissance, has been taken to the studio of a famous painter, Maestro Bernardo, to have a study made of him:

O shame! O dishonor! Never have I endured such degradation as that which was inflicted on me that terrible day. I shall try to write down what happened, though I would rather not remind myself of it.

The Prince had commanded me to seek out Maestro Bernardo who was working in the refectory at Santa Croce, saying he had need of me. I went there, though I was annoyed at being treated as though I were the servant of this haughty man who is no concern of mine. He received me in the friendliest fashion and said that he had always been greatly interested in dwarfs. I wondered: "What has not interested this man who wants to know all about Francesco's intestines and the stars of heaven? But," I continued to myself, "he knows nothing of me, the dwarf." After further amiable empty words he said that he wished to make a picture of me. At first I thought he meant my portrait, which the Prince perchance had bespoken, and I could not help feeling flattered. Nevertheless I replied that I did not wish to have my likeness reproduced. "Why not?" he asked. I answered, as was only natural. "I wish to possess my own face." He thought this strange, smiled somewhat, but then admitted that there was something in what I said. But, even when unreproduced, one's face is the property of many, in fact of all who look upon it. And here it was a question of a drawing of me which should show my shape, and therefore I must take off my clothes so that he could make a sketch of my body. I felt myself grow livid with wrath or fear (I know not which prevailed), and they both shook me so that I trembled all over.

He noted the violent agitation which his outrageousness aroused in me and began to say that there was no shame in being a dwarf and showing it. He always felt the same deep reverence for nature, even when its caprice created something out of the ordinary. There is never any disgrace in showing oneself as one is to another person, and nobody really possesses himself.

"But I do," I cried, beside myself with passion. "You don't possess yourselves, but I do!"

He listened to my outburst with perfect calm, he even observed it with a curious interest which agitated me still more. Then he said that he must begin —and drew nearer to me. "I can't bear any offense against my body!" I shrieked wildly, but he took not the slightest notice, and when he realized that I would never strip of my own free will, he prepared to undress me himself. I managed to jerk my dagger from its sheath and he seemed very surprised to see it gleaming in my hand. He took it away from me and laid it carefully down a little distance away. "I believe you are dangerous," he said, looking thoughtfully at me. I felt myself sneer at this remark. Then, placid as ever, he began to take off my clothes and exposed my body most shamelessly. I resisted desperately, fought with him as for my life, but all in vain, for he was stronger than I. When he had completed his vile task he lifted me onto a scaffold in the middle of the room.

I stood there defenseless, naked, incapable of action, though I was foaming with rage. And he stood some distance away from me, quite unmoved, and examined me, scrutinizing my shame with a cold and merciless gaze. I was utterly exposed to that outrageous gaze which explored and assimilated me *as though I were his property*. Having to stand like that and submit to somebody else's scrutiny was such a degradation that I still burn with shame to think that I ever was forced to endure it. . . .

I have never hated the human race so much as during that ghastly hour. *My hatred was so alive* that I almost thought I should lose consciousness, everything went black before my eyes. Is there anything more vile than these beings, anything more detestable? [Emphasis added.]

The above story illustrates how the rage and the hatred is directly proportional to the powerlessness of the dwarf. Interestingly enough, Edgar Allan Poe wrote a short story, "Hop Frog" (Poe, 1956), also based on the theme of destructive hostility aroused in a powerless dwarf-jester in a king's court. After a particularly humiliating event the dwarf conceived of a plan to destroy the king and his seven ministers. The story details this plan and its final enactment during which the king and his courtiers are burned to death.

Other dramatic examples of hostile responses by individuals who have inadvertently been rendered powerless can be taken from both fact and fiction. President Kennedy, symbolizing the strength of the American nation, was assassinated by a man who had not been able to find a place in American society. The destruction of Othello through the far more subtle, but no less hostile acts of Iago portrays a parallel situation. Shakespeare describes how Iago, deeply resentful over the fact that Othello did not make him a field commander, a position he believed he deserved although he was unable to protect what he considered his right, set out to destroy his master. In this case, the hostile act was carried out without a trace of violence on Iago's part. He played on Othello's particular weakness, jealousy, to destroy him completely. Both examples show how the aggressive individual may take territory from the defenseless without realizing it, but the response is nevertheless forthcoming.

VIOLENCE

The observation that Othello was the victim of Iago's hostility (Desdemona in this case was not the object of Iago's destructiveness, but only a tragic pawn in his hostile ploy) in spite of the fact that Iago accomplished his aim while committing no violent act himself, draws attention to the necessity of carefully distinguishing between the terms *violence, hostility, assertiveness,* and *aggression.* In daily as well as in scientific language these words are often used interchangeably. Specifically defined, violence indicates an explosive use of force, an attempt to damage or harm with the use of destructive weaponry. It refers to a particular way in which a territorially relevant action is carried out. In other words, violence is just one of the means by which an act of aggression, hostility, or assertiveness may be accomplished. Although violence is often used in actions which are either aggressive, assertive, or hostile, it is not a necessary component of any of them. Hostility, aggression, and assertiveness can be carried out in many ways, and numerous examples of all three illustrate how they have been perpetuated with calmness or even gentleness.

ANGER

There remains one final term, *anger,* which may create confusion concerning our notion of hostility. The word *anger,* and its milder form *irritation,* refers to a person's emotional state. Both words indicate a complex set of feelings which are prone to occur when an individual is ready to fight or at least when he would like to fight. Anger is not a behavior. It is a feeling which may or may not accompany certain behavior patterns. Anger is therefore very similar to words such as *rage, anxiety, tranquility, joy,* or *pleasure.* A person may feel angry or even appear angry without this in itself being a characterization of territorial behavior. One can feel angry while one behaves in an assertive, an aggressive, or a hostile fashion, but one can also behave in all of these ways without experiencing a feeling of anger. One can be extremely hostile and destructive while feeling and appearing at the same time very calm and without anger. This is convincingly described in Truman Capote's book *In Cold Blood* (1966).

To summarize the distinctions which we have made and which are relevant to aggression, assertiveness, and hostility, we can say that all three of these terms refer to actual territorial behavior. Violence, on the other hand, indicates only one of the possible ways in which any of these territorial purposes can be pursued, whereas anger is only one of the many feelings which one can experience in the course of such actions.

Hostility and aggression are not directed exclusively toward people or objects, but also toward the realm of ideas. An aggressive approach to ideas involves exploration, a search for truth, and the expansion of knowledge. It is recognized by open-mindedness, as well as by the pleasure which the individual derives from advancing into new realms. The aggressive person is open to, and eager for, that which is new. The hostile approach to ideas, on the other hand, is a destructive one. It seeks to distort or disprove anything that is contrary to the preconceived notions that the individual has held. It is prone to occur when the individual's identity is maintained by rigid and dogmatic concepts which, by their very nature, are hard to defend or whose security is dependent on a certain social, political, or intellectual system. It is not surprising, therefore, that anything that challenges such notions is likely to evoke a hostile response. The late psychologist George Kelly was the first to draw attention to this hostile approach to reality (Kelly, 1969). He did so by comparing it with the behavior of Procrustes, a mythological figure from Greek antiquity. Procrustes was a man who, as Kelly describes him, offered shelter to the weary travelers passing through the region where he lived. He treated his guests well, offering them food and hospitality. When it was time to retire, he would show the guest to a room containing a bed where he could sleep in comfort, or so it seemed. Procrustes had one peculiarity. After the guest had fallen asleep, Procrustes would return to the room and "adjust" the guest to the bed. If the guest was too long for the bed Procrustes felt obliged to cut off his feet; and he stretched him to the appropriate size if he was too short. The hostile approach to ideas is like that of Procrustes to his guests. It adjusts reality to one's preconceived notions rather than accepting and absorbing facts as they appear.

Aggression, assertiveness, and hostility refer to different sets of behaviors. An individual may display each of these types of actions at one time or another. However, in the course of his life a person tends to acquire a certain style, or what psychologists call a certain response disposition, a tendency to respond one way rather than another.

The predilection, however, of one form of behavior over another is readily concretized in the language. For instance, one often hears such statements as: "Bill is an extremely aggressive person," or "Janine is a very hostile woman." Such statements are condensations of more complete sentences. Saying that Janine is a hostile woman really means that Janine is a person, who, up until now has engaged in a lot of behavior which can be characterized as hostile. The condensation of the sentence, although serving a practical purpose, unfortunately also leads to serious confusion, for hostility is not a personality trait of the individual but rather an aspect of his behavior.

The implication of equating behavior preference and personality type is that in order to rid Janine of her hostility she has to change her personality completely. As a matter of fact, Janine is continually given to know that her hostility is a serious defect. Others admonish her, "Don't be so hostile—just think positive thoughts, and try to be sweeter and kinder." Unfortunately, being kind and sweet are feelings that are incompatible with the resentment Janine experiences at being continually harassed by the aggressions of others, especially since Janine sees herself as helpless or inadequate in the face of such attacks.

Hostility, resentment, and destructive impulses are frequent targets for psychiatric intervention. Commonly, the approach to such problems is to provide insight into the infantile roots of these feelings and to help the patient recognize their inappropriateness in his present life context. Our observations on territoriality lead to a more direct approach to the reduction of hostility. Hostility is the result of a person's inability to defend his territory. *Hostility, therefore, is eliminated when the individual learns to counter specific territorial invasions with an immediate assertive response.* No amount of contemplation, insight, or understanding can undo the individual's resentment when he has failed to defend the territories that are important to him. The person who wishes to reduce his hostility level needs to learn assertive skills, and he must either seek out a coach or start practice on his own to improve those skills, just as a person wishing to speak French needs to find a teacher and learn the language. To spend his time in search of insight into his reasons for not learning French before seems rather inefficient. The contemplation of past reasons for present behavior is interesting—at times even fascinating—but it is hardly a promising approach to behavior change.

Janine's hostile behavior, then, will lessen and her angry feelings subside only when she has learned to use an alternate set of behaviors. If, for instance, she were taught to turn back aggressive incursions into her territory with direct assertive responses, she would no longer perceive herself to be inadequate and defenseless; thus, not only would her hostile behavior automatically fall away, but also the feelings of rage that result from the inability to maintain territorial integrity.

Each act of aggression evokes a reaction from the individual who stands to lose. This response can take several forms. The most effective reaction—assertiveness—confronts the aggressor directly in an attempt to protect or regain the area under attack. Sometimes this response can be delayed, but long postponement reduces its effectiveness. The less a person is able to defend his territory, the more likely he is to respond with an attempt to destroy his opponent and the opponent's territory rather than to reconquer a specific terrain.

CHAPTER 6

SHARING TERRITORY
WITH OTHERS

Try to have a secret with him. Something that, in the whole world only you and he know of. You will be feeling, then, that he is you and you are he.

Isak Dinesen*

Man is a social animal and sharing is, if not innate, at least so thoroughly ingrained in his behavior pattern that he views the hermit as a curious phenomenon to be either ridiculed, institutionalized, or deified. Although human beings have a strong need to maintain their privacy, their desire to form alliances with their fellows is even greater. This tendency has important, practical benefits, for it allows the individual to increase the size of his territory through cooperative venture, to ease its maintenance through joint management, and to relax in the security that springs from common defense. In fact, it could be argued that the individual can only emerge in relative independence because of the security provided by the group to which he belongs. When the community is safe, the individual can be born.

The word *sharing,* like so many terms with important, positive connotations, has a wide range of usage. It may refer on the one side of the spectrum to the casual show-and-tell practices encouraged by primary-school teachers and which might be more precisely denoted by the term "to display." On the other side of the spectrum it stands for the profoundly meaningful exchange between two people in an act of complete trust which may alter the course of each of their individual lives. In our territorial context we will use the term *sharing* to indicate *the acquisition, management, and defense of a common territory by two or more individuals.*

**From *Ehrengard.* New York: Random House, 1962, p. 41.*

For simplicity's sake we will label such shared territory with the term *co-territory.*

Some important practical differences prevail between a regular territory and co-territory. To begin with, sharing a territory demands that an individual subordinate some aspects of his behavior to the dictates of the group with which he shares. Sole ownership carries with it the privilege of using the area in a manner of one's own choosing. Co-territory extends the same benefits to the co-owners, but does so in a more restricted fashion. The lone wolf who lives in his own house by himself can do whatever strikes his fancy—throw darts at the paintings, carve his name in the furniture, or tear the place down if he wishes to follow such an impulse. The member of an exclusive club, although privileged to use its facilities, has to restrain himself from such unusual inclinations and keep within the limits of behavior deemed proper by the membership.

The very presence of restrictions on certain behavior relative to any particular territory should alert the individual to the fact that he does not have exclusive ownership over that particular area and that it is shared with others. *When a person feels that he needs approval for certain actions within a given territory, or if his approval is sought by someone else, the territory is a co-territory.* This observation, although seemingly obvious, is nevertheless of practical importance, for it can facilitate the sorting out of many interpersonal difficulties. If, for instance, a woman's actions evoke her husband's anger, she must first check whether her actions involve a co-territory, and if so, whether they are a transgression against the agreed-upon limitations. When an individual observes approval-seeking behavior in himself, he similarly needs to ask whether it is indeed true that the other person has a legitimate claim to co-ownership over the territory involved. If the claim is not legitimate, then he is making an important mistake in seeking approval, for in doing so he extends co-ownership to the other. If one wishes to share, approval-seeking is, of course, logical, but frequently an individual inadvertently gives away that which he does not intend to, an act that is likely to lead to conflict at a later time.

Seeking advice has serious ramifications, as it implies an invitation to share territory. At times the invitation becomes a teasing game with a hidden agenda. Eric Berne (1964, pp. 116-117) describes this game as "Why Don't You—Yes But."

> White: "My husband always insists on doing our own repairs, and he never builds anything right."

Black: "Why doesn't he take a course in carpentry?"

White: "Yes, but he doesn't have time." ...

Red: "Why don't you have your building done by a carpenter?"

White: "Yes, but that would cost too much." ...

· · ·

YDYB can be played by any number. The agent presents a problem. The others start to present solutions, each beginning with "Why don't you . . .?" To each of these White objects with a "Yes, but . . . ." A good player can stand off the others indefinitely until they all give up, whereupon White wins. In many situations she might have to handle a dozen or more solutions to engineer the crestfallen silence which signifies her victory . . . .

Territorially speaking, White is asking advice by complaining, and in doing so invites territorial sharing. Co-territory means coresponsibility for management, and therefore Black and Red start to make suggestions to solve the proffered problems. White, by her replies of "Yes, but . . .," is actually defending the territory against Black and Red, while at the same time reissuing the invitation to share by bringing up further difficulties. Black and Red try time and again to set the co-territory in order, but each time are successfully rebuffed by White, who has no intention of giving up an inch of ground. Black and Red eventually withdraw, feeling irritated and defeated, while White, who has actually been engaged in capturing Black's and Red's psychological space (the hidden agenda of the game) by using shared territory as a decoy, moves on triumphantly, her territory intact.

LARGE GROUPS

Co-territories may vary widely in the number of people that share in the ownership, ranging from two, as in the case of a home owned by a married couple, to all of humanity, as in the case of the planet earth. The relationship between the owners of these co-territories varies with the number of participants and progresses from the most intimate to the completely impersonal. One can portray the realms in which each individual lives by a series of circles varying in size. The largest of these represents the world, of which one is a co-owner through his membership in the human race. This territory provides some minimal privileges for all human beings, such as the right to breathe air, to sail the oceans, and, with some restrictions, to travel across the land masses. The privileges are extremely limited, quite tenuous, and profoundly impersonal, governed by general rules rather than by individual arrangements. Inside of the first big circle one may imagine a smaller one that stands for the particular nation of which one is a citizen. The rights and privileges which come with co-ownership of this area are considerably more extensive and simultaneously more exclusive than those of the first circle. Noncitizens do not share in them unless they have been accepted as guests through the extension of a visitor's visa. Although each citizen has access to his country's privileges—for example, he may use the public parks, the beaches, the highways, and the public transportation—he is extended this access only on the condition that he abide by the rules which the community has set for the usage. He is not allowed to cut down the trees in a public park, walk around naked in the streets, or break the traffic rules on the highways.

Inside the second circle one can draw numerous other circles, some smaller, some bigger, some inside each other, some overlapping, some entirely separate. They may represent co-territories that one gains access to through membership in service clubs such as the Lions or the Kiwanis, through membership in a church, or by being an employee in a company. Other circles may represent the area one shares with a family, one's spouse, a friend, or a business partner. Each individual, then, shares with different people and numerous groups in a wide variety of co-territories, each of which carries with it certain privileges and restrictions. *The smaller the number of people with whom one shares a particular co-territory and the more personal the relationship between the partners, the less is the use of the area guided by well-established, clear rules and regulations.* Of necessity, formal rules have usually been established for larger groups of people, but when only a few individuals get together to establish a co-territory, be it in business, recreation, or marriage, the rules have to be worked out personally, informally, and more often than not through a good deal of conflict. When two parties jointly own a boat, each of them is allowed to use it within certain limitations and obligations, such as responsibility for the upkeep of the boat and the agreement that mutual consent is necessary prior to altering the property or selling it.

Bob and Fred decided to pool their money and buy a cabin at the beach which each of them desired to have but neither of them could afford by himself. They made the purchase and agreed on a plan which stipulated that each of them would have the cabin on alternate weekends and for a full month in the summer. Both were to leave the cabin cleaned up and in good repair after each use. Not too many months went by before Bob noticed that Fred apparently had a considerably different idea of the meaning of "cleaned up" and "in good repair" than he himself. Bob confronted Fred with the fact that he was not keeping his part of the bargain and told him that unless things would change the partnership had to be terminated. We will not pursue the particular way in which these two men settled their conflict. This very common example does, however, point out that in the process of sharing a territory between individuals a compromise arrangement acceptable to all parties involved has to be worked out if the venture is to be successful.

Public territory is theoretically equally accessible to all members of a community that owns it. In actuality, however, many unofficial and unorganized subgroups stake out special claims on what is supposed to be a public area and exclude others who are rightfully co-owners. One of the dominant features of the lives of the culturally deprived and the socially unsuccessful is their limited membership in these types of informal subgroups, which give special access to various co-territories. Thus, these areas in effect remain restricted to certain privileged members of society (Lyman and Scott, 1967). Sometimes the restrictions simply result from the fact that certain areas, although public, require some amount of money in order to reach them. For instance, the cost of transportation excludes many groups from the state parks. The seas and lakes, although open to everyone, require a boat to be used to the fullest. Other restrictions are not based on financial barriers. In European countries and to a lesser extent in the United States a person's social status is readily judged by his language; mistakes in grammar reveal his social class and close the door to the territory of many subgroups, just as racial background does in South Africa.

Acts of discrimination that rob individuals of areas of which they were supposed to be co-owners are not perpetrated by the affluent part of society alone. When a well-dressed individual ventures inside a neighborhood tavern of a slum area, he is likely to heave a sigh of relief once he finds himself in the street again, having quickly realized that he had strayed into a place where he did not belong and was not welcome. Ignorance of existing opportunities also keeps many from sharing in those areas to which they have a legitimate claim.

IMPACT OF CO-TERRITORIES

Security. Co-territory, like individual territory, has an impact on security, identity, and freedom. Of these three, security is most obviously affected by group membership. In a group one can anticipate that every member will cooperate in the defense of the co-territory, and, as a consequence, one never stands alone in the task of holding out against the rest of the world. The tight-knit family unit in which every individual knows that his territory is co-owned by the whole family and that any attack by an outsider will bring every member to his defense, provides such safety. Similar security is derived from belonging to a small village in a rural area of Western Europe or being a member of a tribal unit in the highlands of New Guinea (Read, 1965).

It is extremely important to provide for co-territorial arrangements in our society in order to enhance the security of each citizen. Oscar Newman's study on *Defensible Space* (1972) draws attention to the fact that especially in crowded cities it is essential to use architecture and street planning in such a way as to create areas which are shared. He shows that when a suitable territory is adequately marked and becomes the common property of a neighborhood, it leads to a change in the attitude of the local residents. The residents begin to take care of the area and "to plant gardens and define the areas immediately adjacent to their houses. Concern for the maintenance and safety of the street appears to be universally shared by residents. Every Saturday morning a different group of residents gather to give the street a thorough cleaning" (p. 61). Sharing of common property also fosters the tendency to common defense. "For example, almost any type of behavior can occur on a city street: loitering, dancing to a transistor radio, leaning against cars, and begging. Within the confines of an area, defined if only by a change in surface texture or a grade level, the range of possible behavior is greatly reduced. It is, in fact, limited to what residents have defined as the norm. All other behavior is incongruous and is so understood and dealt with" (p. 63). In order to create a communal spirit, therefore, one needs a public territory which a group of people can readily identify as being under their jurisdiction.

Identity. Also an individual's identity is affected by group membership. Sharing in the privileges which come with co-ownership makes him aware of the ways in which he is different from outsiders. At the same time, it underscores that he is similar to the other members of his group. The identity which he derives from co-ownership, therefore, is a group identity rather than a completely individual one. It creates that peculiar state in which, on the one hand, the person loses his individuality, his autonomy, and his self-directedness in the context of the group, while, on the other hand, he experiences a strong sense of uniqueness through comparison with outsiders. Such identity is best symbolized by a uniform, which helps erase ingroup differences and accentuates the distance from outsiders. Consider, for instance, the trappings of the members of the American version of the Hare Krishna sect which has sprung up in recent years. These principally fair-skinned young people with their exotic dress and shaven heads, their public chanting and the use of noisemakers are both audibly and visually immediately identifiable to anyone who has seen or heard them before. Not all uniforms are this extreme, and many are specifically designed as in the case of nurses and soldiers. Some are traditional, such as the broad-brimmed hats, bonnets, and simple dark clothing of the Amish community. Some may evolve under the pressure of fashion, be it dictated by the whims of a Parisian haute couturier (the New Look, Mini, Maxi) or the teen-age peer pressure in high school (bobbysox and saddle shoes, waffle-stompers, bleached jeans, pea coats).

In a more general way, individuals seem to become similar to one another in their identity to the degree that they share territory. From time to time one comes across an old married couple who have shared, in a real sense, the major part of their lives; their home, their children, their hopes, and their disappointments have been equally their common concern. The striking aspect of such a couple is their similarity; gradually their identities have approached each other. However, no sharing is ever complete and no two identities ever become the same. Our observations concerning the impact of co-territory on one's identity reveal an interesting tendency: *If one does not wish to acquire an identity similar to that of someone else, it is wise to avoid sharing any territory with him.*

Freedom. Group membership also enhances a person's freedom because it provides access to co-territory which one could never manage alone. This added freedom, however, exists only within the borders of the group territory and, as was mentioned earlier, within the confines of the group rules. Paradoxically, group-earned freedom also restricts one's individual freedom, for it reduces access to certain other areas. This loss, in general, is the price paid for group membership. The more exclusive the group the greater are the sanctions leveled against a member when he breaks the group rules, and the higher the barriers against his moving into the outside world. The Duke of Windsor belonged to a very exclusive group, namely, the Kings of England. He nevertheless chose to marry a divorced commoner and thereby was forced to abdicate his throne. He chose to live abroad as an exile from his family. No official invitation to visit the Royal House in England was ever extended to his wife until after his death.

The positive impact of exclusive group membership can be exemplified by the community of Hutterites in the United States. The Hutterites have an unusually low incidence of schizophrenia, the predominant psychosis in the United States. Joseph Eaton and Robert Weil (1962) relate how only nine Hutterites out of 8,542 ever manifested delusions, hallucinations, and other recognized symptoms of schizophrenia. The number of depressions, on the other hand, was quite high. As schizophrenia is a condition usually thought to be associated with lack of identity and security, whereas depression is related to the loss of hope and a sense of guilt, this observation lends support to the hypothesis that membership in an exclusive co-territory strengthens security and identity but reduces the freedom of access to new territory. In other words, the Hutterites know who they are, feel secure in their daily existence, but have little hope for new challenges or opportunities and are not supposed to dream of the land beyond the borders of the community.

The impact of shared territory on the individual's identity, security, and freedom is not limited to areas usually seen as highly desirable. The alcoholic who has landed on skid row soon acquires co-ownership over a new area which he shares with other alcoholics. This area includes, among other things, the drunk tank in the county jail, hardly a desirable place. The psychiatric patient who is committed to a hospital soon shares a particular physical space with other patients, but also some unusual privileges (Green, 1964, pp. 46-47):

> "Sometimes I hate the people who made me sick," Carla said. "They say that you stop hating them after you've had enough therapy, but I wouldn't know about that. Besides, my enemy is beyond hating or forgiving."
>
> "Who is it?" Deborah asked, wondering if it could only have been one.
>
> "My mother," Carla answered matter-of-factly. "She shot me and my brother and herself. They died; I lived. My father married again, and I went crazy."
>
> They were hard words, and stark, with no euphemisms such as one always heard outside. Starkness and crudity were two important privileges of the hospital, and everyone used them to the fullest. To those who had never dared to think of themselves, except in secret, as eccentric and strange, freedom was freedom to be crazy, bats, nuts, loony, and, more seriously, mad, insane, demented, out of one's mind. And there was a hierarchy of privilege to enjoy these freedoms. The screaming, staring ones on Ward D were called "sick" by others and "crazy" by themselves. Only they were allowed to refer to themselves by the ultimate words, like "insane" and "mad," without contradiction. The quieter wards, A and B, were lower on the upside-down scale of things and were

permitted only lighter forms: nuts, cuckoo, and cracked. It was the patients' own unspoken rule, and one learned without benefit of being told. B-ward patients who called themselves crazy were putting on airs. Knowing this, Deborah now understood the scorn of the rigid, dull-eyed Kathryn when a nurse had said, "Come on now, you are getting upset," and the woman had laughed, "I'm not upset; I'm cuckoo!"

These otherwise unappealing types of group membership nevertheless do provide a special co-territory, which may be an important reason that individuals persist in group memberships even when they appear highly unrewarding to outsiders. Some time ago we had a patient to interview, a professional safecracker, who had just been paroled after serving out his tenth jail sentence. He was in his late fifties, intelligent, and quite pleasant. Over the course of 35 years he had lived no more than three or four years as a free man. He was a rather introspective person and volunteered that he felt far more comfortable in jail than he did in the free society. He did not like jail; he did not enjoy the confinement, but he belonged there, he had his place and his reputation among fellow inmates and guards. He often longed for the freedom of the outside world with its many opportunities and pleasures, but each time he was discharged from prison he felt out of place and without a sense of security. In a matter of days he would return to his old profession, seeking contact with his old cronies, starting up new bank robberies which soon led to a new arrest and imprisonment.

An individual who has gained access to, and finds his identity and security through such socially unacceptable groups cannot be successfully rehabilitated unless he can leave the old group and *join* a new one. He must be provided with access to a new territory and assisted during the transition phase in coping with the unavoidable insecurity and loss of identity. Halfway houses, group living programs in which the transition is eased by the presence of people who have made the transition themselves, have been most effective in such efforts. Daytop Village, a tightly organized group living unit for ex-heroin addicts which is completely staffed by ex-addicts, is an excellent example of such a program (Bassin, 1967).

GROUPS OF TWO

Thus far the focus has been primarily on large groups which share a variety of territories and which one joins either through a formal process or by an accident of fate. Now we will turn to that far more intensive and personal process of sharing in which two individuals establish exclusive, joint ownership over the most important realms of their lives. As this process is not entirely structured by special social routines, the co-ownership depends on the efforts of the two individuals for its successful formation, consisting of the establishment of a trusting union in love or friendship which facilitates the mutual sharing of a territory without the loss of autonomy. The best example in Western society is the establishment of the marriage partnership. Aside from the present confusion as to the necessity for or the benefits derived from this embattled relationship, it is reasonable to conclude that the society feels so strongly about this cooperative venture as to try to guarantee its success by legally sanctioning its existence, granting its members privileged status in the society as a whole, and discouraging its failure. We will use the process of marriage to exemplify the mechanics involved in developing an equitable relationship in a shared territory.

SELF-DISCLOSURE

Boy meets girl and if the chemistry is right courtship follows. Aside from the usual courting behavior involving a myriad of ploys and counterploys whereby each lover beguiles, entices, cajoles, and mesmerizes the other with posturing and flattery, the vital process of *self-disclosure* begins to take place. *Self-disclosure is a stepwise procedure whereby one individual reveals himself to another.* This process usually starts out with the disclosure of neutral items, and if the signals from both sides indicate that no harm is intended, then each person may reveal additional aspects of himself which make him more vulnerable. He may admit a mistake, talk about events that he is not particularly proud of, tell of his hopes, show his feelings—all of which the other could use as weapons of attack in a territorial skirmish. If, instead of abusing this information, the other responds with the same degree of openness, the process of disclosure can continue. The information conveyed is not in itself essential. The specific content serves as a vehicle to demonstrate to the other that he is lowering his defensive barriers and that his level of trust is increasing. If either individual shows the slightest inclination to attack the other, the process stops or is reversed. Most contacts stabilize, therefore, while disclosure remains at a fairly superficial level.

Occasionally the self-disclosure process moves on and a friendship is established. This friendship implies the tacit agreement that neither individual will abuse the information obtained in the process of opening up and, moreover, will assist in protecting the other's weak spots. Self-disclosure is a process which some individuals engage in more easily than others.[1] The presence of one individual who feels comfortable in taking the lead greatly helps in the process (Jourard and Landson, 1960). By the same token, a person who self-discloses easily is more prone to establish warm and close relationships with others (Halverson and Shore, 1969). Self-disclosure also influences personal space in that it reduces the distance at which the self-disclosing individuals feel comfortable with each other (Savicki, 1970). The ultimate in this process is reached when self-disclosure leads to a level of intimacy which includes complete openness of the psychological as well as the physical aspects of the couple.

Returning to the courting twosome, we find them at the point where they have decided to get married. This agreement is announced in the form of an engagement by means of which the society at large is informed that a couple wishes to enter into the privileged relationship of marriage. The society licenses the marriage and eventually a ceremony is performed in which the contract is publicly agreed to. A common territory has been formed and, paradoxically, the co-territorial struggle begins. People readily agree that marriage is a give-and-take affair, but which territory to give and which to take is not so simple a decision. After the honeymoon is over, or perhaps even before, many pedestrian questions need to be answered: What side of the bed do you want to sleep on? Who will turn off the alarm clock? Who gets up first? Who makes breakfast? Who decides what will be on the breakfast menu? If the wife comes from a dry cereal and orange juice background and the husband from a bacon and eggs one, an agreement will have to be made on the breakfast menu before too many breakfasts have passed. If both parties are adamant about this question, a battle is inevitable before a compromise can be reached. Again, the husband may evoke great consternation in his wife by using her tweezers to clean his fingernails, and the wife may cause shivers of rage in her husband by using his best wood chisel as a screwdriver. The wife may spend hours in the kitchen preparing a sumptuous dinner for her husband only to have him ask her what is the funny-looking stuff smeared all over the meat; or the husband, bursting with enthusiasm, may show his wife a

---

[1]Hamid Hekmat and Michael Theiss (1971) found that self-actualizing people are much more prone to engage in behavior of self-disclosure than individuals who are low on that particular scale.

painting he has just bought for the living room, only to have her collapse on the couch in a fit of laughter.

These incidents may seem small and unimportant, but it is from such threads that the intricate fabric of co-territory is woven. The process of self-disclosure has brought the two individuals to a trusting and open relationship and has led to moments of intensely intimate sharing. This openness, one of the major rewards of marriage, must continue, but the additional factor of assertiveness must be added so that a fair and equitable compromise can be reached which preserves and enhances the individuality of each partner while strengthening the marriage relationship at the same time. Thus, both parties assume a double burden: each person must give of himself, yet at the same time protect his own rights. As a relationship of trust has evolved through self-disclosure, both partners have become keenly aware of each other's weak spots and sensitivities. In the unavoidable conflicts, which occur when they establish their own areas of relative control and autonomy within their joint territory, the temptation will be great and at times irresistible to use this privileged knowledge as a weapon. Each partner is confronted with the need to establish control over what seems to him or her like an appropriate share of the co-territory, but *at the same time both partners will have to respect each other's integrity if a relationship of trust is to survive.* This delicate balance is *the crux of marriage: to effectively preserve one's own interests relative to one's partner and yet to maintain a basis of trust.* It is a difficult task, and no one succeeds completely or all the time.

There are moments of tragedy in every marriage when in the course of a legitimate struggle, one of the two suddenly lets go of a remark that he knows will hurt the other deeply. The first time such indiscretion occurs constitutes the first threat to the existence of the marriage. Ordinarily the process of being married involves repeated events such as these, each followed by a gradual or dramatic reestablishment of trust, depending on the couple's style, and eventually, if everything goes well, an increased care not to undermine the partner's integrity. If events take a less favorable course, each attack may unleash an equally vicious counterattack resulting in a protracted destructive battle which destroys the fabric of trust that holds the marriage together. For a constructive marital relationship, therefore, it is necessary for both partners to defend their own territorial needs but to do so by fighting fairly, by direct assertive confrontation concerning the specific areas under dispute and *without using the privileged information obtained in moments of trusting intimacy.*

TREATIES

The process of building a good marriage relationship takes several years during which there will be arguments, hard feelings, dramatic scenes, or periods of silence and tension. Fair fighting techniques and good faith on both sides will lead to compromises which are acceptable to both partners. Such a compromise basically includes, "O.K., I'll give a little bit here, but I will take a little bit there and expect you to give up about as much as I do." In this manner each skirmish leads to some degree of settlement with either a formal or an unspoken treaty to seal the dispute. From now on the husband will not refer to his wife's boeuf bourguignonne in disparaging terms, and the wife will not clip articles out of the newspaper before her husband has had time to read it. She will check in advance whether the budget can stand the purchase of a new outfit, but the selection will not be up to him and negative comments about it will not be one of his prerogatives.

Unfortunately, in some marriages these initial skirmishes do not lead to treaties, but persist as smoldering feuds which every once in a while erupt into open and prolonged destructive warfare. In other marriages, one partner simply refuses to fight and immediately gives up all territory that is contested, which amounts to a withdrawal from the relationship. There are also marriages in which one partner lays claim to all the territory involved and refuses to compromise on any issue. Whatever the case, an imbalance in the territorial division creates tensions which, if they persist, are serious liabilities for the relationship and for the family as a whole. *In marriage winning all the battles means losing the war.* If either partner attempts to grab the major part of the co-territory, he engages in a very dangerous act, for he will unavoidably get a counterattack, and probably in the area where he is most vulnerable. To be sure, the counterattack may be a long time developing or may take devious forms, but it will occur. If the husband constantly criticizes his wife's cooking, he should not be surprised if its overall quality deteriorates and he finds that he is eating hot dogs six times a week and canned spaghetti on Sunday. If the wife nags her husband about his lack of drive, she may find that he spends every evening sitting in front of the television set; or if she insists on treating him as if he were a "darling little boy," she should not be surprised if he responds by becoming irresponsible and spending a great deal of time away from home.

If one partner leaves the other too little room, the other will expand his or her territory elsewhere, either by neglecting the family for an endless string of social or business activities, by pursuing the path of extramarital affairs, or by following whatever avenue for expansion is open.

The following is an example of the subtle and mutually destructive way in which a co-territorial imbalance may evolve. Two young dentists, both intelligent and ambitious, met during their student days, fell in love and decided to marry. Both completed their training, but soon thereafter the woman became pregnant and had to interrupt her career plans while the husband continued his studies. In rapid succession, two more children were born and the woman had to devote all of her time to raising the family. The husband, in the meantime, completed his specialization and found a job in a university where he engaged in practice as well as research. During this time his wife continued to keep up with the professional literature, but the husband systematically blocked any career pursuit that she may have had in mind. She still talked about scientific topics and discussed ideas she had read, but he responded by not taking her interest seriously and by showing her, in his attitude as well as his responses, that he regarded his own knowledge far superior to hers and that he did not appreciate any claim to expertise on her part. He cut short any discussion of part-time jobs for her, pointing out that her responsibility was with the children. In short, he effectively eliminated the professional realm from her life. When she got married her professional pursuit had been a major part of her territory with a promise of expansion, but now, several years later, her husband had even closed off all her access to his own professional realm which she now could no longer consider her co-territory either. The wife had failed to fight back; she gave up reading the professional literature, and she completely deferred to the husband's "superior knowledge."

To fulfill her life, the wife devoted all of her energies to the new territory that she had gained, that of housewife and mother. She was a meticulous housekeeper and spent an inordinate amount of time with her children, involving herself in all of the details of their daily life, playing with them, teaching them, and catering to their every wish. She now began to expand her motherly care to her husband. If he had a minor illness she seemed to almost enjoy it and took care of him hand and foot. When he came home at night she would see that he looked tired, would encourage him to sit in his chair, have a drink, and read the paper while she was busy around the house, making the dinner and taking care of the children. Before long a new pattern evolved: When father came home, she would tell the children to be quiet and not bother him for he was tired. Father would settle back in his chair and read the paper. Mother would feed the children in the dining room and bring father his dinner on a tray. After dinner the children would go to their rooms or mother would help them with their homework, while father took a brief nap in his chair. When the children were taken care of, mother would bring a cup of coffee to father, telling him what the children had done during the day, chattering incessantly about the little details of the housewife's everyday events. Soon, however, the husband seemed to tire of this routine, looking around the room with a vague sense of discomfort. Eventually he would feel a desire to escape from the room and when this tension had become unbearable, he would excuse himself and withdraw into his study to do some reading in preparation for the next day.

This case clearly illustrates a destructive series of events which started when the husband took a vital territory away from his wife, to which she eventually responded with acquiring a new realm. In turn, an important part of the co-territory was taken away from the husband, who, under the guise of his wife's motherly concern, ended up totally dispossessed of his home and, more importantly, of his children. The only space in the home left to him was in his chair and his study. The case is of special interest in that the whole process took place without any overt, violent action on the part of either individual. Territory was taken by both sides without a shot being fired. Neither partner realized that important territories were changing hands, but both felt extreme discomfort and irritation in the relationship. If the wife had been cognizant of the fact that her professional sphere was being taken away, she might have put up a battle and the outcome would have been different. By the same token, the husband who was being conquered by kindness might well have insisted on his right to come to the table and have normal parental contact with his children, had he recognized the process.

TRUST AND LOVE

Thus far we have focused the discussion on the process through which two partners work out the relative autonomy and the mutual obligations which each of them will have within the co-territory. Even if this process is complete, a great amount of overlapping control and joint responsibility still remains, and for the harmonious handling of this realm trust and love are of particular importance. We have already implied that *trust refers to a state of affairs in which a person believes that the other will respect and, if needed, protect his territorial integrity.*

Trust is a relative process. Robert may trust a teetotaler in his wine cellar but at the same time would not think of entrusting him with any secrets; however, Robert may consider such secrets safe with another friend whom he would not leave alone with a bottle. Trust does not only vary with the person one is dealing with; it also depends on the state of affairs in one's own territory. If an individual feels *firmly in control of an area* and cannot conceive of any way in which he could be dislodged, he would have little trouble inviting strangers in and allowing them to inspect every detail of it. A person who is thoroughly confident of his own professional competence does not hesitate to display that his knowledge has some deficiencies. He does not feel that his authority is undermined by the admission that he hasn't read a certain book or is not familiar with a specific reference. On the other hand, a person who is less convinced of his mastery would be more inclined to protect his control over the area by a pretense of competence. He would try to hide such deficiencies in his knowledge.

The above discussion implies the following hypothesis: *The more firmly one feels in control of an area the more easily he admits someone else to it (or the less defensive he is of it), and what is the same, the more easily he trusts others with it.*

Although most individuals have some areas which they master in a comfortable and firm way, it is equally true that each person has parts of his territory that he rules in a very tenuous fashion. These are his weak spots, his Achilles' heel, which he is least likely to expose to the attack of others. He will admit the existence of these areas only to his most trusted friends.

Love can be defined as the counterpart of trust, that is, the resolve never to violate the territorial integrity of the other.[2] If one has entered into a relationship with another person and, proceeding with the process of mutual self-disclosure, has arrived at the point where both know each other's most vulnerable areas but also feel sure that the other will not use this knowledge to attack, then one has a relationship of trust and love. *Trust* implies knowing of the other's love, and *love* is the resolve to honor and safeguard the other's territory. Insofar as one loves another person,

---

[2]The word *love* has many meanings. We have given it a particular definition in a territorial context. As such it comes closest to *agape*, brotherly love, and has little in common with romantic love or erotic feelings.

one takes pleasure in seeing his territory expand and watching his grasp over his possessions increase. Thus the parent who loves the child derives his greatest joy from the gradual expansion of the child's territory as he tries out new skills and explores new frontiers, gradually expanding his mastery over his world.

To be loved is a precious commodity. It provides the basis for trust in others and it creates a most comforting sense of security and peace. It is small wonder, therefore, that much effort is expended to obtain the other's love. This effort, however, reveals at the same time a peculiar, paradoxical aspect of love as we have defined it. To coerce the other to do something, to force him, is an attack on his autonomy. It will reduce rather than increase the other's trust. It will evoke a response to defend his own territory rather than the inclination to protect that of the person who sought his love. Love, therefore, is more likely to come forth if one does not feel attacked in any way; in short, when he trusts his partner. Love and trust form a complementary relationship which is most likely to come about if both partners seek to protect each other's integrity. In other words, by strengthening one's own love the other may—but does not have to—respond in kind. *This fact underscores the problem of the insecure person who feels most desperately in need of the other's care and who, by his attempts to force the other to give his love, is least likely to obtain it.*

In considering love and trust it should be remembered that these terms do not indicate permanent characteristics of human beings, but rather a more or less temporary state of affairs. Two people may have a loving, trusting relationship one moment, and only an instant later, whether by accident or intent, one of the two may violate the other's territory and immediately the scene changes from the quiet pastoral tableau to a battleground. Love and trust become lasting aspects of the relationship between two individuals only because of their personal commitments. When each of them sticks by his resolve to protect the other's integrity under all circumstances, trust can be preserved.

Individuals who have trusted each other completely can have the most intense conflicts when their relationship disintegrates, for each knows that the other, who has now become an adversary, has direct knowledge of all his vulnerable spots and is therefore in an extremely powerful position. When one couples this phenomenon with the fact that an individual will put up the greatest struggle to protect his most important territory, it is no wonder that two people who once were friends and lovers attack each other so viciously when the relationship dissolves. Louis Nizer gives a convincing description of this point in his book *My Life in Court* (1963, pp. 173-174):

Litigations between husbands and wives exceed in bitterness and hatred those of any other relationships. I have represented defrauded businessmen who fight their deceivers for fortune and power. I have seen them pour out their venom against their opponents until they suffered heart attacks or were ulcerated. I have witnessed struggles for the protection of copyrighted property, where the pride of authorship, being dearer than life itself, consumed the creative artist. I have seen public figures libeled or accused of wrongs which could wreck their life's work, strike back at their detractors. I have observed men with spotless reputations who were indicted, suffer nervous breakdowns. I have witnessed children sue their fathers to deprive them of their businesses, or brothers engaged in fratricidal contests without quarter. I have seen defendants in antitrust suits beleaguered by plaintiffs seeking treble damages or defending themselves against Government actions aimed to break up their enterprise, painstakingly built over a lifetime. I have participated in will contests in which relatives were at each others' throats for the inheritance.

All these litigations evoke intense feelings of animosity, revenge, and retribution. Some of them may be fought ruthlessly. But none of them, even in their most aggravated form, can equal the sheer, unadulterated venom of a matrimonial contest. The participants are often ready to gouge out the eyes or the soul of the once loved, without any pity whatsoever.

A man whose sense of honor may be punctilious and whose restraint under extreme provocation may be admirable, will unhesitatingly insist on making charges against his wife which, even if true, would not be entertained by any decent man, particularly against the mother of his children. A woman who all her life has been kindly and gentle may turn so vengeful against her husband that she will write obscene and poisonous letters to his friends, create violent scenes at his office, confront and physically attack him in public places, have him arrested, and write anonymous accusations to the Treasury Department. Either may disregard their children's welfare by making them pawns in the battle, filling their ears with loathing for the other. There is no limit to the blazing hatred, the unquenchable vengefulness, the reckless abandonment of all standards of decent restraint, which a fierce matrimonial contest engenders.

One of the implicit demands of Western marriage in this century is that both partners will share a major part of their territory. Division of labor and responsibility, division of authority and control, through precise role definitions of the male and the female, have been minimized, whereas sharing on the basis of trust and love has become a goal in itself. Such expectation, largely stemming from romantic ideals, fed by a long history of romantic literature—a literature which, though rich in description of the trials of love, has added little realistic knowledge as to how couples can go about creating a constructive life together—has placed a horrendous burden on the young partners. As if the task of creating a life together were not difficult enough, the partners are bound to experience it as a failure unless an intense relationship is created and maintained. Marriage in this form is planned for failure. Practical couples will find a *modus vivendi,* and gradually arrive at a division of territory which is acceptable. They enjoy the occasional moments of sharing trust and love as high points of the relationship, just as they regard the perhaps more frequent periods of struggle and isolation as unavoidable low points. Those, however, who have been indoctrinated by the hearts-and-flowers fantasy of their culture must soon experience their own relationship as a failure and in bitter disappointment may start a search for a more idyllic liaison.

To round off the discussion of sharing we need to mention that not all sharing is sharing of territory. There is one particularly important type of sharing which occurs on occasions when two people experience a moment of perfect communication. At such a time they know exactly what the other means, feels, and experiences. A slight gesture, a few words, or the exchange of a quick glance, are sufficient to establish such a bond. Edmund Bolles (1972, p. 55) writes of such a moment of sharing, which happened to him while he was in the Peace Corps in Africa.

> One question that still puzzles us is why the genes of language were so successful that they became a universal characteristic of man. . . .
> One possible reason is the universal power of language to make people feel they share a bond. When my two African friends told me the word for "father" in their tribal language was "dadi" and I replied the American word was the same, a feeling of kinship swept through the three of us. This sense of intimacy is the qualitative difference between the effect of animal cries and speech. It justifies the success of language and allows us to feel a tie with a hitherto hidden and private mind.

Such communication is often part of the relationship of trust and love. It represents that knowledge and understanding of one another which perhaps is only possible when each person can unfold himself, reveal himself without fear of the other, when all power struggles have been completely abandoned. This experience is very rewarding, but in its very nature it is a fleeting state of affairs which occurs as an occasional high point in a relationship.

CHAPTER 7

CRITICISM, PROTEST, LAMENT, AND COMPLAINT

What injures the spirit is having someone always on your back, beating you, telling you what to do and what not to do.

Don Juan, as quoted by *Carlos Castaneda**

Viewed from the perspective of human territoriality, several common interactions which are a frequent source of difficulties between individuals emerge in sharp relief and reveal their nature as stumbling blocks to genuine human communication and cooperation. Two types of such behavior that often lead to fruitless cyclic patterns in interpersonal relationships lend themselves particularly well to a territorial exposé; they are criticism and complaint.

CRITICISM

Few individuals appreciate being criticized. Most, however, find it necessary on occasion to comment on the behavior of someone else in a way which is apt to be construed as critical. Criticism is something, therefore, that a person frequently finds necessary and reasonable to inflict on others, but which he considers quite unpleasant when directed at himself. Since most everyone is keenly aware of the painfulness of criticism, people are forever trying to find ways in which criticism of another person can be made more palatable. An employer racks his brains thinking up subtle means of telling an employee to change his behavior

*From *Journey to Ixtlan.* New York: Simon and Schuster, 1972, p. 12.

without hurting his feelings, and a wife devises new and ingenious ways to inform her husband that she doesn't like the way he tells jokes at parties.

Criticism, defined in Webster's dictionary as "finding fault; censuring; disapproval," *is a straightforward invasion of another person's territory, for it seeks to influence him to comply with the critic's preconceived notions of proper behavior.* An individual frequently finds himself in situations in which a direct assertive response to criticism is made difficult because he believes that the other has a right to such comment since the criticism is made in his own best interest. This "constructive" criticism, as it is called, must be scrutinized to ascertain its social implications.

CONSTRUCTIVE CRITICISM

The term *constructive criticism* implies that the disapproving comments one person gives to another will help him improve on his shortcomings. When such comments are made in a teacher-student relationship, they can be very useful to the student who desires to acquire certain skills in order to advance to a higher level of proficiency in the field he has chosen. If a teacher is showing a pupil how to play the violin, he will, in the course of the training, have need to disapprove of certain ways in which the student holds the bow or counts the meter. In this way he makes corrections in order to let the student become aware of specific habits that will keep him from gaining mastery of the instrument. The central feature of this situation is that the student determines the goals he wishes to attain or the territory he seeks to expand, and will therefore give qualified individuals the right to comment on relevant areas. In this way he hopes to gain skills or information. If, however, the violin teacher begins to make correctional remarks about the student's attire or his manners, the latter will soon become very unhappy, for he has not engaged the teacher for his expertise in these areas and therefore does not appreciate the unsolicited comments. In other words, the teacher has invaded a part of his territory uninvited.

Constructive criticism can occur, therefore, in the context of a teacher-pupil relationship. This relationship does not have to be a formal one of pupil and professional teacher; one party must simply know something that the other wishes to learn. Thus if a son knows more about stream fishing than his father, the father will let the son correct his fishing technique because he recognizes the son's superior skill and wants to acquire his know-how. In this sense, the son is his father's teacher and no territorial invasion occurs if the son sticks to the topic of stream fishing.

In many instances, the role of teacher is assumed without anyone having asked for it. If the would-be teacher starts handing out advice or commentary on another's habits, tastes, or ideas, the reluctant student will soon become irritated and uncomfortable. Constructive criticism in these instances is a form of self-righteous meddling in which the goals are being determined by the teacher and not by his student. In other words, one individual decides unilaterally that the other needs improvement, and he tries to impose his own ideas regardless of the wishes of the other.

From a territorial perspective, true *constructive criticism* is basically *teaching which extends the territory of the recipient and his mastery over it.* However, when one is forced into the pupil role, part of one's adult, independent role is taken away and one's freedom and personal initiative curtailed; in other words, one suffers loss of territory.

CRITICISM IN A TERRITORIAL STRUGGLE

Except for its use in a legitimate pupil-teacher situation, criticism serves primarily as an instrument or a weapon in territorial struggles. It can be used in two different ways: as a means of expanding one's territory and as a defense against an invader.

Criticism as a means of taking territory. Bob is driving the car and Joan is sitting beside him. Bob is a conscientious driver who has given Joan no reasons to distrust his skills. However, Joan finds it very difficult to be dependent on someone else and she much prefers to be in the driver's seat herself. As a consequence, she is continually scanning the surroundings for potential dangers. As they approach a stop sign she says sharply, "Watch out, there's a stop sign!" A little later at an intersection she warns Bob that there is a car approaching from the right. Still later she tells him to be careful because the road is slippery. Her statements are basically critical, for they imply that Bob is incapable of good driving.

In the above example, Joan wishes to take over Bob's territory. Sitting in the driver's seat gives Bob the responsibility for driving. By accepting the seat next to Bob, Joan has conceded that she is a passenger, not in control of the car. When Joan, nevertheless, tries to control Bob's driving, she is invading his territory and, quite predictably, Bob will give some form of angry response to this invasion. Several conclusions can be drawn from the situation: (a) If an individual is about to criticize another, he must first decide whether he will encroach on the territory of someone else. If encroachment is indeed apparent, he might do well to pause and determine the cost of such an attack, for unfailingly a counterattack will follow. Does he really want the battle? If the decision is affirmative and he decides to try to conquer this piece of territory at all cost, then it is prudent to consider whether criticism is the best weapon, or whether a more direct approach to the issue might be more fruitful. (b) If an individual is being criticized, he must first determine if the criticism is an appropriate one, based in a teacher-student relationship, or whether it is an invasion of his territory. If the latter is the case, then he must decide whether or not to give ground.

In the above illustration, Bob may decide that driving the car is his responsibility and tell Joan something like, "Joan, I am trying to drive the car with care. I don't wish to endanger your life, so when you're a passenger in my car you'll have to leave the driving to me." If this does not work he may go one step further and say, "Joan, if it is impossible for you to be comfortable as a passenger while I do the driving, it is perhaps best if you don't ride with me any more and either take your own car or go with someone else." And, of course, the final stance is, "Joan, I won't take you along any more if you don't stop your back-seat driving!"

This kind of response may seem fairly drastic, and yet it is far more useful than what frequently happens if the line is not drawn so tightly. For example, if Bob and Joan are married and if Bob has not assumed a firm and assertive position, they might arrive at the unpleasant and destructive—but not at all uncommon—situation wherein each time they go somewhere they engage in the same battle. When they leave Bob knows that Joan will make comments about his driving, and therefore he is already angry the moment he enters the car. In his anger he may be more prone to drive carelessly (after all, he will get nasty comments anyway), and Joan will feel increasingly justified in responding to her own tensions by making comments and giving warnings.

In many families this struggle leads to a situation wherein the driver sits in silent irritation with an occasional angry outburst in response to an almost continuous flow of critical comments from his partner, usually called *nagging*. Nagging is a very unpleasant interchange and a fruitless one at that. It is a state of continuous border war in which no one makes any gains or gets any closer to a solution. One usually blames the nagger for this pattern and such blame is partly justified, but it is equally the fault of the person who did not clearly and unequivocally either defend his territory or give it up. Nagging can only be maintained if the person who is being nagged does not make a final and definitive stand.

Criticism as a defense against an invader. Bill is a somewhat reckless driver who frequently switches from one lane to the other, routinely exceeds the speed limit by five or ten miles an hour, tailgates other cars, and passes on blind corners. Jan, his passenger, is very uncomfortable with this situation and begins to make critical remarks: "You're going too fast"; "You're following too close"; and "Why don't you put your turn signals on when you change lanes?" All of these statements are made in the hope that they will make Bill improve his driving, but in reality all they accomplish is that Bill becomes annoyed and his driving, if anything, gets worse.

In this example, the comments made by Jan are a defense against the invasion of her territory by Bill. In driving carelessly Bill endangers Jan's life, which is an attack on her core territory, her body and her total existence. If Jan were driving she could make the decisions whether or not to take the additional risks, but with Bill at the wheel she does not have the chance to make this choice. She is his victim; her autonomy has been reduced. This invasion of territory angers Jan and her critical remarks constitute an attempt to regain her ground. The example leads to two observations: (a) If a person is being criticized, he first needs to determine whether or not he has invaded the other's territory. If he finds that he has been guilty of such an attack, he should either withdraw graciously (in this case drive carefully) or prepare to accept the consequences of such an invasion (the critical remarks in this case). (b) If one feels inclined to criticize someone else, one must first check whether one is functioning legitimately as a teacher to a pupil. If this is not the case, one next needs to determine whether or not he is responding to an invasion of his territory, using criticism as a defensive weapon.

As a general rule, criticism is not a very effective defense. The most successful response is to deal directly with the problem. If Jan, for instance, would say to Bill, "Bill, your driving frightens me. I'd appreciate it if you would slow down and drive more carefully, because I don't wish to be killed," she would have spoken directly to the point and would have given Bill a chance to consider whether or not he wanted to act on her request. If he decided to do so the problem would be solved. If he chose to disregard her appeal Jan could proceed with, "Bill, will you please let me off at the next gas station so I can call a taxi; I don't care to risk my life driving with you."

Most people would like to be nice and avoid scenes; therefore, it is not easy to make such direct statements. Nevertheless, if one's purpose is to safeguard one's life, then the direct approach is the most functional and most likely to lead to results. Criticism is less effective precisely because it is devious, and implies that one is not fully self-assured and not entirely willing to defend one's ground. Criticism has much in common with hostility, in that it uses round-about methods to accomplish its goals. It represents a shift from a direct defense of the territory itself to an attack on the self-esteem of the opponent.

CRITICISM UNDER THE GUISE OF BENEVOLENCE

Criticism is often dressed up in the guise of benevolence. "I'm saying this for your own good"; "I feel that it's my duty to tell you"; "I believe I'd be neglecting my responsibility to you if I didn't tell you"; or, "I love you very much, and it's because of my love for you that I'm concerned with what you're doing. I hope you'll take what I'm going to say as a sign of that love." The foregoing are all variations of the same theme. One invades someone's territory and at the same time displays a banner which reads, "I love you and am doing this for your own good." During World War II Nazi forces occupied small countries like Norway, Denmark, Holland, and Belgium with the excuse that they had not come to capture them but, rather, to "defend" them. The people of these countries were being "liberated from the corrupt governments that ruled them." This stance may have succeeded in making the Nazis feel better about their attack, but it did not fool too many of the people in the occupied countries.

Most of the time the victim of the "benevolent" attack will disregard the banner and respond to the attack with irritation or anger. In that case the invader will react with righteous indignation, "Here I tried to help you but all you do is get angry with me!" As a result of this maneuver the attacker obtains a noble sense of self; perhaps he will feel like a martyr if he has been able to convince himself that he is in the right, which places the other beyond the pale. Occasionally, however, the victim is deceived by such propaganda, in which case he finds himself in a most unpleasant bind. On the one hand, he feels an impulse to answer with anger, but on the other hand, he perceives the need to respond to what he has taken at face value as a sign of love. The person who is so misled finds himself in a quandary which does not permit a satisfactory response, a situation that he experiences with discomfort and anxiety.

The recognition that criticism, except in certain specific instances, is always a means of carrying on a territorial struggle exposes the excuses as irrelevant. If an individual finds himself in the process of making a criticism "for the good of someone else" he must be aware that he is actually invading that person's territory and that the cover of love is only a clever trick which does not give him the right to feel righteously indignant if the other quite appropriately responds in an assertive manner to the invasion.

DISGUISED CRITICISM

Criticism, because of its general negative reception, is often couched in subtle or disguised forms. A rather common example is the question: "I wonder why you keep on driving too fast if you know that it is dangerous?" A more complicated disguise takes the form of an interpretation: "I have the feeling that you are trying to punish your mother when you are driving dangerously." Communication between individuals is complicated and confusing at best. It seems most advisable, therefore, to reduce that complication by making assertive statements rather than offering criticisms either directly or in disguise. Individuals in the helping professions are especially prone to manipulate their patients and clients by means of subtle disguise and clever forms of the "it's for your own good" excuse. The professional, therefore, needs to focus systematically on his communications to avoid such maneuvers, for they always imply a territorial invasion.

An ingenious individual can conceal a criticism in many other ways: a tangential comment; a remark about someone who is absent, but which pertains to the party present; or drawing attention to an article in the paper about smoking to tell a smoker that it is a bad habit. The fact that these criticisms are covert has the advantage for the recipient in that he can simply pretend not to understand the hidden message. They are nevertheless territorial attacks.

SPECIAL INSTANCES OF APPROPRIATE CRITICISM

If a contractor hires a carpenter and observes that this employee does a sloppy job, he will show him what he is doing wrong and expect the situation to improve. If the carpenter's work does not improve, the contractor will fire him. This relationship is not a teacher-pupil one, and yet the criticism seems justified. In fact, it is a *particular situation of territorial definition.* In a sense, the employer pays the employee a salary to *manage* a part of his action territory, and in exchange the employee gives the employer the right to control a specific part of his life. The contractor says to the carpenter, "My territory is too big, I need you to help me manage it. I will pay you so much for so many hours for your expertise." The carpenter, in accepting this offer, says, "My special expertise is carpentry, and I will rent this ability to you for so many hours at such and such a wage." If the carpenter does an inadequate job he is not living up to his contract, and the contractor's specific criticisms may help him correct any errors he is making. Here one must emphasize "specific criticism," for all too often the critical remarks run over into areas not included in the contract. The contractor may notice, for instance, that the carpenter has not countersunk the nails. He has the right to call this omission to the attention of the employee and expect the carpenter to correct his error. However, if he says, "Hey, you stupid idiot! Why can't you ever do anything right? Get your fat rear over here and countersink these nails! And while I'm thinking about it, don't come back tomorrow unless you have gotten rid of that stupid beard; you look just like a bum!"—he has clearly overstepped his authority and invaded the other's territory. Being an employer does not give him the right to comment on anything that was not in the original agreement. In the above example, the justified criticism of failure to countersink the nails gets completely lost in the extraneous criticism of intelligence, general ability, physical size, personal appearance, and social status. Since criticism is appropriate only insofar as it pertains to the actions which are relevant to the territory that has been leased to the employer, the employee has every right to defend himself against attacks which fall outside the work agreement. Of course the employee is often in a poor defensive position and the employer has the worker over a barrel, unless there is a labor shortage, in which case the situation is reversed.

Frequently, friction between employers and employees occurs because the contract is not clear and means one thing to the employer and something else to the employee. The employer, as well as the employee, fare best if there is a clear definition of the contractual obligations they have to each other. This clarity is especially important in an era when traditional patterns are changing. In the past, a teacher in the public school was expected to dress in a fairly conservative manner. Today, a far more casual attire and a variety of beards and mustaches can be seen in the classrooms. The teachers insist that personal appearance is a private matter, whereas the school principal may still feel that decisions regarding it are his to make. Unless the teacher and his supervisor can arrive at a general agreement on the obligations implied in the contract, one can anticipate serious conflict.

The employer, then, has the right to criticize the behavior of his employee only in those areas that the employee has contracted to him. Anything else amounts to an invasion, and the employer must anticipate either a direct counterattack if the employee is an assertive person, or subversive, hostile retributions if the employee is unable to respond openly and directly for fear of losing his job. Such subversive or hostile attacks may take the form of slowdowns, small accidents damaging the employer's property, carelessness with his supplies, lack of enthusiasm and drive, continuous small infractions of the rules, and the like. In any case, the employer will ultimately pay a price for overstepping his boundaries.

A situation very similar to the one described above (but in which no exchange of money is involved) occurs if several people are engaged in a common task. A group of individuals working together to get a political candidate elected, a team of baseball players trying to win the pennant, and a group of mountain climbers scaling Mt. Everest are all in a task-oriented situation. Ordinarily such a situation involves a division of labor. Each member of the team has certain expertise and is responsible for a specific segment of the shared territory. Insofar as the overall goal is too big for one person to obtain alone, each individual is also dependent on the expertise of the others to help him reach it. In this way each member gives up a part of his autonomy to the others. In the case of the mountaineering group, each climber depends on his companions for his safety and will therefore not hesitate to correct the actions of another if he fails to do his job or does not do it adequately. Here again, the criticism must be specific and not stray across the boundaries of the agreement. Thus it is very important that each person in the team have a clear understanding of his duties and the extent to which he is allowed to rely on others. The more precise the definitions of this division of labor and the more homogeneous the understanding of it by the members of the team, the less likely it is that friction will occur and the more readily appropriate critical comments can be exchanged.

A discussion of criticism must be based on the assumption that one can recognize it when one encounters it. Often there is disagreement between individuals as to whether a certain comment was critical or not. The person who responds to the comment as if it were a criticism is then considered hypersensitive. Some remarks are simply misperceived and so misunderstandings occur. From a practical point of view, it is most useful to take the response of the person receiving the comment as the determining factor: If he responds as if criticized, then to him criticism has taken place. If the person seems hypersensitive, there are good reasons, some of which will be discussed in Chapter 8.

Similarly, a person needs to take his own feelings as a point of departure. Irritation and dismay arise when an individual *senses* his territory is being invaded. This irritation should alert him, therefore, to the possibility that someone else is moving in on his ground, even if he does not at the moment clearly see which area is under attack. If one is the recipient of kindly rendered "good advice" and one feels irritated in spite of the apparent good intentions of the other, it would be prudent to consider whether the provider of the advice is perhaps extending a criticism in a disguised fashion.

Taking the response of the other, or, for that matter, of oneself, at face value, one can avoid confusion by asking the following questions:

1. Is it a teacher-student situation? If so, does the teacher stay within the limits of the area which he is to teach?
2. Is it an employer-employee situation? If so, is the criticism within the boundaries of the contract?
3. Is it a cooperative venture? If it is, are the criticisms consistent with the agreed-upon division of responsibilities?

If none of these situations pertains, one is dealing with a territorial conflict in which criticism serves as a weapon. One can clarify the conflict further by deciding whether the criticism represents an aggressive or a defensive maneuver, after which the selection of an appropriate response is a relatively easy matter.

Criticism and even more so its chronic form, nagging, has a rather low effectiveness in spite of its ubiquitous usage. Statements about personal feelings or demands communicate more clearly than do critical remarks. Parents may wonder whether it is possible to raise children without being critical. Although this topic will be dealt with extensively in Chapter 8, it may be stated here that even in child-rearing criticism has little utility. Criticism is unpleasant and as such it may be judiciously used in certain circumstances as a punishment for undesirable behavior; as a means of settling territorial differences, however, it is of little value.

PROTEST

Protest involves a direct expression of a person's or a group's discontent with a certain state of affairs. In territorial terms, it is a warning that contains the message, "You are on my property; get off!" Frequently, this warning statement is accompanied by an elaboration which justifies the protester's claim to the territory under dispute. Protest is ordinarily made directly to the transgressor; *it is an immediate confrontation* and, as such, does not make use of third parties. *Protest is not a request.* The other is not asked to have the kindness to leave the area under dispute; he is told to get off or else. It is made from a position of actual or pretended strength and displays a willingness on the part of the protester to follow up his warning with effective action. Ordinarily the course of events is as follows:

1. The protest is made.
2. a. The protest is accepted, apology given, ground vacated; or
   b. The protest is completely rejected and the claim is denied. Subsequent to the rejection the protest will fizzle out if adequate strength for action is not available, or a next and more active step is taken by the protester either by a publicity campaign, by seeking stronger allies, by a boycott, a strike, court action, or even a physical take-over of a concrete amount of space; or
   c. The protest is partially accepted, and a period of negotiations ensues during which new boundaries are set and a mutually acceptable treaty completed.

Here, as in all situations of territorial struggle, acts of hostility are likely to occur if one of the parties operates from a position of real or assumed weakness. Bombings, sniping, as well as police brutality are examples which are all too familiar. The practical handling of protest lies in the answers to the following questions:

1. Which territory is being disputed? Because a hidden agenda often exists, it is essential to determine precisely what the protester is after.
2. Does the protester have a reasonable claim to the territory? Even if the protester is not the owner of it at the present time, does his total life situation make control over this territory necessary? This assessment is vital, for if control over the disputed ground is essential to the protester he will undoubtedly use all the strength he can muster to acquire it.
3. What is the actual strength with which the protester can back up his

threats? In spite of the fact that one may believe that the protest is unjustified, it is impractical not to carefully review the forces of the opponent.

4. How important is the territory to the present occupant? Is it vital to all his operations? Does the protest entail the loss of a small area only, or does it involve a major decrease of control over a vast area?

5. What kind of forces can be maximally brought to bear against the protester?

After careful review of all these factors, one can determine whether one has a chance of success, if the size of the territory under dispute is worth the amount of effort involved in holding onto it, and what the potential results of each course of action would be. This procedure provides at least a reasonable basis for either making a protest or designing a response to it. The choice of action ultimately depends on one's objectives. That which one anticipates will best advance his goals will be the preferred course of action.

This discussion of protest has centered on social confrontations, but the pattern is essentially the same in the more common one-to-one situations, be it a wife who protests the husband's being late for dinner, or the neighbor who objects to the deposits made on his lawn by the dogs from next door.

LAMENT

A lament is an outcry of sorrow resulting from a serious loss; through it the individual in desperation and loneliness seeks the comfort and the consolation of sharing his feelings with another human being. The appropriate response to such a lament is not to try to convince the sorrowing person that he does not have a basis for his lament (if he truly had a loss of vital territory nothing is gained by trying to deny such a loss), but rather to give support by allowing him a temporary dependence on the comforter and by extending understanding and sympathy (giving him free access to the comforter's psychological space). The person who has suffered an irrevocable loss has experienced a sudden sharp reduction of his territory. During the period of readjustment he can be helped by allowing him temporary expansion in other areas. The person who has just lost a loved one through death will not respond to those who attempt to convince him that he should look on the brighter side, for such advice implies, in part, a critical attitude toward the legitimate sorrow of the lamenter (hidden criticism). Through such advice the lamenter will lose even more territory and consequently suffer increased sorrow.

The lamenter is helped the most by those individuals who allow him to confide in them, to communicate with them, in other words, *who give him free and unreserved access to their psychological space.* After a certain period of time during which the sorrowing person will have had the opportunity to adjust and reorganize his domain, he will gradually become less and less dependent on the psychological space of others for his territorial requirements. At this time he will be more receptive to their attempts at helping him reestablish himself as an independent human being.

If one is to help a sorrowing person one must first know *how much territory he has lost, over what period of time, and the amount of vital resources he has left to work with.* The degree of despair a person suffers will depend on a combination of these three factors, as will the time needed for his recovery.

Mr. Jones, age 52, was a man who built his whole life around his family. He was still very much in love with his wife and was enormously proud of his three children. The oldest girl was 20 and engaged to a young man whom Mr. Jones was also very fond of. One Sunday Mr. Jones, his wife, their three children, and his future son-in-law were driving to the beach to go swimming when Mr. Jones swerved to miss a squirrel that ran into the road. The car went out of control, crossed the center line and hit a truck, head-on. Mr. Jones was badly hurt, but all the others were killed. In the briefest period of time Mr. Jones lost all of the territory that he held vital to his existence. He recovered physically but was unable to recover emotionally. He was discharged from the hospital but was readmitted to the psychiatric ward because of repeated attempts at suicide. Psychotherapy proved useless. Drug therapy also failed to change his basically hopeless orientation. Whether a person in Mr. Jones' position ever recovers from so complete a loss of all he owns and values may at least in part depend on the maintenance of some form of human contact. The lament, the verbal or perhaps silent plea for compassion in a moment of feeling totally lost, can be one avenue by which this contact is established. Mr. Jones was in the unfortunate situation of being dealt with by medical personnel who saw his despondency as a psychiatric illness. They treated him with medication and therewith implied that he should not be that depressed. This closed off the one possible avenue for return to the human community: to be given time to grieve in the safety and protection of a fellow human being who understands the depth of one's feelings.

A much less grim example of this principle can be easily recalled by any parent who has turned a household inside out and searched every inch of garden and neighborhood for the grubby remnants of his child's beloved blanket, while his offspring howled in abject grief. An essential part of the child's territory is missing, and no amount of candy or ice cream will persuade the child to go to sleep without it. Any attempt at substitution will be angrily rejected. The parent who has not had the wisdom to keep a piece of blanket stowed away for just such an occasion will probably have to hold the child in his arms until he sleeps and even stay with him through the night until the child has made up for the loss. To an adult a blanket may seem like a rather insignificant example of a territory. However, one only has to observe how much time the child interacts with it to realize its magnitude. The trauma involved in the loss of the blanket depends, therefore, on the relative size of the territory which the child still possesses.

COMPLAINT

A complaint is neither like a protest, a direct attempt at obtaining or regaining a territory one claims; nor is it like a lament, a communication of the sorrow one feels after a devastating loss of territory. It has, however, some degree of similarity to each of these behaviors. Its uniqueness can perhaps best be brought out by means of an example. The following is taken from a letter to the newspaper columnist, Abigail Van Buren:

> Dear Abby: While attending a lecture, a strange gentleman (?) sitting on my left started to smoke a pipe. I don't like smoke of any kind, but thought he would soon quit, so I said nothing. Instead of quitting, he continued to puff away while the smoke wafted in my direction. I took out my handkerchief and started to "fan" the air in front of me hoping he would take the hint. He pretended not to notice and kept right on smoking.
>
> Then, the woman on my right turned to me and said sharply, "Please madame! You are distracting me with all that motion! If the smoke bothers you, either tell the fellow or move!"
>
> I was dumbfounded. I said nothing, but I moved. However, I was so upset I didn't stay for the end of the lecture. What do you think about smoking during a lecture? Was I out of order for fanning myself? And was the woman out of order for complaining that I was distracting her?   —Smoked out.

Dear Smoked: The gentleman was no gentleman. He should have asked permission from his immediate neighbors before smoking.

However, since his smoking bothered you, you should have either moved or asked him to please stop. (Your "fanning yourself" was a hint which he probably caught, but chose to ignore.) The woman on your right did what you should have done in the first place—told your neighbor that the smoke bothered you. Moral: If someone infringes on your rights, tell him!

In spite of the gentle tone of "Smoked out's" letter, it exemplifies a complaint about the two people that bothered her. The complaint is directed to Miss Van Buren, which points up the fact that complaint, as opposed to protest, does not involve a direct confrontation with the person most involved in what one is complaining about, but is rather directed toward a third party.

ASSERTIVE COMPLAINT

The quality of the complaint varies with the appropriateness of the third party chosen as the recipient. It ranges from the futile effort of a *helpless complaint* when the third party is a total outsider, as was the case with the letter sent to Abigail Van Buren, to something that comes close to a protest and which we call an *assertive complaint.* The latter occurs, for instance, when a parent does not like the way a teacher is treating his child in class and goes to the superintendent of schools to complain.

The court system is society's formalized authority toward which one can effectively direct one's assertive complaints about another citizen. In essence, the complaint includes a statement that someone else has taken something away—either a right or a property—and a request that the authority will take steps to remove that person from the disputed territory or have him make equivalent amends. The court system has the purpose of avoiding major, direct, and violent confrontations in territorial struggles. Arbitration by a powerful, neutral third party is meant to result in a just and equitable solution to territorial conflict, and it is a basic rule in any society to abide by the final decisions of its judicial body. Complaints directed to such an authority are not basically different from any other direct territorial confrontations, except that they are handled in a manner which is rather impersonal, more systematized, and less violent.

One could argue that the violence level within a free society is inversely related to the accessibility, efficiency, responsiveness, and integrity of its judicial system. The individual who has no faith in or is ignorant of the availability of an effective social appeals system will be inclined to take matters into his own hands. Thus it is conceivable that both citizen and police will use violent means to settle disputes when they despair of the judicial system's ability to insure their rights.

Anarchy—pure autonomy and right by might—is in practice so fraught with inconvenience and danger to the individual that para-judicial systems of justice are quickly organized to make up for the absence of an effective social redress system. Every man against every other man, a grim state of equality, is replaced by a system of group strength against the undesirable behavior of the few. Constant violence is reduced when a hierarchy is established, territory is allotted each person, and all are protected by group agreement. Internal peace is then established so that the group and its members may thrive.

HELPLESS COMPLAINT

To expand the perspective on the nature of complaining, we turn to history. In the early Middle Ages life in Western Europe had become a hazardous affair. The empire of Charlemagne was crumbling as his successors quarreled after his death. The Saracens threatened from the South, the Magyar horsemen from the East, and from the North the Vikings raided the shores and penetrated inland on the rivers with ever more devastating attacks. The central control of the king did not suffice to cope with these dangers and "only the local lord and his castle could provide any security for most subjects of the empire" (Strayer, 1968, p. 18). Simultaneously, there was a collapse of the clan institutions, the extended family groups which previously had provided protection to its members and had avenged injuries. These conditions increased the need for new safeguards, and "many free peasants thus gave themselves, by an act of commendation, to the protection and commands of a powerful lord who often took their land and became their landlord" (Hintze, 1968, p. 27). In this way was was created the personal dependence of the defenseless citizen on the powerful vassal who owned the fortification (Schlesinger, 1968). (A vassal was the owner of land, including the people on it. He received such an estate from a more powerful lord in exchange for loyalty and services. Ultimately this overlord remained the owner of the land, but as he needed to rely on his vassals and their military contributions for the maintenance of his own dominion, the vassal became a lord in his own right, all powerful on his own domain.) As a result of these events developed the feudal system of Western Europe in which the lord owned the land and the people on it and was responsible not only for their protection, but also for maintaining order, holding court, and determining what was the law (Strayer, 1968). That the ownership of a large territory is not without its drawbacks is well expressed by Strayer in his description of the feudal times: "On the other hand, any important accumulation of private property almost inevitably becomes burdened with public duties. The possessor of a great estate must defend it, police it, maintain roads and bridges and hold a court for his tenants" (p. 14).

In territorial terms the serf was a person who, *because he was incapable of protecting his own territory,* gave the control and the defense of it to someone else. As a consequence, he lived safely but in a state of complete dependence. If someone were to encroach on his property, steal his cattle, or abduct his daughter, he would have only one defensive recourse: the ruling vassal. He would go to the fortress, seek admission to his master, and, when given the opportunity, he would *complain.* Since he was totally dependent on the mercy of his master, who decided on the laws, he needed to convince him that he, his faithful servant, needed and deserved his protection. The serf would have to plead, portray his pitiful situation, and hope that help would come his way. This was truly a *helpless complaint.*

This brief excursion into the early Middle Ages suggests that complaints of the helpless variety—and these are the ones we will focus on because they tend to give the greatest difficulties in interpersonal contacts—are rooted in the complainer's feeling that he is incapable of defending his own territory. Complaints derive from a basically dependent stance. They imply that the person feels that he does not have the power either to expand his territory or defend it against intruders. In short, there is an imbalance between the territory he desires to have and his capability to defend it. Paraphrased, the complaint would sound something like this: "I want to keep my territory which is too big for me to defend, so you defend it for me. You're big and strong." Or, "My territory is too small, I want more. I can't conquer it myself, therefore, you give me some of yours because you have more than enough."

From a territorial perspective, the chronic complainer emerges as an individual who occupies a territory greater than he can defend or one who claims more than he has means to acquire. Lacking the confidence in his own territorial skills, he implores the help of others. The modern complainer, however, unlike his precursor in feudal times, does not consider giving the territory itself to his protector. He likes to have his cake and eat it too: rely on someone else for the management and yet maintain the autonomy of ownership. Similarly, the complainer may depend on someone else to provide him with additional property or privileges, without a willingness to pay the price for the benefits that come with such dependency. In a peculiar way, therefore, the person on whom the complainer becomes dependent ultimately turns out to be the loser.

RESPONSES TO THE HELPLESS COMPLAINT

The above observation has some interesting consequences. Usually it is concluded that the chronic complainer is insatiable. No matter how much one gives him, he wants more; and the more he gets, the more he complains. He can never be satisfied, and eventually he drives away all who sought to help him. If the previous assumption about the complainer's territory is correct, then the reason for his so-called insatiability is obvious. If his complaint results from the fact that he cannot defend or manage the territory he has, how can he be expected to manage and defend an even greater amount? As a matter of fact, one could anticipate that *the more territory he is given, the less he will be able to defend it and the more he will complain.* In addition, since the ability to defend territory depends on a wide variety of factors, including mastery of the territory, control over it, and confidence in one's own defensive skills, it becomes apparent that helping the complainer decreases rather than increases these abilities. When a person acquires a new domain through his own effort, he also gains confidence in his own strength. If he learns to manage this new territory he expands his arsenal of skills, and if he defends it well he learns to be self-reliant.

If a person is tempted to respond to a helpless complaint with the "gallant" act of coming to the rescue of the "downtrodden," he might do well to stop and consider the consequences of such an act. In our culture there has evolved the righteous expectation that one good turn deserves another in the sense that the rescued person owes the rescuer something—a reward, a favor, or at least gratitude. This expectation is apparently not a universal response to rescue, however, as this example taken from *The Devil Drives,* a biography of Sir Richard Burton, shows (Brodie, 1967, pp. 75-76):

> ... The colonel, seeing a native struggling in a river, orders the workmen on the bank to save him. When none springs to the rescue, he strikes at them with

his whip, instead of properly offering them a rupee, to which, Burton tells us, they would have responded instantly. The Sindians flee the whip, and the colonel is forced to dive in the water himself. Once rescued, the native, instead of thanking him profusely, says, "Sahib, you have preserved me, what are you going to give me?" The Englishman, recoiling in anger, refuses him charity, whereupon the native begins cursing him. The story ends with the now thoroughly outraged officer swinging his whip at the man whose life he has just saved.

We do not mean to imply that one should not come to the aid of those in distress; we simply wish to alert the would-be rescuer to the fact that such activities frequently create unexpected obligations.

Another factor may dissuade one from taking up the cause of a helpless complainer. The respondent to a complaint might expect gratitude for his altruistic behavior, but he is more likely to receive hostility instead. Dependence always implies a loss of autonomy, and the complainer experiences such loss when he receives help. Being in no position to defend himself against this loss, he will find a secret resentment generated inside himself. *Whenever one person makes another helplessly dependent on him, he makes an enemy rather than a friend.*

However, one does not always make enemies by giving assistance. In a relationship of friendship and mutuality in which there is equality and balanced interdependence, such problems do not occur. Elizabeth I of England was a ruler who brilliantly used the balance of power, both in international politics and in personal relationships, to further the goals of her reign: peace and prosperity for England and a secure throne for herself. She surrounded herself with strong and able men to whom she gave much loyalty, freedom, and responsibility. Elizabeth Jenkins comments on this genius for leadership in her book *Elizabeth the Great* (Jenkins, 1958, pp. 185-186):

> ... She was not, it was true, a woman whom men would die to possess, as Chastelard had died for the chance of possessing Mary Stuart; she was self-willed and dictatorial, and she had none of that capacity for sexual passion which, if it is strong enough, will, in a man's view, carry off these or any other failings. Yet she had qualities that aroused the admiration and emotion of men. She was brilliantly responsive; she met with comprehension and sympathy a wide range of interests; anything, indeed, that interested the men about her, interested her. Pale and frail, glittering with jewels, in long, narrow bodice and inordinate skirts that looked fit only for a garden lawn, she rode so fast that it alarmed the Master of the Horse responsible for her safety, and danced and

walked as if she could never get enough of rapid motion. But, active and domineering though she was, *one of her strongest claims on men was her dependence on them.* She excited those whose ambitions and hopes were the same as her own, *and she made them understand she could not do without them.* Her ministers groaned at the amount of work she exacted and at having to spend their own money in the public service; they exclaimed that they must retire, or at least take a holiday; but the queen could not spare them, and they were with her till they died or until she did. . . . [Emphasis added.]

THE CHRONIC COMPLAINER

If an individual must deal with a chronic complainer, either because he is closely associated with such a person or because he makes his living dealing with complaints professionally, several avenues are open for him. The first step, obvious but easily neglected, is to determine if one is dealing with protest, lament, or assertive or helpless complaint. As the appropriate response to each of these behaviors is entirely different, it is time well spent to make this differentiation. To facilitate the differentiation, a brief summary of the major characteristics of each of these patterns follows:

A *protest* is made to the appropriate party, the one with whom the conflict exists, and it originates in real or assumed strength on the side of the protester. By definition, therefore, a protest is never brought to the office of a counselor, for he is always a third party. However, the patient may protest against his therapist once they have begun their interaction. In fact, this kind of behavior, disconcerting as it may be to the counselor, should be recognized as a sign of the patient's strength.

A *lament* is an outcry of sorrow, the result of a specific loss; it seeks the comfort of human communication rather than the solution of a problem.

An *assertive complaint,* although directed to a third party rather than to the opponent, is like a protest in being the result of a specific dispute, and it aims at an assertive solution of the problem. Many of the clients who seek legal assistance come in this manner and are therefore best helped through an approach which aims at arbitration.

A *helpless complaint* is closer to a lament than to protest in that it seeks to induce compassion and readiness to come to the rescue. However, it is different from the former in its apparent cause. It results from relatively minor problems and adversities and not from one specific major loss. As it stems from a basic stance of helplessness, it is usually embedded in a chronic pattern of complaining, and neither comforting nor attempts at arbitration result in its reduction.

The chronic complainer, who has forged this pattern into a life style, makes up a substantial part of the clientele of physicians and psychotherapists. He is known by many names: to the physician as a "pain-prone patient" or less flattering, "a crock"; to the transactional analyst as a person playing the game of "wooden leg" or "yes, but"; to the offices of Workman's Compensation and Social Security as a person who seeks a pension with insufficient objective evidence of a handicap. After one has clearly established that one is confronted with a *helpless complaint,* it is time to make a choice of strategy, provided that one wishes to reduce such complaining behavior. First, one must look at the territory of the complainer to see which area he handles competently and which he manages poorly. Any areas which are inadequately managed should be curtailed, or, if possible, eliminated. If the area remaining turns out to be too small to occupy the individual's time and interest, a fact which shows itself in the person's attempts to expand once more, one can channel the available energy in a direction where the complainer has shown talent and capability before. The cardinal point is this: Never allow the person to expand beyond the realm which he handles competently.

In a lawyer's office, one of the junior partners seemed to have an inclination toward chronic complaining. He was dissatisfied with his secretary who worked too slowly, angry with his superior for not giving him enough authority, envious of his colleagues who got more interesting cases to handle, and so on. A response that certainly would fail to remedy the complaining would be to replace his secretary, give him additional authority, and more interesting cases. A successful solution was to limit his work to one area, copyright law, which he knew well and had handled well in the past. He was gradually given increased authority in this area, while all other types of work were channeled to his colleagues. The restriction created a drastic change in his behavior with an almost complete disappearance of complaints.

The second approach to dealing with chronic complaint, and which follows from our observations, seeks to increase the complainer's skills in management and defense of his territory. This change cannot be accomplished by "helping" the individual. On the contrary, that will only further reduce his faith in his own capability. The situation is similar to the one that prevails for the socially underprivileged. Simply receiving the rights and benefits of a society gratuitously cannot result in the same sense of accomplishment and power as when such rights and privileges are gained through forcefulness and from a position of strength. The same holds true in child-rearing. One does not assist in the development of an assertive human being by giving the child everything he wants whenever he wants it. The child who is given the opportunity to gradually conquer a territory of his own against the resistance of his parents and other grown-ups will arrive at adulthood with confidence in his own capability and strength. The resistance must be stiff enough so that the child has to try hard, but not so fierce that he is always defeated. The parent who offers no resistance to his child's wishes is as destructive to his offspring as the one who consistently repels the child's attempts to gain ground.

Attempts at teaching the complainer to manage his territory more effectively include the actual coaching in skills necessary for the task. In doing so, one has to bear in mind that the *person learning new techniques must have actual practice in the skills he needs and not just the theory.* The "you should learn to keep a budget" or "you should learn to tell your mother-in-law to shut up" must be replaced by actual, supervised practice. In order to gain proficiency and mastery over any area, it is necessary to repeatedly go through the steps required until they have become a routine. Some of the babbling that an infant engages in for months prior to actual speech is not random noise, but the practice of those sounds he will need to form words in the language in which he will be speaking. The child who has finally learned to walk has been working up to this activity for weeks, first by learning to stand and balance, then move and balance while holding on for support. His first steps may not be the epitome of elegance and grace, but they are part of the gradual process leading to ever-increasing mastery over his world.

A psychiatric treatment program has come to our attention, which, although not by design, seems to use both of these territorial approaches to the helpless complaint. This is an experimental rehabilitation program initiated by Dr. Johan Verhulst, described in his book *Pokers-pelgeneeskunde* (1972) at the University of Louvain, Belgium; and although it is based on a different rationale, its methodology seems directly relevant to our discussion of complaining. Only those patients are admitted into this program who could be characterized as the most extreme example of complainers, individuals who have been totally incapacitated by all sorts of physical complaints of which they have suffered for many years, and have been intensively studied and treated by competent physicians without success and without ever finding evidence for an actual disease process which could explain the complaints. As a matter of fact, no patient was accepted in this program unless he had been completely unable to engage in any form of employment for at least five years. In the medical profession this type of patient is notorious. Every doctor has had him in his office and, as success with him is almost nonexistent, the doctor soon becomes irritated and refers him on to a colleague. The frustration of the physician is particularly great because such patients tend to present themselves with a display of expectation and hope that this physician, in whom they have great faith, will at last rid them of their ills. However, as soon as the doctor gets involved, he is confronted with a sophisticated version of the "yes, but" game: Nothing the doctor tries works. Every medication he prescribes gives terrible side effects. When he resorts to operations he will find that he relieves the symptoms for approximately two weeks, and just as his hopes are rising high, the complaints suddenly come back. These experts in complaining are taken into Dr. Verhulst's rehabilitation program and treated in a most unusual way.

Throughout his stay in the program the patient is treated with a great deal of kindness and consideration. Immediately after admission the message is conveyed to him that although he has a serious problem, he will eventually get better. He is often told, "One of your problems is that you try too hard. You will get better, but you shouldn't hurry; take half a year, or a year, or five years if necessary. You will get better, but don't push for it." This approach, which, on the one hand, accepts the total dependence of the patients and, on the other hand, does not press them to resume their responsibilities, undermines their usual interaction with doctors. Not being able to fall back on the familiar pattern of behavior, the patient invariably becomes depressed and anxious.

At this point the patient is completely disengaged from all activities on the unit. He is completely taken care of by the staff, in that no area of autonomy, responsibility, initiative, or control is left to him. In other words, all action territory is denied him. From this zero point he is gradually allowed to take over certain functions one by one if he expresses a desire for them. Anytime, however, that an area is added and complaints appear, the new area is taken away for a limited period of time.

Through this gradual process, which in actuality goes quite rapidly, the patient is allowed to expand his territory step by step until he has reached complete rehabilitation. Simultaneous with the expansion he is given assistance in learning effective management of his new responsibilities, including a careful rearranging of the marital situation through family therapy. When the patient finally is allowed to go home, he is instructed to come back to the hospital immediately if any symptoms reappear. Most individuals return several times, but thereafter they maintain their newly gained freedom without complaints. This program has proven highly effective where others have completely failed. Although it was not designed on territorial principles, it seems to provide an excellent support for the ideas which we derived from looking at complaining from a territorial perspective.

We have looked at the problem of chronic, helpless complaining from the side of the recipients. It is the complainer himself, however, who suffers most as he experiences himself as incapable of handling his own problems, feels compelled to seek help, and yet knows of his mounting resentment toward those around him. Perhaps by careful scrutiny of his own territorial situation, pinpointing which areas he cannot handle and which skills he is lacking, he can reorder his priorities, eliminating nonessential areas where he finds himself to be overextended. At the same time he may seek training which will increase his management abilities in those areas that give him the greatest gratification and that he wishes to maintain.

CHAPTER 8

TERRITORIAL IMPORTANCE

One Man's Trash is Another Man's Treasure.
Caption on the business card of a second-hand store

Each person rates the importance of the various parts of his territory in his own unique fashion. That which one individual defends with utmost vigor, another gives away with pleasure. In daily life, one becomes aware of the degree to which a person values a specific part of his territory by the vehemence with which he responds to a threatened or actual invasion. If one has acquired the habit of looking for the various possible responses, such as direct assertiveness, hostility, or expansion in a different direction, one is not likely to overlook the implication of such behavior.

What makes an area so important to one person and not to another? Why is it that one individual cannot concede an inch, while another gives freely of what he has? To answer such questions and to handle interpersonal relationships effectively, it is particularly useful to explore the importance that a person attaches to the various parts of his territory. A charming example of territorial importance is drawn by A. A. Milne in a poem about Sir Thomas Tom of Appledor, "The Knight Whose Armor Didn't Squeak" (Milne, 1955). In this epic Sir Thomas is described as a rather cowardly person who avoids all confrontation if possible. Whenever he rides out to survey his realm and notices the approach of another knight, his inclination is to hide. One day as he is resting in a ditch, he becomes aware of something peculiar about a passing horseman:

. . .
Sir Thomas raised a cautious ear
  And listened as Sir Hugh went by,
And suddenly he seemed to hear (or not to hear)
  The stranger made a nicer sound

> Than other knights who lived around.
> Sir Thomas watched the way he went—
>   His rage was such he couldn't speak.
> For years *they'd called him down in Kent*
>   *The knight whose armor didn't squeak,*
> And here and now he looked upon
>   *Another knight whose squeak had gone.*
> He rushed to where his horse was tied,
>   He spurted to a rapid trot,
> The only fear he felt inside
>   About his enemy was not
> How sharp his sword, how stout his heart,
>   But, has he got too long a start? . . . [Emphasis added.]

Sir Thomas, emboldened by the force of his indignation about Sir Hugh's usurpation of an area so dear to his heart, overpowers his rival, removes his armor, and dumps it in a nearby pond with the result that,

> . . .
>
>   So ever after, more and more,
> The men of Kent would proudly speak
>   Of Thomas Tom of Appledor,
> The knight whose armor didn't squeak,
>   Whilst Hugh, the knight who gave him best
> Squeaks just as badly as the rest.

Knowledge about territorial importance will help prevent one person from blundering into areas which are most vital to another, thus avoiding the blistering counterattacks or subtle malice which such ventures will inevitably bring about, as well as the pain inflicted on the person for whom one cares. Although the importance of territory can be recognized by the intensity of the response, it is often possible to determine the value of a specific territory ahead of time, thereby eliminating most of the hassles that arise because of carelessness and impulsiveness. Being engaged in a territorial skirmish without any awareness of the worth of the area under dispute is like playing chess without knowing the value of the pieces. In chess, the king and queen, which are of the greatest value, are always defended to the maximum of each player's capability. In life, however, the value of the pieces is influenced but not decided by agreement or tradition. Territorial value is a subjective matter which depends on many interrelated factors, the most important of which will be discussed separately.

OVERALL TERRITORIAL SIZE

The larger a person's total territory, the easier it is for him to relinquish peripheral segments of it, or to state it in opposite terms: *The smaller the territory, the greater the importance of any part.*

A young woman had the ill fortune of having been born with a somewhat less than average intellectual endowment to a family in which every other member was both ambitious and capable of a high level of performance. The girl's development, which may well have been very satisfactory in another setting, was tragically inadequate under these circumstances. As everyone else was more able, she had no responsibilities with which she was entrusted, generated no ideas to which the others listened, and evolved no skills which the rest of the family valued. In fact, she seemed to have no psychological space or action territory whatever in this family, except for one small niche that over time she had carved out for herself: Every night after dinner she cleaned the kitchen and did the dishes. She did not do them well, but her mother appreciated the help and she vaguely recognized that it was of some importance to her daughter. One evening a peculiar event took place which led to the young girl's admission to a psychiatric hospital. The day had been somewhat strained because of conflict between the parents. In the evening, after a rather tense dinner, the girl went to the kitchen to do the dishes. Perhaps because of the tension in the house, perhaps by sheer accident, a plate slipped out of her hand, landed on two crystal glasses, and shattered them. At just this moment the mother entered the kitchen and, startled by the sudden noise, yelled, "You stupid thing, you can't even wash the dishes without breaking them! I will have to do them myself from now on!"

The mother's reaction may seem like a simple expression of anger. There is hardly a family that has not witnessed such an event at one time or another, and yet, in this case, it had drastic consequences. The girl flew into a rage, threw down another plate she had in her hands, swore, and ran out of the kitchen to her own room where she first picked up a table lamp and then a radio, crashing both of them violently to the floor. Then she sat down on her bed, sobbing, and when the startled parents caught up with her, her speech was totally incoherent. They tried to calm her, to tell her that mother didn't really mean what she said, but no degree of comforting had any effect. Eventually they called the doctor, and the girl was admitted to the hospital where during the first days she uttered incomprehensible sentences, repeating over and over that she was dead and that the people around her were dead, a sentence no one really understood.

The implication of this example is that if an individual has an exceedingly small territory, he cannot take any risks with it, for when he loses it he may have nothing left, and *having no territory at all is equivalent to not being alive.* The recognition of this principle gives some insight into the behavior of individuals whose life sphere is extremely restricted. A. H. Esser describes a patient on a back ward of a state institution who was mute and without function within the group. He had one tiny territory in the day-room, however, to which he laid claim. When this area was invaded—regardless of the reason—even if a nurse was trying to give him medication or food, he would strike out at the intruder (Esser et al., 1965).

The unfortunate girl described earlier derived her identity and security from an action territory, however small it may have been. Most of the time a person has access to all major types of territory, but occasionally there is an exclusive reliance on one of them. If this area of primary importance happens to be psychological space, it makes the individual especially vulnerable, because of its temporary nature. In addition, psychological space is by definition dependent on the attention of others, and a person who relies exclusively on it cannot therefore tolerate being alone, for that automatically means that all of his territory has fallen away. Albert Camus describes the dandy as such a person. The dandy always provokes others in order to gain the attention needed to sustain his life: "The dandy, therefore, is always compelled to astonish . . . he compels others to create him. . . . For the dandy, to be alone is not to exist" (Camus, 1965, p. 52).

The need to sustain a grasp over psychological space may well account for the behavior of some members of certain groups whose provocative actions and appearance seem designed to attract attention to themselves, rather than their cause. A radical student leader told of his conversion to the ranks of protester when one day, as a lark, he decided to march in a picket line carrying a sign. He went on to describe that "Suddenly I got the feeling of *this is it. When I felt the eyes of the crowds focus on me, a new feeling of self made me feel alive in a way I had never experienced before!"*

The predominant importance of a particular type of territory, and its effects on interpersonal relations, played a major role in the lives of a couple that sought help for serious marital problems. Their relationship was all but destroyed because of the unfortunate fact that the wife was primarily dependent on psychological space, whereas the husband placed the utmost importance on privacy retreat. The intensity of the involvement and the absorption of her husband's attention were so essential to the wife that she overwhelmed him completely from the moment he would enter the home. As he valued his privacy above all else, enjoyed being immersed in his thoughts or going on walks by himself, he experienced her behavior as an invasion and responded with building higher and higher walls around himself and withdrawing behind them. Although this response served to save his own security, it destroyed the foundation of his spouse's existence. The result was that she attempted to break through his defenses with ever more violent means, only to be met with ever-thickening ramparts. At the time the couple sought help, this conflict had gone to the point where the wife alternated between uncontrolled rage and the sense that she was dying, while the husband had become bitter and isolated, forever vigilant, expecting to be attacked.

Problems which result from too small or too limited a total territory suggest a strategy for change either by means of expansion or diversification. The simplicity of this formulation does not, of course, mean that the process is easy. To enable the girl who depended on dishwashing for her sole area of autonomy to expand her territory would require a long process. First, she would have to learn skills with which she could slowly increase her area. This process would involve working with the other family members to have them yield some ground. Many steps would need to be taken, but the steps are neither mysterious nor impossible. The awareness of this type of territorial situation will prevent the therapist from foundering together with the patient in the quagmire of misunderstanding the roots of the patient's exclamation that "everybody is dead!" In the case of the couple, the vicious circle can be reversed if each partner, recognizing the predicament, first takes steps to change his own situation. Thus the wife could acquire an action territory of her own, reducing the need for her husband's attention and thus allowing him to lower his defenses.

CENTRALITY OF THE AREA

Even if an individual has a considerable amount of territory, he may have certain areas which are of inordinate importance to him. *The centrality of a specific area is a major determinant of the importance it holds.* By the term *centrality* we mean to indicate that *a particular area interlocks with many other parts of the person's total territory in such a way that those other areas would become inaccessible with the loss of the central one.* The concept can be exemplified by the rather peculiar organization of France.

In that country, Paris holds a position of extreme centrality. All of the country's administration, commerce, and communication is channeled through Paris first and thereafter dispersed to the rest of the country. As a consequence, France is very vulnerable, for if Paris were taken or destroyed by an enemy, all of France would become an unmanageable chaos. General de Gaulle's realization of this may have accounted for his proposal for decentralization, a proposal which led to his resignation as President when it was defeated in a public referendum. On an individual level, the unusual degree of centrality of one area leads to the same type of vulnerability.

A widow lived alone with her young daughter. She had a fairly active life with many friends with whom she often had coffee. She participated in school-related activities, PTA meetings, and from time to time she played bridge with acquaintances. She was a devoted housekeeper and spent a good deal of time reading, which was one of her favorite pastimes. When the daughter graduated from high school, the mother was proud of the fact that she had been accepted in a well-known Eastern college. The mother worked hard to get everything ready for her daughter's departure, and she seemed in good spirits when she saw her off at the airport. Yet a week thereafter she became listless, almost unresponsive to the friends who visited her; she had no appetite, she was restless at night, and showed no interest in her environment. Several days later some concerned friends took her to a psychiatrist, who diagnosed a serious depression and placed her in a hospital.

The loss of her action territory relative to her daughter constituted the loss of a central part of her territory. All other areas of importance were closed off with the disappearance of her maternal role. School affairs no longer had any importance to her. As topics of conversation with her friends had usually centered around the activities of her daughter, the lack of daily contact with her made the conversations rapidly dry up. In addition, talking about her daughter was a painful reminder of her absence. She had been an immaculate housekeeper, but now it seemed purposeless to clean a house when no one shared it. In the past she had enjoyed grocery shopping, but now it became apparent that the pleasure of shopping was dependent on the preparation of the meals which were her daughter's favorites. Without realizing it, this widow had built her life in such a way that every part of her territory had become tied in with her role as a mother. *Losing this role constituted the loss of a central part of her territory, leaving her extremely little, if any, accessible realm of importance.*

The above example illustrates the risk that one runs when no *independent territorial areas* are maintained to fall back on following a loss. This type of organization makes one extremely vulnerable. As a consequence, the central area becomes of vital importance, and it should, therefore, be treated with great care. The recognition of such centrality suggests that an individual take steps toward the development of some new and independent areas in order to prevent future problems. This development is of special importance if one is bound to lose the central territory sooner or later, as was true in the widow's case. *Decentralization is an important strategy if one wants to increase the security of his territory.*

It is ironic that extremely unfortunate circumstances sometimes provide such diversification. During the conflicts between Catholics and Protestants in North Ireland, the incidence of depression and suicide fell off drastically, especially among those who lived closest to the upheaval (Lyons, 1972). The same was observed during World War II. If one considers depression to be a consequence of the loss of a central territory, the hypothesis suggests itself that the independent action territory associated with the social upheaval reduces the centrality of other areas, thus making the individual less prone to depression.

ACCESSIBILITY OF NEW TERRITORY

The ease with which a person can abandon an area depends on the accessibility of new territory. An analogy drawn from the animal world portrays the broad applicability of this statement. The little hermit crab, weak-bodied and vulnerable, uses a borrowed shell to keep him safe and secure. He laboriously carries this small fortress with him on his sojourns in search of food. Under certain circumstances, after coming across another shell and finding it unoccupied, he may decide to investigate if it is more suitable to his needs than his present abode. After much poking, feeling, and fussing around, he will try the new shell on for size. This maneuver is usually followed by a thorough reappraisal of his old home, which he reenters. Then he reexamines and tries the new shell once more. This ambivalent process continues while he carefully ascertains the merits of each shell. Finally he reaches a decision, selects one of the shells, and goes on his way.

Several years ago, after a springtime outing to the beach, we brought home with us about two dozen hermit crabs, a quantity of sea water, and a large number of empty shells. We put the crabs and empty shells in a flat container with the water and settled down to see what would happen. After a brief period of timidity the crabs began to crawl about. Encountering great numbers of empty shells, they were soon engaged in a veritable orgy of shell swapping. At first we were fascinated by this frenzied spectacle, but as it showed no sign of let-up we grew bored and drifted away, realizing vaguely that we had somehow created a monstrous situation that could only lead to an evil end. Returning after several hours, we found that a few rugged characters were still dealing in real estate, but the rest were lying about shell-less in a moribund state. We quickly transferred the few survivors to a container which more closely resembled their natural environment. Order being restored, we were able to keep this group alive and seemingly healthy for some time.

Aside from the hazards of too many alternatives, if an individual is aware of many possibilities open to him and trusts in his own capability to carve out a new niche after he has lost the old, he will not find the loss of any part of his territory too great a threat. However, when a person no longer believes in his future and his possibilities, when he despairs of ever again knowing the joy of expansion, he has no choice but to hang tenaciously on to what he has and to spend his days in fear that that which he treasures will be taken away from him. If the widow in the above example had had new territory accessible to her, the departure of her daughter would have opened up a whole new slice of life and the loss would not have left her in despair, but rather in the vigorous pursuit of new possibilities. Instead of being committed to a psychiatric ward, she would have been registering for classes at the university or interviewing for a new job. The accessibility of new territory is a critical factor influencing the importance of a person's present realm, his vulnerability, and his defensiveness.

The availability of new areas is dependent on the *territorial style* a person develops in the course of his life. This style lies on a continuum between two poles. The one extreme reveals an emphasis on the management of the territory which one possesses, aiming at an ever-greater control and an ever-stronger defense of it. At the other pole is a style that develops little attachment to the territory over which one has control, and whereby satisfaction is derived primarily from the process of expansion. Both styles have serious drawbacks which, in their extremes, outweigh their advantages. The person who seeks an ever-greater control tends to reduce his territory rather than to increase it, for the smaller it is the better he can manage and defend it. However, having such a small territory with no available alternatives makes him automatically more vulnerable, a vulnerability which in turn leads to increased defensiveness. This vicious circle may end with a man living as a prisoner in his own carefully built fortress. By the time he recognizes that he has lost his freedom, he may find it very difficult to break out of his own heavy walls, except in an explosive way. Understanding of this vicious circle throws some light on the strange events one reads about from time to time concerning a person who has led an exemplary life and who has been recognized as an outstanding, stable citizen, but who suddenly breaks out of his pattern in a most irrational and destructive way.

A typical example, as reported in a West Coast newspaper, described how a young man had situated himself with a gun on a bluff overlooking a highway and sniped at passing cars, seriously wounding several people. The arrival of the State Patrol resulted in a brief exchange of shots followed by silence. On investigation the police found a 17-year-old boy who had committed suicide with his last bullet. He had been known in school and by his parents as a model child. He was hardworking, earning straight A's in school, and had recently become an Eagle Scout. His schoolmates saw him as extremely straight, and no one would have predicted this sudden, irrational behavior leading to tragedy.

A different way in which an ever-greater control over one's territory can be obtained, relying on management rather than defense, is exemplified by the virtuoso. A cellist, for instance, may literally spend all his time perfecting the control over his instrument, to the neglect of all other aspects of his life.

The person with the opposite style, who develops little attachment to the territory he acquires and who readily abandons it in search for that which is new, may become an aimless wanderer forever in a hungry search, losing himself in the excitement of acquisition like the drug user in the whirl of the LSD intoxication. Such a person remains a guest in life, for whenever he momentarily settles down he accepts neither obligations nor restraints and "keeps his bags packed," ready to leave at a moment's notice when his freedom from restraint is threatened. In the end he suffers a deep sense of loneliness and alienation which comes with being homeless. As he looks around he sees his fellow men as strangers. They all seem to move purposefully with goals and responsibilities. They seem to know what is going on and he does not. He stands aside as an outsider, an observer, interested perhaps, but not a part; he may wish to join the others and become one of them, but the possibility of assuming a definite place with responsibilities, obligations, and commitments frightens him.

Why does he fear this commitment? There may be many different reasons. Perhaps he does not believe in his own management capability, or he may fear that he cannot defend himself and that others will take any territory he has gained away from him, which may seem worse than having nothing to begin with. Perhaps it is a way of defending his privacy. He travels, as it were, through life incognito. There may be moments when he cuts through his isolation as he encounters wanderers like himself, for strangers who meet in transit can freely visit and exchange ideas as each of them knows that he will travel on tomorrow and will never meet the other again. Unavoidably, the person will experience a sense of loss that comes to those who do not know who they are. Knowing who one is derives from having a territory to which one is committed. Only the individual who settles down, who shares the hardships as well as the pleasures, who takes responsibilities, makes commitments and keeps them—only he, who occupies a definite territory among his fellow men, acquires an identity and ceases to be a stranger. It is small wonder, then, that the wanderer, bereft of such identity, may suddenly attach himself with great abandon to some group movement, perhaps a fanatic religious sect, a commune, or another place which will provide a home in order to cut through the unbearable isolation, even if doing so may be at the price of the total loss of his independence.

The dichotomy between the two life styles is not a new observation. These two aspects of man, which, to some extent, are combined in every individual, have long been recognized. Being at the one pole is akin to the occasional experience of being at the center of one's universe with a deep sense of the possible, dizzy with one's freedom in the awareness that one can truly choose. It has to do with the sense of abandonment to the moment, of dissolving, as it were, in the activity that one undertakes, like the Zen master who becomes at once the bow, the arrow, and the target (Herrigel, 1971). The other experience is like the common fantasy of living in an impenetrable fortress, complete ruler in an obedient domain, easily repelling any attempt to break through the defensive lines. The nineteenth-century philosopher Nietzsche discriminated between the *Dionysian* and the *Apollonian* aspects of art (Nietzsche, 1927). The Dionysian aspect, exemplified in music, indicates man's surrender to the existence of the moment and is associated with such terms as becoming, possibility, growth, choice, absorption, spontaneity, and present. Its opposite, the Apollonian aspect, represented by the art of sculpture, captures the structure of the moment, freezes the form, and renders it forever unchangeable. It has greater affinity to words like structure, control, unchangeability, eternity, carefulness, and management.

The extreme of each position brings with it disadvantages of considerable magnitude. Some middle ground, in a balance which suits the individual, has the greatest promise of combining some of the advantages of both. As a matter of fact, many people derive their greatest joy from a keen awareness of a combination of expansion of their territory and the acquisition of the skills that provide mastery over it. This combination of new skills and new opportunities creates a deep sense of involvement, of being alive, as well as a pervasive sense of identity, a feeling that one is, indeed, a strong, unique individual. This balance is perhaps best symbolized by a fountain, for it combines structure and motion.

An interesting parallel exists between these two territorial styles and the two major drives which some psychologists believe to motivate human behavior. The one category serves the maintenance of security and the preservation of the life of the individual as well as that of the species, whereas the other supports the pursuit of newness, what one could call curiosity or the exploration drive.

The sadist, who lives in an extreme mode of territorial control, is a person who is challenged by the uniquely free spirit of another human being. The other is always elusive, and the sadist obtains his most intense pleasure at that brief moment when the other seems to be totally under his control. Such a person once described that he had his moments of greatest satisfaction when he saw the terror in the eyes of the woman he controlled. A book by John Fowles, *The Collector* (1964), convincingly describes a young man who lives totally immersed in such a style of life, a style he resorts to because of his deep sense of vulnerability. In the course of the book he imprisons a young woman whose *esprit* has both fascinated and challenged him. He locks her up in the basement of a country home where he observes her and where she eventually dies, just like the butterflies he catches and pins up in his collection. It is a terrifying book, for it tells how one man's need for control destroys the life in another human being. His action toward his prisoner is an extension of his overall life style. He treats her as an addition to his territory and handles her in essentially the same way as the rest of his realm of existence, by carefully controlling her. In this respect, John Fowles' novel correctly portrays that the young man is not acting out of sheer viciousness, but rather, in a fashion consistent with his life style.

The central premise of the present discussion is that the accessibility of new territory is a major determinant of the importance one attaches to that which he already possesses. The person's life style, whether loaded on the Apollonian or on the Dionysian side, has an important bearing on this accessibility. Each style leads to a characteristic restriction. The Apollonian extreme seeks complete control over an ever-shrinking area; the Dionysian opposite ultimately leaves nothing but the privacy of body and thoughts, beyond which lies dissolution into chaos.

The recognition of the advantages and the disadvantages of each life style affords a person the opportunity to take stock and scrutinize to which extent he has relied on either. There is no reason to assume that one is born with one style rather than another. On the contrary, each individual reaches his particular balance through a process of learning. A person can change, therefore, if he anticipates that this would bring more favorable consequences. If he finds himself too far over on the side of control and territorial constriction, he might begin building new bridges toward the future by the exploration of new possibilities. The individual who has neglected to make firm commitments to the management of any specific territory may find it to his advantage to assume such responsibility and set out to learn the skills needed to manage one area effectively.

Shifting one's emphasis in life style is easily described, but perhaps not so readily accomplished. A move in either direction brings with it certain discomforts. To move towards new possibilities means to live more dangerously. It involves sticking one's neck out—taking risks. This move opens opportunities, but it also brings with it great uncertainties. To change style in this direction requires giving up control over many areas of one's life, with the implication that the future becomes less predictable. There is no way around it—such a shift creates anxiety. A shift in the opposite direction means making commitments and assuming responsibilities, which implies reduction of certain freedoms. It means tying oneself down to specific parts of a territory. This change, too, creates apprehensions, including increased vulnerability, more chance of failure in responsibilities assumed, knowledge that some escape routes have been closed off, and perhaps a global sense of the loss of opportunity. Life presents an intriguing paradox. On the one side there is the exhilaration and the joy of becoming, which is inseparably tied to the anxiety concerning the unknown, while on the other side there is the safety, the certainty of controlling a small, familiar, securely maintained territory which offers few surprises, induces little anxiety, but which precludes real growth—potentially a world of ennui and calcification.

THE SEARCH FOR SECURITY

Implied in the last section lies another factor which has a bearing on territorial importance. *The relative importance of one's territory increases with the greater need of security.* To the extent that an individual perceives himself as vulnerable and the environment as dangerous and hostile, he will hold on to an area that he knows best and can defend optimally, for here he has some degree of safety.

Mr. Jones, a 34-year-old man, who has been characterized by his psychiatrist as an obsessive-compulsive neurotic, feels extremely uncomfortable when anything is outside his control. In his small apartment everything is immaculate, the newspapers are stacked in exact order, and each object has its own place. Lately, since a conflict with his mother, Mr. Jones has felt increasingly uncomfortable and somehow extremely vulnerable. When he walks in the street he's afraid that passers-by will cough and cover him with germs. He has begun to avoid crowded places such as elevators and restaurants and therefore has to take care of his own meals. Sometime later he begins to worry about the possibility that the people handling the food in the stores may contaminate the products, and he now limits himself to canned and frozen items. Gradually his sense of being vulnerable intensifies, and he now rarely leaves his room. When he does not show up at the homes of his relatives for a week, they come to look for him and find him standing in the corner of his room, unable to move beyond an area of several square feet, convinced that some hostile force will descend on him and destroy his life.

The sense of vulnerability, whether it stems from past experiences or from an extreme threat of the moment, affects both the accessibility of new territory and the size of what one holds at present. Vulnerability, therefore, is an important link in the circular process which leads to ever-greater defensiveness. It is usually not possible to determine whether a person has a constrictive territorial style because he has learned to fear the world around him or whether the sequence is the other way around. Practically, the sequence is of little consequence, for the more important question is which avenue is most available and promising for leading him out of the impasse. Perhaps it is possible to reduce the danger quality of the outside world by establishing communication that can lead to the formation of a trusting alliance. Simultaneously, however, an expansion of the territory, coupled with training in skills of management and defense, should be fostered.

THE ELEMENT OF TIME

Time, the relentless dimension, although silent and unobtrusive, determines the meaning of every human event in an all-pervasive manner. Ingmar Bergman's classic movie, *The Seventh Seal*, shows a scene in which an actor who is a member of a traveling stage company is being pursued by Death. He runs through the forest, hides behind bushes, and finally finds safety in the top of a tall tree, or so he thinks, for when he looks down a moment later he shivers at the sight of Death, who is methodically sawing through the trunk of the tree.

> "But you can't do that, I have a performance tonight."
> "Cancelled," is the grim, emotionless answer of Death.

When an individual is confronted with his own time limitations, all events suddenly show themselves in a different light. Things which seemed of the greatest importance a moment ago now have become futile or even ridiculous. When one projects his daily worries against the endlessness of space and time, he cannot help but feel humility in the recognition of the relative unimportance of his territorial conflicts.

Shifts in time perspective are often employed by writers, film directors, and other media manipulators to enhance a plot or resolve a dilemma. William Golding uses this device to great effect in his various novels. In *Lord of the Flies* (1959) the reader is first introduced to a group of young boys who have survived the crash of an airplane in which all adults have perished. The boys, left without a higher authority to comfort them and settle their disputes, are at the same time suspended without a future and with no audience to judge their actions. As the author zeros in on their actions in greater detail, time seems to slow down and disengage from the ongoing process of a larger world. The boys are soon embroiled in petty rivalries and quarrels. The reader begins to experience them not as children but as adults playing out the moral game of good and evil. In the end, the only surviving member of the rational group, Ralph, is hunted by the superstition-driven gang of red-haired Jack, who, armed with pointed sticks, mean to kill him. Ralph flees, his attackers pursue relentlessly, remorselessly. Time stands still and the tension of the moment becomes unbearable (Golding, 1959, pp. 345-348):

> Ralph screamed, a scream of fright and anger and desperation. . . . He shot forward, burst the thicket, was in the open, screaming, snarling, bloody. . . .

They were all running, all crying out madly. He could hear them crashing in the undergrowth and on the left was the hot, bright thunder of the fire. He forgot his wounds, his hunger and thirst, and became fear; hopeless fear on flying feet, rushing through the forest towards the open beach. . . .

He stumbled over a root and the cry that pursued him rose even higher. . . . Then he was down, rolling over and over in the warm sand, crouching with arm up to ward off, trying to cry for mercy.

He staggered to his feet, tensed for more terrors, and looked up at a huge peaked cap. It was a white-topped cap, and above the green shade of the peak was a crown, an anchor, gold foliage. . . .

A naval officer stood on the sand, looking down at Ralph in wary astonishment. On the beach behind him was a cutter.

The officer looked at Ralph doubtfully for a moment, then took his hand away from the butt of the revolver.

"Hullo."

Squirming a little, conscious of his filthy appearance, Ralph answered shyly.

"Hullo."

The officer nodded, as if a question had been answered.

"Are there any adults—any grown-ups with you?"

Dumbly, Ralph shook his head. He turned a half-pace on the sand. A semicircle of little boys, their bodies streaked with coloured clay, sharp sticks in their hands, were standing on the beach making no noise at all.

"Fun and games," . . .

The officer grinned cheerfully at Ralph.

"We saw your smoke. What have you been doing? Having a war or something?"

Ralph nodded.

The officer inspected the little scarecrow in front of him. The kid needed a bath, a hair-cut, a nose-wipe and a good deal of ointment. . . .

Other boys were appearing now, tiny tots some of them, brown, with the distended bellies of small savages. . . .

"Who's boss here?"

"I am," said Ralph loudly.

A little boy who wore the remains of an extraordinary black cap on his red hair and who carried the remains of a pair of spectacles at his waist, started forward, then changed his mind and stood still.

A crunch of dismay strikes the reader. One moment the boys are bigger than life and the next they have been reduced to children playing games. The quarrel which filled the mind becomes unimportant when viewed against the panorama of ongoing time. Mankind, which tends to experience and therefore respond to life as a series of disconnected incidents, is as often confounded and dismayed as well as relieved and comforted by such glimpses of eternity.

Time has a different significance for each of the three types of territory. Psychological space, which is totally constituted by the moment, gains its importance largely from the duration of that moment. One can define psychological space as the product of attention and time. Maximally, a person can have all of the attention all of the time, but he will generally have to be satisfied with some of the attention for some of the time. People have an amazingly keen perception of the amount of time during which others deserve their attention. If, during a panel discussion, one of the members holds forth for a longer period than the audience judges appropriate, their displeasure becomes immediately apparent by the growing degree of restlessness, coughing, and whispering. It is as if by these means the audience is taking back the psychological space that the speaker is undeservedly appropriating. If, in a classroom, one pupil repeatedly asks questions or in other ways draws an unusual amount of attention from a respected teacher, he is likely to be ostracized by his peers. The amount of time a person may draw the attention of a group depends on his status. An authority may lay claim to this attention for a long time because he "owns" that much psychological space, but if a less important individual tries to do the same he should anticipate an assertive counterresponse—if not an outburst of hostility—as many a poor performer on the stage or in the lecture hall has found out to his regret.

The time dimension also has an interesting impact on private domain, especially when it is shared with others. In a family home each person has the right to use the bathroom as his privacy retreat for a limited time, but taking two hours for a bath is often more than he has a right to and is apt to evoke anger and protest from the other family members. A person who uses a public telephone booth to have a long and detailed conversation while a line of people forms to take their turn, risks considerable hostility. Even the privacy of one's own thoughts has a time limitation on it. An individual may withdraw in fantasy, concentrate on a book, or read the evening paper, but if he spends all night doing this he is claiming too much privacy by the usual standards of those around him. After some time others will begin to intrude, asking questions, starting conversation, or making distracting noises.

The way in which an individual uses his time basically falls within the realm of his personal autonomy. In a sense, therefore, time itself becomes part of his action territory. Anyone who carelessly disposes of another's time is, therefore, guilty of an aggressive act for which he should expect an angry response, whether it be assertive or hostile. A most common example of this is the annoyance which results from having to wait for someone else who is late for an appointment. The feeling of impatience derives from the anger which is evoked when someone else uses one's time without permission and without appropriate consideration.

The experience of time and the time perspective varies from person to person. For some, time is primarily concentrated in the present, whereas for others time is imbedded in a continuity which reaches to various distances of past and future. Some individuals lead their lives as if their personal existence will have no end, but others live with the continuous awareness that it may come to an abrupt closure at any moment. The Apollonian life style is associated with an emphasis on duration and continuity, with the unavoidable weight of long-time commitment and perhaps the implicit desire to freeze the world into an unchangeable, eternal state. The Dionysian, on the other hand, is associated with the experience of time as the exciting whirl; time as duration and continuity is eliminated, while the dynamic aspect of the moment is accentuated.

The individual's unique sense of time determines in a major way the importance of his territory. If his time perspective is short, he is bound to attach less significance to a specific area than when it is long-range, for if he looks far into the future he connects an endless number of consequences to his activities. These consequences will unavoidably increase the significance. If a person lives within a short time span, he can afford to impulsively abandon areas which, to others, may seem of great importance. The discrepancies between the ways in which time is perceived lead to great differences in the weight given to territorial importance and are bound to result in conflict. For instance, when an extremely Dionysian individual invades the territory which is very dear to the heart of an Apollonian person, to the Dionysian it may be incomprehensible why anyone would make such a fuss over trivial matters. The Apollonian may look at the same situation, outraged over the lack of sensitivity displayed by so blatant an aggressor.

This discussion of factors which determine the importance an individual attaches to any part of his territory is far from complete. The vicissitudes of each individual's life may exert influences in highly unpredictable ways. The value of an area may be based on very personal concerns or on such mundane matters as money or fame. A group of young rock musicians had fallen into the pattern of "jamming" together. They enjoyed the fun of playing and singing, as well as each other's company. In due time they became quite good and were often invited to play at social events. Then came an offer to play professionally and, not much later, a lucrative recording contract. Without planning it, the music which had been a minor part of their lives became the central, most important area for each of them. It now involved fame and fortune. The previously harmonious friendship between the group members now came under tremendous strain. Each began to worry whether he was getting his rightful share of attention and money, and whether the others were playing well enough to allow the whole group to rise to the peak of popularity. The bass player was thought to be weak by several members, and, in discussion between them, the idea of replacing him came up. Soon the previous harmony was destroyed by angry arguments, and after a brief period of success and promise the group broke up, leaving each of its members alone in the struggle to establish himself.

Other unpredicted events may suddenly enhance or decrease the value attached to parts of a territory. Illness may take away all possibility of an individual's participation in work. As a consequence a hobby may now become the center stage of his life. By means of a series of poorly planned maneuvers a person may find himself in a corner, having burned all his bridges behind him. The last foothold he has left now becomes immensely important and any opponent would do well to realize this. Many unforeseeable events affect territorial importance, and the introduction of new elements into a situation may lead to a shift toward a hitherto unfavorable balance. In one's personal life, as well as in professional work with a client, it is often by means of the ingenious application of this principle that fortuitous results are obtained.

CHAPTER 9

TERRITORIAL RIGHTS

Quod Licet Jovi, Haud Licet Bovi [The privileges of Jupiter are not
allowed to the cattle].

Old Roman Proverb

We hold these truths to be self-evident, that all men are
created equal, that they are endowed by their Creator with
certain unalienable rights, that among these are life,
liberty and the pursuit of happiness.

Declaration of Independence

The human struggle over coveted territory always poses the question of
who holds legitimate right to the area claimed by both sides. Whose claim
should be supported and whose not? Many individuals occupy territory
they feel they have no right to, whereas others seek access to areas which
traditionally have been closed to them. Ethical questions arise, such as: Is
it good or bad to be aggressive and invade somebody else's domain? Is the
"good person" the one who is satisfied with a small territory, or is the "best
man" the one who "wins" by taking as much space as he can get away
with?

We have deliberately refrained from moral judgments concerning
territoriality, primarily because, in our view, only those individuals having
a direct pipeline to the "truth" would be capable of such an omnipotent
stance. In our experience, such a claim to the truth usually serves the
purpose of supporting one person's position and is not likely to coincide
with the truth of the opposing party. "God is on our side" is a slogan used
with equal conviction by all nations engaged in a war, and anyone who has
seen the flaming indignation and righteousness engendered on both sides
of a childhood squabble, for instance, in a quarrel about the right to sit by
the window during a trip to the corner market, will appreciate the

fruitlessness of any attempt to decide *a priori* what is right and wrong in
territorial matters. Claims and counterclaims to possessions and privileges
must be constantly reevaluated and negotiated.

If one avoids choosing sides and looks at territorial conflicts with a keen
interest but without a stake in the outcome, one cannot help but recognize
that, in spite of the absence of a universal standard, each of the parties
involved holds strong convictions as to his rights to the area under dispute.
Much of the time the foundation for a specific claim is as vague as the
feelings about its rightfulness are tenacious.

Ideas about division of territory change drastically with time and place.
Many rights which seemed self-evident in the past are hard to conceive of
today. Only 200 years ago most European countries found it self-evident
that the right to govern a country was determined by the accident of birth.
The child of a monarch became the next monarch because it was his blood
right. At the same time, on the American Continent a group of men signed
the Declaration of Independence, which denied the right of kings and
stated that it was self-evident that each man had a right to life, liberty, and
the pursuit of happiness. Although it was self-evident to the drafters of this
remarkable document that each person had such rights, George III
evidently thought otherwise, and sent his army to instruct the American
Colonies that, to him, such an idea hardly seemed desirable, let alone
self-evident.

Rights and privileges concerning any territory are always either given to
an individual or taken by him. They may be given by the society or specific
group of which he is a member, or by a particular individual. They may be
acquired through great effort or with relative ease, after sharp confrontations, reasonable negotiations, or clever machinations. When the actual
division of territory coincides with the notions of all parties involved
concerning the areas which they can rightfully claim, one has the good
fortune of living in a state of interpersonal or social tranquility.[1] However,
as soon as two or more individuals lay claim to the same area, a conflict
arises. In the struggle which results from such a discrepancy, both parties
will attempt to justify their position to the best of their ability. The success
which these efforts meet can be calibrated by the expressions of right-

[1]Consistent with this view is the observation of Syunzo Kawamura (1967) that there is
relatively little conflict in monkey troops in their natural state but that one must expect a
great amount of fighting when one brings a number of individuals together to establish a
troop artificially. In such situations the fighting continues until the internal structure has been
clearly established.

eousness from the side of those who find their claims unjustly obstructed and the signs of guilt in those who, with obvious ambivalence, hold onto a territory which deep inside they fear belongs to their opponent.

A letter from an irate mother to her son may serve as an illustration. Separated from his mother by the full width of the continent of the United States, the son had been in the habit of traveling with his wife and children to his home town in order to visit with his mother during Christmas vacation. This particular year, however, he decided to postpone the visit, mainly because of financial pressures. Having explained his decision in a letter, he received an immediate reply in which his mother expressed her indignation and staked out her claim, "If you don't want to come to see me this Christmas, I can only conclude that you find it no longer necessary to give some consideration to your mother. As far as I'm concerned, if that's the way you feel, you and your family may as well forget about ever visiting me again. . . ." The letter leaves little doubt about the mother's sense of righteousness concerning this particular claim to her son's time and financial sacrifice. In spite of the threat, the young couple decided to stick by their decision and wrote to the mother that they would come over during the summer and not at Christmas time. Although the son intellectually recognized that this decision was a correct one, he experienced a considerable degree of discomfort and was not able to acquire the same sense of tranquility about it as his wife. Instead, he was plagued by a vague and disquieting sense of guilt.

Whenever individuals seek to resolve disagreements about territorial claims—regardless of whether it is a matter between a few individuals or a vast process involving all of society—they will seek to find firm foundations for the correctness of their position in many different ways. Most of these fall in a limited number of categories. We will attend to each closely, with the recognition that specific styles of justification may facilitate the negotiations for acceptable territorial settlements.

TRADITION

Some years ago a professor in a university commanded great respect. As he entered the classroom the students, who were all properly dressed in tie and jacket, stood up and would remain standing until asked to be seated. The classroom was the professor's domain and he had complete control over it. He could exclude a student from a class for not wearing proper attire, and accept, with good grace, the praise of his colleagues for this forthright defense of propriety. The professor, without really thinking about it, accepted as self-evident that he had the right to both respect and obedience. The students appraised the situation in exactly the same way, for they knew that the classroom was the professor's bailiwick and admission to it was completely at his discretion. This example shows the importance of tradition for the amount of space one person affords another, as well as the changes that occur over a period of time which affect this allocation. Today, the same classroom is more nearly the property of the students. In fact, the professor comes close to being the students' guest, who is treated with courtesy only as long as his performance pleases them, a situation which many professors wholeheartedly endorse. Whether or not the present allocations are superior to those of the past is irrelevant; rights change as old traditions crumble and new ones take their place. As a consequence, demands that were once the prerogative of the professor now amount to invasions of student territory. If a professor would try to exclude a student for not wearing a tie, he would find himself embroiled in a battle which he could not win. In a society undergoing rapid changes, it is easy to fall behind in one's appraisal of which territory is currently being claimed by whom. The old order may believe itself in possession of certain powers, while the rights to them have already slipped out of grasp. At the same time, the new establishment may overestimate the degree to which fantasies have become reality and, as a consequence, claim territories that are still firmly in the control of others.

PRECEDENT

Territorial rights, like laws, are changed by precedent. The person who yesterday had to sit in the back of the bus may show that he has the right to sit where he will. The woman whose action territory was limited to homemaker may prove that she can also hold her own in a discussion of nuclear physics. Civil rights and women's rights are hotly contested areas where ancient traditions and expectations are undergoing extensive and laborious changes in which adherents of the old ways are experiencing painful loss of territory—while the new establishment is suffering equal anguish for want of fully developed managerial skills to handle the territory acquired. As opposed to a static society wherein civil disorder is at a minimum, the modern democratic society abounds in anger, indignation, foment, excitement, and—despite the battle fatigue—great expectations.[2]

The rearrangement of territorial boundaries depends primarily on the pioneers who aggressively take possession of an area hitherto closed to them, and who, in so doing, create *the precedent* on which a new tradition is formed.

The fact that precedents create a new definition of rights explains the vigor with which specific areas are defended in spite of the fact that these areas themselves may seem of little importance. It is not the loss of the one area at a certain time which is feared so much as the establishment of the other's rights to all such territories under similar circumstances. The parents of a teen-ager who has just obtained his driver's license may vigorously resist his driving his friends to a movie, not because they are opposed to his driving to this one specific event, but rather because they fear that the precedent will make him think he is co-owner of the car. Elizabeth I of England was loath to put her cousin, Mary Stuart, to death because to behead a crowned queen on the basis of a judicial procedure would set a precedent which would undermine the sacrosanct nature of royalty itself and, in the end, threaten her own reign.

SQUATTER'S RIGHTS

Even if a person has no basis to support his claim to a specific territory, he will hold on to it with great tenacity and with considerable personal conviction if he has been allowed to occupy it for an extended period of time. If the occupation has persisted very long, he will find such broad support for the continuation of his presence that one could say that the duration of the occupation itself has established the right to it. This right can best be labeled the *squatter's right*. Ultimately, all traditional rights in

---

[2]J. H. Huizinga, in his famous description of the late Middle Ages, *The Waning of the Middle Ages* (1954), paints for us a picture of a static society much in contrast with the one today. People's place in the community was clearly defined. Not only was society divided into three major strata—clergy, nobility, and the so-called third estate—but in addition, every group, every function, and every profession was seen as a separate state. This order was experienced by the man of the Middle Ages as "the right order," a holy structure, in which every man had the status that God had intended for him, and where the hierarchy on earth was only a reflection of the hierarchy of the powers of the angels in heaven.

society are a derivative of squatter's rights. When a territory has been occupied by certain groups over a period of many generations, everyone becomes so accustomed to the state of affairs that it never occurs to anyone to question it. In a monarchy it is accepted that the throne rightfully belongs to the descendants in the family line. Obviously, the oldest ancestor of the royal family took the kingdom over either by force or device and planted himself on the throne as a squatter. This tenuous background of the right to the throne can make understandable the eagerness of its occupants to legalize it through the blessings of the Church or, even more drastically, by claiming a direct relationship to God, as in the case of the Japanese emperor.

In the more pedestrian aspects of daily life, one encounters the same phenomenon. Anything which is allowed to go on for a long period of time generates certain rights for the squatter. If a person routinely lets his neighbor use his lawn mower, he will find himself in a difficult spot when he decides that he wants to discontinue this practice. Although it is clear that the neighbor doesn't have the slightest legal right to the lawn mower, he may nonetheless become angry, hurt, and offended when he is no longer allowed to borrow it. A young woman, mother of several small children, has the good fortune of living across the street from her own mother. Over a period of years she has relied on "grandma" for much of her children's care. As she matures, however, she begins to realize that she would like to take over more of the child-rearing responsibility herself, for by now she has developed ideas which are frequently at variance with those of her mother. When she contemplates the steps needed to move more actively into her own role as a mother, she realizes with considerable discomfort how much actual territory her mother has taken over in the family. She has allowed this situation to continue for such a long time that her mother has automatically acquired squatter's rights. To dislodge her now would mean a major effort resulting in hurt feelings, anger, and frustration—in short, a real territorial conflict between mother and daughter.

The degree to which a person recognizes the reality of squatter's rights is shown in the fact that he usually feels guilty when he proceeds to take back the area which he allowed the other to keep for extended periods. He should think twice before allowing anyone else to occupy some of his territory for any length of time, for even if it is understood that such privileges are only temporary in nature, with the passage of time the squatter's rights inevitably become established.

IDEOLOGY

In the course of history new ideas about the nature of man and the universe in which he lives spring up. These ideas, if successfully incorporated in the fabric of a culture, become part of its ideology.

Social psychologists have supported the observation that man has an extremely strong tendency toward what is called "cognitive consistency" (Feldman, 1966; Festinger, 1957). This term means that man always seeks to bring his ideas and actions in line with each other. If he is convinced that his neighbor is a nasty, selfish person who hates children and he observes him in the process of consoling a little child who hurt his knee in a fall off a bicycle, he might think, "That is just a phony show of sympathy to impress others." In this fashion he will bring the discrepancy between his opinion and the observed behavior back into line: The neighbor *really* is nasty and hates children. Anything that does not fit into a person's expectations is startling and will lead to an effort to reestablish consistency.

This quality of man influences the evolution of claims to territorial rights. In a time when man believed that God was the distributor of rights, it was consistent and therefore perfectly acceptable that God had allocated the greatest power to the king. The monarch's territory was respected because it was based on God-given rights. By the end of the nineteenth century the notion was prevalent that all men were equal and that God had meant them to have equal rights. Looking to the future one can conjecture that as new notions about the nature of man evolve, there will be simultaneous and consistent changes in the ideas people hold concerning human rights. Insofar as the notion that all men are born with equal rights ultimately goes back to the belief that God willed it that way, society would be left without a final justification for such equality if that belief system should fall away. This in turn could lead to new and unforeseen notions about territorial rights. Whatever the future outcome, it is safe to state that *territorial rights will change in a manner consistent with the views of the social order prevalent at any given time.*

It is interesting to pursue the hypothesis that major social upheavals are the result of profound changes in the ideas concerning territorial rights. As long as there is a general agreement as to rights among the members of any community, there is peace and stability. However, if, with the passing of time, these ideas change for some of the people and become increasingly incongruous with the actual situation, tensions will rise as the opposing groups become gradually more and more uncomfortable with the territory they occupy. Those who by the new standards possess too much will develop a vague sense of guilt, whereas those who judge themselves to have too little will become more and more angry and dissatisfied. These changes in attitude can perhaps explain why certain kings lost their zeal of leadership and became ineffectual in the defense of their thrones. Louis XVI in France and later Czar Nicholas II in Russia displayed a lack of decisiveness that eventually cost them their lives, as well as their crowns. This inadequacy in leadership must naturally follow when the leader himself no longer believes that he is the chosen one, the person who has a moral right to guide the destiny of his people. In this case the sense of guilt undermines the resolve to defend the disputed territory with full vigor, whereas a militant sense of righteousness serves to stimulate the determination of the underdog.

The French Revolution can be seen as the most profound single social upheaval which attempted to bring actual territorial divisions in line with the prevailing ideology. It will serve therefore to exemplify the process of changing territorial rights. The royalty of France had a long and illustrious history of opulence and ostentation which was rivaled only by the splendor of the Church. Both of these institutions worked together to keep their wealth, rights, and power intact. For several hundred years the leadership of both estates, although corrupt, was able to keep the people in their place of poverty, obedience, and servitude.

As time passed, doubts as to the absolute right of bishops and kings crept into the consciousness of the members of the ranks of both these social orders. Religion gradually lost its hold over the minds of the ruling class, and this change filtered downward to the lower strata of society. Several years before the outbreak of the revolution Napoleon wrote in his diary: "The priests are no longer to be feared in our time; they lost all their power on the day when their supremacy in science passed to the laymen" (Napoleon, 1910, p. 162). The intellectuals of the enlightenment suggested that the peasant be given a better break in life. The king became less and less sure of his own rights and, therefore, became less and less able to take his own administration and power seriously. As the royalty became increasingly apologetic about their rights and excesses, the common people became more and more hopeful and insistent with their demands for a greater share of the wealth. In 1776 the Americans won their independence from England. New hope was fired in the hearts of the instigators of equality in France. At the same time the queen, Marie Antoinette, indulged herself in reckless and flamboyant shows of splendor, which at one time had been accepted by the masses as inevitable, but which now only served to point up the glaring inequality present and thereby galvanized the feelings of animosity even further. A little over a year before the storming of the Bastille introduced the Revolution, Napoleon wrote (Napoleon, 1910, pp. 6-9):

April 1st, 1789. This year has begun hopefully for right thinkers, and after all these centuries of feudal barbarism and political slavery it is surprising to see how the word *Liberty* sets minds on fire that appeared to be demoralized under the influence of luxury, indulgence, and art.

February 8th, 1791, Serve: Everywhere the peasants stand firm; . . . They are ready to die for the Constitution.

July 27th, Valence: Is it to be war? The country is full of zeal, of enthusiasm. Two weeks ago, in a meeting of twenty-two clubs from the three Departments, a petition was drawn up demanding that the king be brought to trial. . . .

May 29th, Paris: I arrived yesterday, Paris is in a state of grave agitation. The national guards on duty to protect the king at the Tuileries have been doubled.

There is a vast amount of desertion among army officers. From every point of view the situation is most critical.

June 20th. Let us follow this rabble! Seven to eight thousand men, armed with pikes, axes, swords, guns, spits, pointed sticks, marched to the Assembly to present a petition. Thence they proceeded to the king. The garden of the Tuileries was closed, and was guarded by 15,000 national guards. They broke down the gates, entered the palace, placed guns in position opposite the king's lodging, smashed through four doors, and presented to the king two cockades, one white, the other tricolour. Choose,—they said,—reign here, or at Coblentz! The king stood it well, and placed a red cap on his head.
How could they let the rabble in [to the Palace yard]? They ought to have mowed down four or five hundred of them with cannon, and the others would still be running.
When I was told that Louis had put a red cap on his head I concluded that his reign was over, for in politics an act that degrades can never be lived down.

The behavior of the king and the army clearly shows the reduced vigor with which one defends a territory once the belief in the right to ownership has been undermined.

RESPONSE TO SOCIAL CHANGE

Our observations have led to the hypothesis that social upheaval occurs when there is a substantial discrepancy between the territorial implications of the prevailing ideology and the actual distribution of territorial rights. This hypothesis has some interesting implications for the possible ways in which one can cope with social change. Our model suggests that the above discrepancy exerts a force in the direction of bringing ideology and territorial division closer together. To prevent change it is necessary to apply a counterforce which of necessity must become greater as the discrepancy grows. On a societal level such counterforce means reliance on an ever-growing police force if the status quo is to be maintained. However, two other avenues can lead to the maintenance of social tranquility. The one goes in the direction of the governmental manipulation of the prevailing ideology in the country by means of isolationism, regimentation of education, censorship, and propaganda. The other seeks stability by making adjustments in the territorial division itself. Obviously the first avenue is open only to totalitarian states. A nation whose government does not have dictatorial powers and therefore can neither maintain the status quo by force nor change the evolution of ideas through propaganda, must take other steps to maintain internal peace. This implies a process of continuous readjustments of rights and privileges at least to approximate the prevailing ideology. The citizens of such a country need to have an avenue available to bring their rights in line with their ideals. As a consequence, each democratic nation will continue to experience the discomforts which come with social change as long as the notions about man and his place in the world keep evolving. The ability to adjust to this ongoing process in the distribution of territorial rights and privileges depends largely on the flexibility of the parties involved. Change always creates a discomfort, and as a consequence one finds a resistance against it in individuals as well as in society as a whole. When the distribution of rights and privileges is altered, it is obvious that some must lose when others gain. Those who stand to lose the most will naturally offer the strongest opposition.

The resistance against the acquisition of new rights by upstart groups is strongest among those individuals in closest proximity to those groups. One finds very little prejudice against the black man in those European countries where there are almost no blacks. The deepest prejudice against the blacks and the strongest resistance against affording them rights exist in areas such as South Africa and Rhodesia, where they far outnumber the whites. In the South of the United States one can observe that the intellectual, more than the unskilled laborer, is inclined to support the claims of the blacks. Affording rights and opportunities to minority groups means providing them with a larger territory. It is, therefore, not surprising that those who are in competition for the same area will exert the greatest effort to prevent change in territory. Those who have nothing to lose in the bargain are the most magnanimous in their willingness to give someone else's holding away.

This perspective on the situation may provide some suggestions toward a strategy for resolving these types of conflicts. It is clear that such territorial struggles simply cannot end until an equitable redistribution has been made. Thus, one could minimize the resistance by those who fear the loss of their own territory by providing them with a compensatory area. For example, one could predict that an economic boom in the South would do more to reduce racial tensions than a steady stream of propaganda or court decisions alone.[3] The court decisions are necessary to create a clear understanding of where the boundaries are, but the economic boom with a plethora of jobs would lead to an easier acceptance of these new territorial allocations.

GUILT

Guilt is an uncomfortable, disquieting feeling which occurs when a person has laid claim to what he believes really belongs to someone else. The guilty individual himself cannot fail to notice such discomfort, and the outsider may also recognize its presence by his overt behavior. Guilty behavior is not limited to man alone. Our dogs, for instance, are allowed in one particular part of the house; here they are free to move as they wish. Occasionally the younger of the two sneaks into other rooms when she thinks we are gone. That she knows very well when she is off limits becomes apparent as soon as she spots us. She cowers close to the floor, looking upward out of the corner of her eye, with a look of such deep guilt that one cannot help but laugh. Human beings can recognize the guilt of the dog because the behavioral display has universal characteristics. The

---

[3]Carl I. Hovland and Robert R. Sears (1970) give some support to this hypothesis by a report which showed an inverse correlation between lynchings and the cotton price.

crouching, the indirect, shifty look, and the lowering of the head are very similar to the behavior of a man caught off limits.

We already mentioned that man's effectiveness in defending his territory is greatly reduced when he no longer believes in his right to ownership of the disputed area, in other words, when he feels guilty. It is quite understandable therefore that *guilt induction* is a frequently used weapon in territorial conflicts.

Guilt feelings are among the most ubiquitous as well as most intensely disturbing of human experiences. They are one of the most frequent reasons that an individual seeks the assistance of a mental health professional. A major difficulty with guilt feeling arises from the fact that in the course of life a person may meet with circumstances that prevent the acquisition of the sense of having certain rights which he is ordinarily expected to have in his society. If the parents have convinced the growing child that his autonomy is limited by the all-seeing surveillance of righteous and vindictive outside authorities such as themselves or, for that matter, God, he may have a particularly difficult time acquiring control over his own life.

A young man had been raised in the Mormon Church. He had a very strict upbringing and the weekly church attendance was regarded as an absolute must. After leaving home and going to college he found that his ideas slowly changed, and eventually he broke away from all organized religion. He stopped going to church, but found himself in a quandary whenever he visited his parents. When Sunday morning came his mother and father would go to church by themselves, for he had told them that he no longer considered himself a church member. Each time that they left he remained behind with an almost unbearable feeling of discomfort and guilt. His parents had never criticized him for leaving the church and yet he felt deeply guilty in their presence. A careful look at the situation revealed that this young man did not really believe that the decision about religious matters was truly within the confines of his own privilege. He knew intellectually that the decision belonged to him, but he still had the deep-seated feeling that his parents should approve of it. Only after he realized that decisions regarding religion were strictly his and that he *had no right* to demand the approval of others, did he gain the kind of assertiveness necessary to leave the parents to their religion and maintain the right to his own views without a feeling of guilt.

The resolution of this type of situation is greatly enhanced if both parties, here the son and the parents, can openly discuss the situation in order to arrive at a mutual understanding of each other's personal rights and freedom. More often, however, the autonomy of the guilt-ridden individual can be gained only by a firm stand and a willingness to accept the resulting consequences. Being prepared to resist use of guilt-inducing techniques by others is of much help to the person who wishes to stand his ground in such situations. Sometimes, however, none of these attempts at acquiring the desired territory—while at the same time maintaining a friendly relationship with the other—succeeds, and it may well be that only a drastic and painful break can establish the necessary sense of autonomy.

Thus, perhaps one of the crucial consequences of our way of looking at guilt is, ultimately, that *the only remedy is revolt.* In revolting, the person takes this stand: "I refuse; I will no longer do it. From now on I will assume control over this area of my life, and anyone who wishes to keep me from it had better be prepared to fight." Just as in a social order where the downtrodden have no avenue open to them except revolt by which they can gain equal rights, the individual must finally rebel against those who have taken dominion over his life and refuse to relinquish it. Although the process has to start with the recognition that someone has usurped his territory, *ultimately it is not analysis or insight, but confrontation that becomes the liberator.*

As an aside, it is of interest to mention the defensiveness which is typically encountered in individuals who feel guilty. This defensiveness is not surprising, for if a person thinks himself to be the unjustified occupant of another's territory, he cannot help but anticipate a fight. The slightest aggressive gesture will be construed to be the sign that the battle is on.

Frequently a person seeks the help of a mental health worker because he is plagued by "abnormal guilt feelings." Some individuals are brought to the psychiatrist's attention, usually by legal authorities, because they seem to lack "appropriate guilt feelings." In professional jargon the former is diagnosed as suffering from a *punitive superego,* whereas the latter are supposed to have *lacunae* in the same. This is but a rather fancy way of saying to the one, "By most people's standards you feel guilty too often"; and to the other, "You don't feel guilty often enough." Assuming that a person assesses whether or not he is off limits on the basis of what he has learned in the past, it follows that both types of problems result from a territorial learning which has been out of step with the mainstream of the society. To get along in the social order with greater comfort, such an individual needs to realign some of his notions. Roughly speaking, it can be said that the neurotic person with an unusual amount of guilt feelings has never learned that he has a right to a fair share of the cake. He has been led to believe that many areas which ordinarily rest under an individual's autonomous control are the rightful property of some authority, be it a parental figure on earth, a general ethical principle, or a god in the sky. The sociopathic individual, on the other hand, never learned to respect the territory of others. He was either not taught that each person is entitled to his own territory in a society, or perhaps he decided not to recognize existing boundaries because he did not feel part of the overall community.

Guilt feelings, then, serve as important indicators of the state of the territory and should be taken seriously as such. It is of little avail for the person to tell himself that he should not feel guilty, for obviously the word *should* only indicates that he has relinquished his autonomy to yet another authority. The logical step to take in order to deal with such guilt feelings is to determine the territory under dispute, decide whether he wants to claim it or not, and take steps to implement the decision.

SETTLING A TERRITORIAL DISPUTE

Any attempt at settling a dispute concerning territorial rights must of necessity be preceded by a clear definition of the area which is being contested. Frequently this effort alone suffices to eliminate the conflict. Often the apparent dispute is over a small matter, but the intensity of the conflict results from a less obvious but larger concern. If Mrs. Jones becomes irate when she cannot find her scissors, the intensity of her anger may seem out of keeping with the triviality of the loss. Why make such a fuss over a pair of scissors? The fact of the matter is, however, that although the scissors is the focal point of the hassle, the real territory lost to Mrs. Jones (albeit temporarily) is the action territory of sewing. By taking her scissors the culprit has effectively obstructed her access to that area.

Once the territory under dispute has been determined, the process of deciding who has a right to which part of it can begin. A young woman, 23 years old, has been living with her parents. She has a job, sufficient to support herself, and she wishes to move into an apartment with a girl friend. The anticipation of the move makes her feel uncomfortably guilty, for she has been told that her staying at home means a great deal to her mother. The major area under dispute is not whether the daughter should move to an apartment, but rather, whether she is free to make all decisions concerning her life or whether this prerogative is her mother's action territory. The discussion about the rights to this territory can be condensed as follows. The daughter says, "I'm over 21, earn my own living, and therefore I may decide for myself how I'm going to lead my life." The mother's counterclaim implies, "I *need* my daughter, therefore I should be able to control her life insofar as it affects me." Once the basis of each person's claim stands clearly under illumination, it becomes fairly easy to decide on the merits of each person's case. Although each party may try to hold on to the territory he desires, the reasonableness of the claims considered against the background of the current cultural situation has an important bearing on the outcome of the conflict. The situation described above would be very different if it took place in certain parts of the Orient a generation ago. A young adult in that position would probably have felt that the correctness of the parental claim was undeniable, as the major decisions in the family remained the domain of the oldest family members. In the American society, most people would take a different stance. Here the parents do not have the right to make major choices for their children once they have grown up. They may express an opinion—they may even give advice if they feel strongly about it—but they cannot lay claim to the territory that is not theirs. As our discussion has shown, there is no absolute norm by which territorial rights can be measured and disputes settled. Each individual will have to assess the situation carefully and make up his mind as to which claims he considers rightfully his. He has to be prepared for the fact that if his appraisal drastically differs from that of the others involved, he will have to convince them of the correctness of his own estimate or be willing to reach a compromise, if a fight is to be avoided.

CHAPTER 10

GENEROSITY, ENVY, AND JEALOUSY

Our knowledge of what the richer than ourselves possess, and the poorer do not, has never been more widespread. Therefore envy, which is wanting what others have, and jealousy, which is not wanting others to have what one has, have also never been more widespread.

*John Fowles**

The actual exchange of territory such as takes place in giving and receiving, as well as desired and feared exchange, such as in envy and jealousy, provides a common source of difficulties in the interaction between people. Some individuals give easily but do not receive well, whereas others find it easy to accept a gift but hard to extend one. This discomfort does not limit itself to material gifts alone. Most everyone knows of a hostess who, when complimented on a delicious and well-prepared dinner, becomes fidgety and mumbles disparaging remarks about her culinary abilities.

The reasons why an exchange creates discomfort frequently remain obscure. Sometime ago in a group session we initiated a game for the purpose of focusing in on giving and receiving. Each participant was to take three coins out of his purse and give them away to anyone he wished to in the circle. Money changed hands rapidly for about five minutes and then the game was terminated. Each individual was supposed to keep what he had at that time. One person protested that he had considerably more at the end of the game than at the start and insisted on returning the excess to the original owners. When he was reminded that the rules stipulated that he keep his profit, he became visibly uncomfortable and

*From *The Aristos.* New York: A Signet Book, New American Library, Inc., 1970, p. 43.

first attempted to give the money to others, but when nobody accepted he simply put the money on the floor and left it there.

A more common example of this type of discomfort frequently occurs in a restaurant. Two couples are having dinner together. They have a good time and engage in an enjoyable and relaxed conversation while savoring the food, until that unavoidable moment comes when the waiter brings a small tray with the check. Suddenly everyone is aware of its presence and the conversation loses its spontaneity. Several stereotyped acts may now follow, which are ordinarily played by the male members of each couple, although occasionally entered into by an anxious wife. Sometimes the bill is actively ignored while each party waits for the other to pick up the tab. Not uncommonly, one person will stealthily put his hand on the tray and draw it over to his side of the table, indicating his intention to pay for it; an exchange follows in which each individual tries to convince the other to let him pay the bill. Occasionally, the bill is directly and aggressively taken by one person who firmly waves aside all protestations and simply proceeds to put down the money. In whatever fashion it is handled, the bill-paying ritual presents a frequent source of discomfort for all participants, casting a brief shadow on an otherwise enjoyable evening.

Much of the imbalance in interpersonal relationships, and even on a broader plane in society as a whole, is caused by the desire for that which belongs to someone else or the fear that one may lose what one wishes to keep. A person may envy his neighbor's car, his financial success, or simply his apparent happiness. Conversely, one jealously guards a precious coin collection, his reputation, or perhaps most of all, his privacy. Envy and jealousy are the words with which we usually indicate the preoccupation with such matters. Recognizing the many and various interpersonal difficulties related to the exchange of ownership, it appears legitimate to approach this matter from a territorial perspective and see whether the insights gained so far can assist in the understanding of this area of concern.

The act of giving is very complex, involving many factors and serving many purposes.[1] Before analyzing the specific territorial aspects of giving, therefore, it is first necessary to determine whether one is dealing with a territorial exchange. When a husband comes home and hands his wife a dozen roses, he is obviously not giving her a part of his territory. However, the true meaning of the act can only be discerned from the context in

---

[1] An extensive survey of the psychological literature on altruism has been provided by Dennis L. Krebs (1970).

which it occurs. If he simply has bought the flowers because of his positive disposition towards his wife, he uses them as a means of communication. He signals to her his appreciation, perhaps his love. The signal has quite a different meaning if the couple has had a fierce argument the day before. In that case, the flowers may be like the white flag of truce raised above the trenches, indicating a willingness to talk about the conditions for peace or perhaps even signaling a gesture of surrender. Under still different circumstances the flowers may serve to soften up the wife for a special favor which the husband is about to ask. In the last case, the gift serves as a weapon in a territorial struggle.

Another fact, which may cause confusion in discussions of giving, is that the word *giving* is frequently used when no actual giving is involved. Giving money to the sales clerk in the store after purchasing groceries is not the same as making her a gift; the word in this case stands for handing over. This is a little less obvious, but equally true, for the many kinds of obligatory giving that are part of social custom. Even such minor exchanges as the annual habit of dispersing Christmas cards to acquaintances and business associates may exemplify obligatory giving. Similarly, giving to various causes such as the March of Dimes is often more obligatory than altruistic.

In considering territory which is either given or received, one fact immediately stands out, but is so obvious that it is likely to be overlooked: *In order to be able to give something one first has to own it.* In further clarifying this general topic we will focus attention on the two extremes by which it is customary to judge the readiness and ease with which a person gives. The one pole is altruism, characterized by the word *generosity,* and is related to such other terms as *openness, charity,* and *forgiving;* whereas the opposite pole is represented by the terms *envy* and *jealousy,* and has affinity to the words *avarice, possessiveness, miserliness, greed,* and *vindictiveness.*

GENEROSITY

With the word *generosity* we wish to indicate *the ease with which a person parts with that which he possesses.* Generosity refers to something about the basic attitude that bears on the manner in which a person gives. To be generous one needs to fulfill a number of conditions which have territorial implications.

The first condition is that one has to have something in order to give. Although this is true, it should be emphasized that one is most likely to be judged as generous if one consistently gives more than is customary, taking into account the relative degree of sacrifice involved. A gift of a million dollars from the billionaire Paul Getty might thus be judged as less generous than $10 from a person whose earnings are below the poverty level. It is a puzzling fact that some people give easily in spite of a rather limited supply of resources. Therefore, the presence of plenty can by itself not account for what is called generosity.

The importance of the specific territory involved bears on the person's ability to be generous. An individual may, for instance, be generous with material goods in spite of a relatively limited supply, because to him the area of concrete property is not particularly important. Now imagine that to this same person psychological space is the crucial domain. One would then expect him to be less generous when it comes to giving up any part of the limelight. As a matter of fact, it may well be that his generosity with material items—which, although important to others, have little meaning to him—serves the purpose of increasing his psychological space. As a consequence, one must conclude that it has little explanatory use to say that some people are generous because they are "good people," and others are not because they are "bad people." We would rather suggest that an individual gives easily of that of which he has plenty and which is of relatively little importance to him. The act, however, is likely to be considered generous when that which is given away has great importance to the one who judges the act. In Chapter 8 on the importance of territory we have more extensively discussed the various factors which determine how important a certain area is to a person. All of these factors have a bearing on the degree to which he can be generous with specific items.

The ability to defend territory also has a profound impact on the ease of giving. A person can freely give only if he can refuse to give; he can freely say yes only if he can say no. An individual can extend hospitality in the real sense of allowing others access to his home only if he is capable of excluding them from his house when he wants to. He can be hospitable only to the extent that he is master of the door which gives entry to his home. In other words, *a person's ability to defend his territory correlates directly with the degree to which he can display generosity.* Generosity, therefore, can be expected from the person who is truly convinced of his own capability to hold on to whatever he considers his own. If guilt feelings have undermined his control over part of his possessions, they have simultaneously reduced his ability to give his possessions to someone else. If a person feels obliged to give an expensive birthday present and could not possibly do otherwise, then he is no longer able to give freely, for in a sense he would simply be allowing the other to have that which he felt to be the other's rightful property in the first place. This rather common state of affairs leaves the individual with the irritation and resentment that unavoidably occurs when something has been taken away from him against his will; for that which seemed to be a gift was, in actuality, taken from him by the expedient means of guilt induction. These observations suggest that the person who can withstand coercion of any kind has the possibility of being generous. Or, more comprehensively, *generosity is dependent on the interaction between the ability to defend oneself, the ampleness of one's resources, and the importance of the territory involved.*

ENVY AND FEAR OF ENVY

Envy, which is the desire to have that which belongs to someone else, is a powerful motivator of human behavior and provides much of the glue that holds society together. In spite of its importance, however, it has received scant attention by the behavioral scientists, or the people whose responsibility it is to deal with social problems. One exception is provided by a recent extensive exploration of the impact of envy on the fabric of society by the German sociologist Helmut Schoeck (1969). We are much in debt to this extremely interesting and systematic study for the ideas about envy presented in this chapter.

ENVY VERSUS DESTRUCTIVE ENVY

Envy covers a very broad range of experiences, from a mild wish to have something which belongs to someone else, to the consuming desire to destroy the very thing that is envied. Although we are probably dealing with a continuum, for the purpose of exploration as well as for the sake of clarity, we will distinguish between two types of envy. The first type is the common desire to have that which belongs to someone else and which could be described with the somewhat archaic word *to covet*. The second type is characterized by a destructive intent. Here the person is no longer satisfied with acquiring what the other one has; instead, his preoccupation is with destroying the other's possession or even destroying or humiliating the individual himself. Whenever we discuss envy in this sense of the word we will add the adjective *destructive* to it. The distinction between covetous envy and destructive envy recalls the distinction we made in Chapter 5 between aggression and hostility; whereas aggression is oriented towards acquiring new territory, hostility aims toward destroying the other's territory or destroying the owner himself. Envy functions as one of the motivators of aggression. When a person desires what someone else has, he may move aggressively to acquire it. The focus of his effort is the desired territory itself. Destructive envy, on the other hand, is comparable to hostility. The focus is no longer the acquisition of the desired object, but the destruction of it or its owner.

The burning desire to destroy the more fortunate has led to many heinous crimes. Schoeck, in a chapter on this topic, gives many examples, one of which is the case of a spinster in Germany who suddenly and impulsively drowned the baby of a friend when she was overcome by an overwhelming feeling of destructive envy. More recently a young man murdered a wealthy physician and his family who lived in considerable opulence in California. The motive was apparently the same—destructive envy. This crime is very different from the type which has as its primary purpose the acquisition of the desired object. An ordinary thief has no intention to destroy that which he steals or to harm or humiliate its owner. He simply wants to have it for himself; and although breaking and entering are illegal, they are, in our terminology, aggressive acts rather than hostile ones.

Paralleling the characteristics of hostility, destructive envy occurs under circumstances wherein the individual, although highly desirous of a specific acquisition, can conceive of no way in which he can gain access to it. In other words, *destructive envy occurs when all avenues of access to a desired territory are effectively closed off.*

It is of considerable interest to observe when envy is evoked. Peculiarly enough, it is not usually created by extreme discrepancy. A person is more likely to envy his neighbor's new car or his two-week vacation in Hawaii than the yacht of the Queen of England or the affluence of a multimillionaire. In academia envy is common among members of the same department, especially where promotions, salary, and academic achievement are involved. At the same time, one is likely to encounter admiration rather than envy when a comparison is made with a world-famous scientist, a Nobel Prize winner from a foreign university. This brings us to an essential aspect of envy which thus far has remained implicit: *Comparison. To feel envy one has to compare some aspect of his territory with that of someone else.* One does not, however, compare himself with everyone to the same extent and in the same manner. Each individual has a *reference group,* which we will define as *those people with whom the individual is in the habit of comparing himself.* One is little affected by the conditions outside his reference group, but discrepancies within the group are bound to create envy.[2] Within a reference group each person has roughly the same rights to territory, and a deviation from the norm, therefore, implies that one has either too much or not enough. Within the group each individual has a keen sense of what is par for him.

FEAR OF ENVY

To explore this situation further it is necessary to pay attention to an important correlate of envy, namely, *the fear of envy.* In every society there exists a strong force which works against evoking the envy of those within one's reference group. There is a hesitation, not equally strong in each individual, to engage in anything that is extravagant or to possess anything that is likely to provoke envy. Many social customs are designed exactly for the purpose of avoiding the provoking of envy. If a man does well financially, he will not ordinarily tell his neighbors about it, especially if they are less fortunate. He may buy a car that is moderate in price, even if he can afford a more expensive one. He may dress conservatively out of fear of drawing others' envious attention. The fear of envy is a strong equalizing force in the community. Schoeck, who studied this matter in greater detail, has pointed out that fear of envy varies greatly from society to society.

The Duke de Baena, who served for many years as the Spanish Ambassador to the Netherlands, observed (de Baena, 1967, p. 12):

> Anyone can live more or less happily in Holland and have a chance of being understood by the Dutch if he is a moderate person, and by using the term "moderate" I mean no exaggeration, no ostentation, no glamour, nothing visibly superior: for what the Dutch do not like and will not take is: *superiority.*
> ... It is quite an instinct in them, when they see or feel that some human creature is growing long wings and preparing to fly to higher regions than usual,

---

[2]An interesting analogy exists with the animal world. Heini P. Hediger (1963, p. 34) has observed that "The further apart two species are in the zoological system, the less is one a threat to the territory of the other."

to bring out those enormous scissors that every Dutchman carries in his inner spiritual pocket and start clipping with great efficiency. No one should be too big, no one should be too powerful, no one should be too proud . . . . This way of living and thinking has brought much benefit to the peace and quiet of Dutch life and mind, because it has been instrumental in steering the Dutch clear of all forms of political excess; but it has also created a climate, in both the political and social spheres, which is incompatible with anything grand or great.

The effort to gain psychological space clearly runs counter to the attempts to avoid envy. In cultures where the fear of envy runs high, one would anticipate that all ostentatious forms of behavior are frowned upon. By the same token, a person who specializes in the area of psychological space will have to throw the fear of envy overboard if he is to succeed.

Among the Sirionos of Bolivia the fear of envy is so extreme that people hide their food and eat it secretly at night (Schoeck, 1969). When a man returns from a successful hunt, he will put on a disappointed demeanor and report no luck, but just outside the village he has hidden his catch which he will retrieve later in the night when no one will be able to see him. Members of the Ik, a mountain people living on the border between Kenya and Uganda, do not even bring food home with them but eat it where and when they find it (Turnbull, 1972). In many cultures, envy can be obliterated by attributing the desirable gains one has to luck. It is easy for a person to tell his colleagues at work that he won a thousand dollars at the race track, but he would probably keep silent about receiving a thousand-dollar raise because the boss appreciates his work.

In some societies envy and fear of envy are such predominant features that nothing can be attributed to luck. Anything and everything that happens results from a definite intent. In such extreme forms envy and fear of it produce a paranoid community where everyone withdraws in a shell of secrecy and where, simultaneously, the ones who hide themselves are suspected of conspiracy. It is quite probable that the witch burnings of the late Middle Ages were partly rooted in this background. People related untoward events to the destructive acts of the envious rather than to the whims of Fate. Consequently, the people who had reason to be envious were automatically suspected of having used black magic to satisfy their malice. Simultaneously, however, it was the envy itself that made the well-to-do equally vulnerable to the witch trials, for once they were established, the destructively envious person had a tool to destroy those who were more fortunate than himself by accusing them of witchcraft.

An interesting concretization of the envious intent of Fate, rather than its neutrality, is the notion of the "evil eye" which is prevalent in some countries in Latin America and around the Mediterranean. More broadly it is found in the concept of the envious gods, a belief which was firmly held by the Greeks of classical times. They were extremely cautious to hide their good fortune and not to seem to squander their wealth, lest the gods notice and take revenge. Homer's epic of the Trojan Wars and of the long, perilous return of Ulysses to his wife Penelope is filled with examples of this orientation. In fact, the long delay in Ulysses' return was caused by the envy of the gods, and the eventual happy ending of his journey only came about because of the help of some gods who were in turn envious of his enemies. In present modern life there are still remnants of this feeling. The habit of knocking on wood when one has said something favorable about his own fate is a practice designed to ward off the envy of the gods.

The above observations lead to some important conclusions. *The fear of envy provides a strong force toward maintenance of the status quo.* Whenever a person deviates from his reference group, he experiences a sensation not too different from that of *guilt,* which makes him inclined to hide his deviation or return to the reference norm. That the above sensation has considerable similarity to guilt can be seen from statements made by survivors of great disasters and concentration camps. Robert J. Lifton (1967, pp. 35-36) gives many examples of such feelings among the survivors of the atom bomb which was dropped on Hiroshima: "From the moment of atomic bomb exposure, the Hibakusha experienced a need to justify his own survival in the face of others' death, a sense of *'guilt over survival priority'* which was to plague him from then on." And further on he quotes the words of one of the survivors who recalls a walk through the city shortly after the explosion: " 'The most impressive thing was the expression in people's eyes—bodies badly injured which had turned black—their eyes looking for someone to come and help them. They looked at me and knew that I was stronger than they. . . . I was looking for my family and looking carefully at everyone I met to see if he or she was a family member—but the eyes—the emptiness—the helpless expression—- were something I will never forget. . . .' "

This description reminds one of the sense of guilt that a person may have when he walks through a hospital ward occupied by patients who are severely handicapped. He feels guilty of having what they so obviously lack. Here again it is apparent that the implied comparison relates to a specific reference group. The survivor of Hiroshima compares himself with all those who underwent the same disaster. An American who is not a member of this group fails to experience a sense of guilt because he survived. By being directly confronted with the handicapped patients, one is forced to include them in his reference group, and one's vague sense of guilt results from this reference group expansion.

The fear of envy provides a strong force toward conformity and social stability. However when the fear of envy and, simultaneously, envy itself play an overwhelming role in the community, the stagnation of the culture results. Fear of envy prevents individuals from deviating from the norm in any way possible, and strangles all originality and personal initiative. Some envy helps to make society work, but "Ubiquitous envy, fear of it and those who harbour it, cuts off such persons from any kind of communal action directed towards the future. Every man is for himself, every man is thrown back upon his own resources. All striving, all *preparation* and planning for the future can be undertaken only by socially fragmented, secretive beings" (Schoeck, 1969, p. 50). We can see an example of this phenomenon on a small scale in the frequently encountered fear of being outstanding in school. Unusually bright students very often fail to put in an effort in order to avoid getting superior grades. Another expression of the same phenomenon is the attempt in many universities to do away with Honors.

REFERENCE GROUPS

In the social upheavals of today, one can discern the effects of envy on the course of events. In the previous chapter we discussed that social revolution takes place when the discrepancy between the sense of territorial rights and the actual territorial division has become too great. We can now expand this idea. If, *within a reference group*, the discrepancies in territorial division are too great, one can anticipate an aggressive or hostile action stemming from the inevitable envy. The matter takes on even greater proportions *if the reference group itself is changing.* If the reference group is stable, then envy and the fear of envy will lead to a relative equalization within the group. If the reference group suddenly enlarges, admitting new members from other groups and classes, a period of tension will result until all persons conform to the new group norm. In other words, if the reference group suddenly expands, envy becomes inevitable and may take on such proportions that extremely aggressive or hostile action occurs. In the previous chapter we emphasized that the conceptualization of one's rights precedes the action: we have now amended this idea to read that the change in conceptualization involves a change within the reference group and that the actions are motivated by the resultant envy.

As John Fowles pointed out in an earlier quote, today's increased familiarity with people of all classes and of all parts of the world must have an impact on the makeup of each individual's reference group. By means of television, but also by direct contact through ever-expanding tourist travel, we can now see how other people live and comparisons become unavoidable. If these observations are correct, one should anticipate that the underdeveloped nations will become increasingly envious of other countries when they become more familiar with the rest of the world through the media of mass communication, as well as by direct observations. If their reference groups expand, envy and subsequent aggressive action will hardly be avoidable.

If one takes into account such results of the communication explosion, and at the same time keeps in mind that by the year 2000 there will be an estimated seven billion people on this earth, whereas the world's resources are only sufficient to sustain one-and-a-half billion people at the standard of living now common in the United States, one cannot help but anticipate trouble for those who have.

We have made a case for the idea that envy leads inevitably to action designed to reduce the discrepancies within the reference group. Those who have too much will curtail, as well as hide, their extravagance, while those who have too little will seek to find a compensation. Several other ideas of interest are generated when one looks from this perspective at some behavior patterns. For instance, one could postulate that the current counterculture's manner of dress and grooming is not so much a reaction to the older generation's values as to the pressures of the new reference groups that have been created through social concerns. The middle-class young person who went to Alabama to help in the civil-rights movement must have become terribly uncomfortable with his own unearned good fortune compared to that of a poor black family he lived with; and as he identified with this new reference group, he allayed his own fear of envy by adopting a clothing style that brought him on a par.

When a person deviates too much from his own reference group but does not want to curtail his aspirations, he has no choice but to leave the group and choose a new one which is more in line with his assets. As a matter of fact, this avenue is the only one open for a person who wants to live independently and creatively. A young man, who was raised in a lower middle-class, blue-collar family, had acquired a more than usual amount of education. He soon found himself down-playing his own sophistication within his circle of friends and family. He keenly sensed that if he claimed more than usual knowledge in discussions with others, he would incur their envy, and he therefore intuitively toned down his own expertise. Unavoidably the time came when he recognized that if he was to make a career for himself in the direction of his interest, he would have to leave the group in which he had grown up and join a more intellectual set of associates, a group wherein his sophistication would be approximately at par with the others. Once he had made this transition, he experienced the comfort of being able to show his capabilities in relationship with his colleagues. At the same time, however, he felt a faint sense of guilt relative to his previous reference group of which he no longer was able to be a genuine part.

Envy is a driving force toward growth and constructive action through the realization of the discrepancy in one's condition as compared with that of others, combined with the perception of a possible avenue by which this discrepancy can be reduced. *If such a pathway is basically absent or appears inaccessible to the individual, the envy becomes destructive,* characterized by the sentence, "If I can't have it then you won't have it either." A most striking example of the latter is the rather bizarre action which was reported about a group of survivors from a shipwreck in World War II. In one lifeboat, those who were driven by hunger and thirst to jump overboard seemed to envy the fact that others who wished to remain in the boat still had a chance of survival (Schoeck, 1969, p. 110):

> That was a strange feature of every suicide. As people decided to jump overboard, they seemed to resent the fact that others were being left with a chance of safety.
> They would try to seize the rations and fling them overboard. They would try to make their last action in the boat the pulling of the bung which would let in the water. Their madness always seemed to take the form that they must not go alone, but must take everyone with them.

One can obviously counter the observation with the many examples of human beings who have sacrificed themselves so that others would have a chance to live. Perhaps it is only to the extent that one feels at one with his fellow man, with a firm sense of sharing, that self-sacrifice becomes a possibility. Thus one can expect such action in a family or a close-knit group where each person guards the integrity of the territory of the others.

One must anticipate destructive action whenever serious discrepancies occur within a reference group while no avenues of correction appear open. Schoeck notes that in the early 1950's the crime rate among the refugees in West Germany who had fled from Communist East Germany was much lower than the one in the United States. As the refugees were far more deprived, this low crime rate was puzzling. He hypothesizes that the low rate occurred because the refugees knew *why* they were poverty-stricken, whereas the poor in the United States had no such justification. From our perspective, it seems equally important that the East German refugees in West Germany knew themselves to be a special group and therefore made comparisons within this group, but the American poor had no reason to single themselves out and consequently had a larger reference group. Schoeck further observes that the situation is aggravated by the fact that the media continuously show the wealth of an affluent society, simultaneously repeating slogans of equality and equal opportunity, all of which is bound to lead to greater envy.

The implied hypothesis is that, on the one hand, crime of the type which takes property from others is bound to increase if the discrepancies within the reference group widen and the individual sees no other avenue open for equalization. Crimes destructive of life and property, on the other hand, are more likely to occur if an individual despairs of finding any avenue through which he may acquire the status of those envied. In order to prevent major turmoil in society and reduce the crime rate, it is then essential that the opening up of new avenues for expansion keeps pace with the ongoing process of reference group expansion. If the latter seriously outstrips the former, problems are unavoidable.

The comparison with a particular reference group provides a strong stimulus toward growth, but by the same token it creates the stage for the possibility of defeat and bitter humiliation. The tragedy which may stem from a comparison with an individual whose territory far exceeds whatever one realistically attains for oneself is exemplified in the painful story of Zelda, the wife of F. Scott Fitzgerald (Milford, 1970). Fitzgerald as a young writer made a rapid and brilliantly successful career that brought him in the limelight of public attention and admiration. He was an excellent craftsman as a writer and his psychological space was near limitless. Zelda destroyed herself in the competition to reach equal heights. She wrote stories and tried a novel; she subjected herself, with iron discipline, to endless exercises in an attempt to become a ballerina; she painted and had an exhibition in New York. She was a brilliant and talented woman, but she always fell far short of capturing the kind of fame her husband enjoyed. The despair over her failures lead eventually to repeated hospitalization in psychiatric institutions. Psychological space in particular has much of an all-or-none quality. Either one has the attention one seeks or one doesn't. The enormity of Zelda's demand, born out of the comparison with one of the few truly successful writers of a glittering era, was at the heart of her destruction.

Finally, if envy provides a positive impulse towards growth, then fear of envy reduces it. For a person to grow he needs to ignore the envy of others, but if he ignores it totally, he should not be surprised at contrary action from those who have less. Some individuals have dreamed of establishing a society without envy, a community in which all men are equal and no one needs to desire that which belongs to someone else. All of our observations on human territoriality make it improbable that such a model would succeed. Even if it were possible, however, it would not seem desirable if one wishes to encourage an evolving culture, for envy itself is a vital ingredient of change.

JEALOUSY

The private experiences of a person who is jealous are closely related to those of an envious individual. As a consequence, the words "envy" and "jealousy," are frequently used interchangeably. We will reserve the term *jealousy* for the *preoccupation with the possibility that something one possesses and values will be taken away.*

Jealousy is the complement of envy. As such it is closely related to the fear of envy but has an added characteristic, the determination of the jealous person to hold on to what he cherishes with all the tenacity he can muster. When an individual experiences his own intense desire to have that which belongs to someone else, he cannot fail to recognize that others may similarly desire some of his possessions. Consequently, a person is likely to be just as jealous as he is envious, although he does not need to experience both at the same time. From a territorial perspective one would expect that the same conditions which make envy possible also are at the root of jealousy. Jealousy is by no means limited to feelings about a sexual partner. A person can be jealous of his property, his privacy, or even his prerogatives; an individual is likely to guard jealously anything which he values greatly. It is then no surprise that a person experiences his most intense and destructive feelings of jealousy when the feared loss concerns the person he "loves." He has made this loved one the most central part of his territory—a possession—the loss of which would leave him with the necessity of totally reorganizing all aspects of his life. Relative to his partner, he is in a vulnerable position, for the existence of this crucial aspect of his territory depends on the other, and not on himself. After all, his partner in reality is not a possession but a free agent who can choose to stay or leave, to be faithful or to deceive. This part of the jealous person's life, therefore, is well protected only to the extent that he is able to trust the other.

Here one is confronted with a paradoxical situation. When a person feels uncertain about his ability to protect his own territory, he experiences himself as vulnerable and the outside world as dangerous. Under such circumstances, his ability to trust is none too great. At the same time, such a person is likely to doubt that his partner is really voluntarily committed to him. Thus a vicious circle is created. The individual who feels insecure in his own abilities to defend his territory will have little trust in the other's desire to remain faithful. He will, therefore, continuously seek to control his partner to make sure that his territory is secure. As doubt is with him at all times, he reassures himself by spying on his partner. In doing so he evokes the kind of responses which will increase his doubts and intensify his controlling behavior. This in turn may lead to the extreme situation wherein the now insanely jealous lover sees no avenue open which allows him to hold onto his "possession." At this point, jealousy and hostility merge into an intensely destructive disposition which may lead the person to destroy his beloved object rather than have it go to someone else.

One conclusion which follows from our model in respect to jealousy is that the reduction in this destructive sentiment can occur only if new avenues towards territorial expansion and defense are found for the jealous individual. It is crucial to reduce the importance of that which he guards so jealously by eliminating its centrality and by opening up alternate areas in which he can evolve and establish his identity. Simultaneously, improving the person's general ability to defend his territory and therewith reduce his sense of vulnerability is likely to raise his ability to trust. Reassurance, on the other hand, the simple process of trying to convince the individual that his jealousy is unfounded, is doomed to failure.

Envy, as well as jealousy, are the feelings of a dissatisfied individual. Much of human behavior takes its impetus from dissatisfaction in one form or another. Dissatisfaction, like envy, implies a comparison, this time not only between oneself and one's neighbor, but between what one has and what one feels one should have. This "should" includes that which one desires as well as that which one feels obligated to desire. An individual is bound to maintain a profound sense of dissatisfaction if that which he acquires always falls short of the reference point that serves as a yardstick. His dissatisfaction is intensified by the reflection it has on his identity; for the expression *"I don't have enough" always has its counterpart in a person's identity as "I am not enough—I am insufficient, inadequate, a failure."* As envy is derived from the comparison with the reference group to which one belongs, so, in a more general way, is dissatisfaction always founded in a comparison. It is possible to cope with envy by changing reference groups. Dissatisfaction may similarly be countered when one is able to recognize the intrinsic impossibilities of ever gaining a state of satisfaction, balance, or tranquility as long as one insists on the same type of comparisons. Recognizing that he is duped by his standards, the individual may rebel and select new points of reference.

It is interesting to speculate how much the general tone of dissatisfaction prevalent in society comes from the artificial reference group created by television and, primarily, television advertisements, which constantly show the viewer new and improved products and imply that if a person is not in possession of such things he or she is not good enough. Vance Packard, in his book *The Status Seekers* (1959, p. 276), refers to this phenomenon of generating dissatisfaction: "A great many advertisers, however, are not content with merely being realistic about class. They want to put some sizzle into their messages by stirring up our status consciousness. In fact, they sometimes playfully call themselves 'merchants of discontent.' They talk profoundly of the 'upgrading urge' of people, and search for appeals that will tap that urge."

Television advertising strives to make women feel inadequate if they do not have a combination of mammary glands of staggering proportions, the waist, buttocks and legs of a young boy, an adoring, simple-minded smile, the look of perpetual bedroom readiness, and the pristine aura of "never-having-been-there." Men are measured by super-sized cigarettes, longer and stronger cars, and the number of the above-mentioned females who writhe and flounce around him in varying degrees of sexual frenzy. The very purpose of advertisement, however clumsy it may be, is to create envy and dissatisfaction. Insofar as it is successful, it generates the tension between the actual state of affairs and a desired one. Although advertisement obviously is meant for those who have the appropriate route of acquisition open, that is, money, it must result in at least as much dissatisfaction among individuals who do not have such access.

Envy and jealousy are human dispositions which, universal as they may be, are generally regarded as unbecoming or even sinful. "Thou shalt not covet thy neighbor's . . . ." is an admonition to suppress even the passing thought based in envy. This is another example of the extremely difficult task which confronts the individual in the Western culture if he is to have peace with himself. The Christian heritage tells him that he should not envy. Yet, envy is an unavoidable emotion which occurs when he recognizes discrepancies in his reference group, and the industrial society in which he lives employs all available means to increase this type of envy. It is extremely important that the individual recognize his own feelings of envy for such feelings signal inequality. Such signals prompt him to review his state of affairs and decide whether he wants to to take corrective action. However, if he has been led to believe that envy is evil, he is confronted with the mind-boggling task of making the feeling disappear and removing the awareness of the existing discrepancies from his attention. Clearly, insofar as society has succeeded in convincing its members that they should not be envious, to that extent it can keep its underdogs from rebelling against inequities. The religious exhortations against envy, in spite of their obvious intention to promote brotherhood among men, have become a force in the maintenance of the status quo and the preservation of inequality. The person who wishes to bring his territorial status in line with his reference group will need to recognize his feelings, including envy, and accept them as a signal that action might be needed rather than as a sign of his own moral depravity.

CHAPTER 11

WEAPONRY

Every man has his own fashion of making war.

*Napoleon**

Human existence can be compared to a battlefield where the individual, following a patchwork strategy and wielding a hodgepodge arsenal, tries to win a place for himself with enough security to allow him relative peace and enough challenge to keep life interesting. This struggle, though not usually in itself the object of a person's life endeavor, is an unavoidable means to the development of his own unique existence. At times such conflicts assume grotesque proportions, and the weapons used by the feuding parties may resemble those of a war between nations. A recent newspaper story portrayed such a situation colorfully: "A bitter six-year feud over two square feet of land between two posh suburban homes has been settled—at least as far as the land's ownership is concerned. The battling neighbors still have damage claims on file for such things as water hose squirtings, trespass complaints, tossing of garbage, and a 400 Watt searchlight which burns above the disputed property. The tiny strip has resembled a demilitarized zone with the overhead spotlight glaring and all the greenery clipped close to the grounds." In spite of the apparent fanatic quality of the above fight, it is rather simple in nature, for the area under dispute as well as the weapons used are concrete and immediately apparent to everyone. Far more frequently, however, individuals are involved in competition for territories that are ill-defined and in conflicts which are fought with weapons of great subtlety. Where human relationships are concerned, it is the latter type of struggles which cause the greatest problems and offer the most stubborn resistance to resolution.

*From *The Corsican, A Diary of Napoleon's Life in His Own Words* (Collected by B. M. Johnston). Boston & New York: Houghton Mifflin Co., 1910, p.27.

169

Perhaps the word *weapon* as we use it in this context may be confusing or even repulsive to the reader. It has the common connotation of "means of destruction." Nevertheless, we decided to use the term *weapon* in order to sharply underscore what we regard as the essence of this word, that is, *a means of defending or acquiring territory*. Furthermore, we believe it to be good strategy to use the term *weapon* because a major purpose of the present discussion is to dispel the notion—which creates no end of confusion in human affairs—that a battle occurs only when there is violence. Many of the most effective conquests are completed without so much as the sound of an adverse word. In some cases, the astute loser may realize—too late—that his territory has been taken by the use of a clever ruse. Much of the time, however, the person is left in a state of uncertainty and dismay, especially if the clever thief, while busily emptying the victim's pockets, succeeds in convincing him that he is being done a great favor. In order to call attention to such common feats of human commerce and to undo the notion that noisy weapons are worse than the subtle, quiet ones, we decided to call the devices used in territorial struggles by the name which we think they deserve: Weapons.

The process of resolving interpersonal conflict needs to start with an analysis of the situation: A description of the territory involved and an inventory of the weapons of which each party avails himself. Although such analysis may appear straightforward, in actual practice it is not always easy, for in the confusion a secondary conflict often arises concerning the fairness of fighting techniques. For example, a couple may be in the throes of a decision about how to spend some accumulated savings. The husband would like to put it into the purchase of a boat, but his wife proposes to remodel the kitchen. As the intensity of the conflict mounts, the wife becomes furious and subsequently bursts into tears, quite in contrast to her husband who remains calm and reasonable. At this point the battle scene changes as the man points out to his spouse that she is behaving in a childlike manner, a thrust which evokes a new outburst on her side, "Who do you think you are with your superior attitude?" For the time being, the original territory under dispute, the dispersement of accumulated savings, is obscured by the secondary confrontation over the choice of weapons. To deal with such situations it is most helpful to recognize the original object of conflict and separate it from the favorite means each partner uses in settling disputes.

Each individual resorts to those weapons which he knows best and which have proved to be effective on previous occasions. This generalization seems obvious, for it is rather foolish indeed to expect that a person would fight with weapons he doesn't know how to handle or which have proved themselves of little use to him in the past. He acquires his own particular repertoire of fighting techniques through the modeling of others in his immediate environment and through personal experience obtained in jousts with a variety of opponents. The obvious result of this learning process is that some people become better fighters than others primarily because they had more skillful masters, more opportunity for training, or simply tried harder.[1] The individual who finds his repertoire wanting can remedy this situation if he finds a competent teacher who will help him to catch up by means of "fight training." There is no substitute for practice and no book can impart this skill. It is, nevertheless, a useful first step to learn to recognize some of the subtle fighting techniques which are frequently used in the interaction between individuals. To be sure, this is a step preparatory to action, not a substitute for it. A clear formulation of the various fighting techniques with which one person confronts another or by which he himself is confronted has several consequences for effective behavior. In the first place, it simplifies considerably the job of devising an effective response to another's fighting skills. Second, an individual is more likely to achieve the desired objectives if he applies his own weaponry consciously and without ambiguity, being completely honest with himself about what he is trying to do. Finally, a keen insight into the techniques used is likely to lead to a more precise appraisal of the consequences of their application. Some weapons are more effective than others; some have consequences which are unpleasant also for the user himself. Pouting, for instance, may be an effective method of getting one's own way, but it usually has undesirable side effects, such as having to live in emotional isolation, perhaps for days at a time.

In this chapter we will draw attention to a variety of weapons and fighting techniques which are often poorly recognized and which emerged from our observations on interpersonal conflicts. The human arsenal is certainly far larger and much more varied than the rather limited sampling which we have included in our description. In fact, each individual places his own personal stamp on the manner in which he con-

---

[1] It is interesting in this context to note the observations of Syunzo Kawamura (1967) and others who have made longitudinal studies of monkey troops. These researchers show that monkeys in leadership positions have learned their social skill from their parents, who usually were dominant also. Thus there occurs a natural formation of a dynasty which comes close to the human situation.

ducts himself when in conflict with his fellow man. We provide our limited analysis not as a catalogue of the entire repertoire, but rather as examples which show how the weapons can be recognized for what they are as they are utilized in each unique situation.

DEFINITION

This clever technique consists of making a defining statement about another. It is a subtle tactic which is often not recognized as an aggressive tool, especially if the definition has a pleasing quality. A professional campaigner for a charitable organization who has cornered a potential contributor may use definitions like, "We know that you are a community-minded person with a genuine interest in the welfare of our senior citizens . . . ." Or, if he is a little more subtle, he might try to work a statement into the conversation about the many people who are vocal about the need for more of these services, but who aren't home when one comes for contributions. This leaves the victim little choice but to define himself as one who puts his money where his mouth is. The individual must therefore put himself on alert for a territorial invasion whenever another person gratuitously defines him. Sentences that are particularly telling are those beginning with "You and I are the kind of people who . . . ," "You and I differ in that . . . ," or "You are the type of person who . . . ." For example, "You are the kind of person who will not give in under pressure" is a statement which might be made by one executive to another during a labor dispute with the union. If this definition is accepted by the second executive, he will have lost a considerable part of his own decision-making power in the situation, and the other has, in effect, taken over a significant part of his territory, that is, his freedom to make any offer he wants to in bargaining with the union. He now can only make offers which the other considers tough. Usually the victim of definition feels a vague irritation, perhaps a slight sense of being compromised, but he may not realize precisely what has happened to him. A person who pays close attention to his own signals (in this case a feeling of irritation) is readily alerted to this technique and can say to himself: "Aha! The old definition gambit! Do I agree with the definition? No! Then I will not be affected by it, and I will bargain with the union in accordance with my own judgment!"

In the daily process of human interaction, individuals continually try to define their fellow men. Definition implies a prediction about the other's future behavior. If one person defines another as honest, it implies that he can lend him $10 without having to worry about getting it back. The definition, therefore, simplifies life. The more one knows a person, the more one has his number, the easier it is to decide how to act relative to him. In short, man reduces the discomfort and anxiety which stem from the uncertainties and the lack of control in daily life by defining whatever he encounters and by trying to keep everything stable. For instance, to reduce his uncertainties about the physical world, he measures phenomena and defines the laws of nature. As human beings are even harder to control, it is small wonder that an individual puts so much effort into defining his fellow man, and at the same time has such a great reluctance to change his definitions once they are established. It is always interesting to see the processes of definition at work in kaffee klatsches and lunch conversations. Large segments of such discussions concern persons known to all of the participants but not present at that moment. During these gossip sessions all participants compare notes to tighten up the precision with which the absent one is defined. The establishment of a definition sets a circular process in motion. If a person is seen as unreliable, for instance, everyone expects him to live in accordance with this definition, and keen eyes watch for behavior that corroborates the hypothesis. By the same token, evidence to the contrary tends to be disregarded unless it becomes overwhelming.

The research of Rosenthal and Jacobson lends unequivocal support to this observation. In one of their studies (1968) they introduced a definition of some first-grade children by means of a fake test report. In this way the teachers were led to believe that certain children should be expected to blossom out during the year. Although the test reports were randomly assigned and therefore had no relation to the pupils thus designated, the power of expectation of the teachers who were given the incorrect notions was such that the children who were so defined did, indeed, do better than the others. The nature of the circular process of definition and self-fulfilling prophecy leads to the conclusion that it takes very little to sustain a reputation once established, but that it requires a dramatic change in behavior to have such a definition revised.

Through the process of definition one person actively attempts to limit the freedom of another. The French philosopher, novelist, and playwright Sartre has been keenly aware of this phenomenon and has devoted much of his writing to it. The freedom to choose one's own life and the freedom to change in the direction of one's own desire stand central in all of his work. The process of definition by others was recognized by him to be the major obstacle to such freedom. In one of his plays, *No Exit* (Sartre, 1955), he has one of his characters express his agony over this confinement of his freedom by the exclamation, "Hell, that's the others." Being defined by others puts the individual in a prison, a hell, deprived of freedom. A global definition which is currently in the process of being exposed and discarded is that of the woman in our society. The nature of femininity has been the subject of many a treatise (usually written by men), and the prevailing popular definitions have unquestionably put a major restriction on the freedom of women and have sharply curtailed their territory (Weisstein, 1970).

The most significant impact which the women's liberation groups can have will be the discarding of such definitions altogether. Little attention is paid to the fact that such a change would be equally liberating to men, for a man's freedom is similarly restricted by definitions which are complementary to those applied to women. For instance, the implied definition of the male as a person who is basically in need of multiple sexual conquests has robbed many men of the freedom to choose their own style of life.

Perhaps the most dramatic awareness of a defining intent is experienced in stage fright. The gaze of the audience freezes, as it were, every characteristic, gesture, or word projected. The performer's autonomy is taken away by the defining look of the other. Only a minor revolt can break this tyranny: "I will not abide by your definition—I will be the master of my own behavior—I defy you!" The remedy of stage fright does not lie in working through hangups (although this may serve as a preliminary); it lies in the defiance of the definition of the other.

One of the most blatant abdications of territorial control occurs when an individual gives others the right to define him. By the same token, one of the most powerful territorial take-overs has been completed when the aggressor succeeds in convincing his victim that he has the legitimate right to pass judgment on him, which is just another form of defining him. If a patient gives his psychotherapist the right to make judgments about the motivations which determine his behavior—a right which the therapist is ready to assume because of his "superior knowledge"—he has given up an extremely substantial part of the control over his own territory. It is perfectly possible for the therapist to accomplish this take-over by means of a benevolent, fatherly attitude, listening to the trials and tribulations of the other with a paternal smile, leaving his patient with the peculiar sensation of being, on the one hand, grateful for the apparent kindness and yet, on the other hand, vaguely uncomfortable without knowing why. Perhaps the realization that territory has been lost may shed some light on this discomfort.

The individual can take a practical step in the maintenance of his autonomy by establishing the habit of identifying all occasions when another person makes a defining statement. Each time a definition is made, he can ask the question, "Am I giving up some autonomy over my own territory to someone else?" If the answer is a positive one, it can be followed immediately by the second question, "Do I want to?" The counterpart of this rejection of definitions is that a person also has no basis for demanding that others entertain opinions and definitions about him which conform to his own wishes. When an individual protects his own territory by disregarding unsolicited definitions about himself, he can hardly deny that it is every man's prerogative to form whatever opinions he chooses. If he, for instance, demands that others think of him as an honest, intelligent, or generous person, he is taking away part of the other's freedom. In other words, a person defends his territory when he rejects or ignores a definition. He invades that of someone else when he tries to control the other's opinion about himself.

SELF-DEFINITION

Just as individuals seek a definition of the world and their fellow man, they often try to define themselves, and for much the same reasons. A person may be inclined to say, "I am the kind of person who . . . ," or "I am honest," or even, "I would never do that," or the more definite, "I could never do that." Take, for example, a person who says, "I could never kill anybody." By the form of his statement he makes a definition: He says, "I am made in such a way that killing a fellow man would be impossible." Such a statement reveals the benefit of the definition; it makes him totally predictable to himself in one particular respect. From now on he can say that he will never kill anyone, for, after all, he doesn't have that capability. Obviously this statement is a nonsensical one. It is possible to say, "I do not ever want to kill anybody," or even, "I solemnly swear that I will never kill another human being," or to be on somewhat safer ground, "I will never kill another person, unless, perhaps, by accident." These statements, although closer to the realm of the possible, have the disadvantage of leaving the future uncertain. By defining himself, a person removes the discomfort that comes with the knowledge that he is unpredictable, even to himself. The fact is that all human beings are able to kill. Whether or not they will do so in the course of their lives depends on choice and circumstances, not on their nature.

Self-definition is sometimes used to provide justification for actions which involve intrusions into others' territory. "I'm the kind of person who just can't keep from telling the truth" may cover a vicious criticism. "I am by nature very temperamental" may be a statement to excuse an angry attack. Self-definitions of this kind claim special privileges, based on "natural" and therefore uncontrollable tendencies.

A person who allows himself to be defined by another gives up some of his freedom; a man who applies a definition voluntarily to himself does the same. The more he defines himself, the more he limits his own freedom for making new, independent decisions. Self-definition gives a person the sense of having rights because he has certain characteristics (Sartre, 1956). An individual who is intelligent, capable, and well organized may rise to a position in life where he is given the right to administer and direct those who are less gifted than himself. Another may gratuitously define himself as a superior administrator and try to assume such rights by virtue of this definition, rather than as a privilege which is extended to him with a certain job. Such a man presents a threat to the territory of others. Most dangerous is the man who defines himself as selected by destiny to bring new order to this highly inadequate world, for such a man believes he has extensive rights—so extensive that he will not hesitate to trample the holdings of others. To those who are trampled it makes little difference whether the "chosen one" prefers ideas of the right or of the left, whether he is an atheist or chosen by God.

It is useful to make a differentiation between self-definition and com-mitment. "I could never kill anybody" is a definition. "I *will* never kill anybody" is an expression of commitment. It is a choice, a personal decision, which the individual is determined to uphold to the best of his ability. He will take responsibility and credit for it, but he also will accept the blame if he breaks his pledge. Commitment, then, is an agreement of a man with himself or his fellow men, by which he determines how he will act in the future. Such a commitment remains at all times his own. When two people marry and they make the commitment to love each other, which is to protect each other's interests and integrity, it remains a daily effort to implement the commitment they have made. A commitment maintains freedom, but allows for no excuses. A man who breaks a commitment can only say, "I and no one else broke it." Commitment encompasses the exhilaration of freedom as well as the burden of responsibility; self-definition removes both.

GUILT INDUCTION

In the chapter on territorial rights we already discussed some of the implications of feeling guilty. In the present context we will underscore how the induction of guilt can be used as an extremely powerful weapon in territorial skirmishes. It appears that human beings feel comfortable only if they occupy a territory which they recognize as properly and rightfully their own. In fact, the effectiveness of a person's defense of his territory is largely dependent on his belief in the rightfulness of his claim to it. If a person succeeds in convincing his opponent of the notion that he has no right to the area under dispute, he has won half the battle.

It should be emphasized again that all of this has nothing to do with the question of the correctness of the claim. The essential feature is whether a person believes in the claim. Once one recognizes that guilt induction is a means of fighting, it comes as no surprise that the opponent fights back, not infrequently employing the same tactics. Many married couples recognize the process set in motion when one of the partners starts the attack. Let's assume the husband is two hours late from work.

"Why are you so late? the dinner is ruined and I was worried sick about you." This is the first guilt induction. The statement means, "By taking two additional hours you took territory that didn't belong to you." The first response is a defensive one:

"I'm sorry I'm late, but I had some important business in the office." In other words, he is saying, "Let's not fight about it, but I do have a right to the territory; it is justified by the business."

To which the wife responds with, "The least you could have done is call me," another guilt induction, implying: "No, you do not have a right to the territory. If you had wanted it you should have called me, then I could have given it to you—if I had wanted to." At this point the husband is stalemated. She has succeeded in convincing him that he had no right to that territory; he experiences guilt, and he is now preparing a counterattack to make up for lost ground.

"Listen, I don't know what you're so self-righteous about. Remember three weeks ago you were two hours late yourself after your meeting with the Women's League." This one hits home, and now the battle shifts to a higher gear.

"Just what I thought! In all these years that we've been married I was late one time and you keep holding it up to me." The implication is, "You think that you can control my life. Well, your claim is unfounded. You are occupying a ground that isn't yours—you are guilty." We will not pursue this circle of aggravation further, but it is likely to proceed step by step, taking in ever larger areas of the couple's life, culminating in a pitched battle and ending in either a stalemate, a new contract, or a giving up by one of the partners (which usually amounts to a temporary withdrawal from the battlefield to return with new weapons when the other is off guard).

An excellent example of guilt induction is given in the movie, "I Never Sang for My Father." This screenplay portrays in a beautiful and moving way the desperate struggle of a man to maintain his own integrity and yet continue his relationship with his father. The son has fallen into a trap because of his wish to make his father happy and, one day, to have a relationship with him of openness and mutual respect. The father, however, has assumed a life style which is controlling and which does not admit the display of personal feelings. He has aggressively taken over the lives of all members of his family, or at least he has tried to do so. When his daughter refused to submit to his control, she was banished from the house, but the son has kept on trying and in so doing lost much of his autonomy. In an intense exchange with his sister he says of his father, "When I am with him I have the sensation that I shrink." The feeling seems appropriate, for his father's controlling behavior reduces him from a mature and independent man to a small boy. His territory is taken away from him, and, as a result, his wish to make his father happy is mixed with an intense hatred. As a consequence, he experiences an unbearable discomfort whenever he is with him, "I can't stay in the room with you for over five minutes!"

In the final scene the son tries to convince the father that he has a right to his own life. The father, however, supports his own claim to the son's territory by telling him that he has worked his fingers to the bone to give his children food and a roof over their heads and an education. He says that he himself was born in poverty, had no father, and lost his mother when he was ten; and, although he has given his own son life on a silver platter, he is now cast off like an unnecessary burden. This guilt-inducing approach had been successful in the past in convincing the son that he had no right to the independence that ordinarily belongs to a grown-up man. But at this final point the son takes the only step left to him if he is to gain his freedom; he severs the relationship just as his sister did.

We will not belabor the issues around guilt, but rather turn to its practical implications for the handling of aggression and defense. The simple conclusion to be drawn relative to aggression is that if an individual seriously wants to take over a new territory, he is well-advised to prepare a strong and convincing support for the claim that he lays to it. As claims to a territory are not based on inalienable rights founded in the laws of the universe or written in the stars, it would seem most useful for the person, in preparing his support for a claim, to keep in mind which currency is presently highly valued and which argument is most likely to impress the particular party he is dealing with. For example, if a person dislikes the smokestack which obstructs his view across the lake and he seeks to convince the community that he has the right to have it removed, he may well find his most potent argument in the current concern about ecology. Certainly the fact that the smokestack is belching out pollutants into the atmosphere may now provide him with the argument that clinches his victory, whereas less than ten years ago it would have been laughed off.

In the process of defending territory a person may proceed as follows. The discomfort of guilt is easily recognized. However, instead of using such a futile response as trying to convince himself that he is not guilty or seeking to reduce the guilt by atonement or escaping into diversionary activities, he would need to begin with the understanding that this feeling is a sign that somebody is disputing the rightfulness of his ownership. Before going any further the individual needs to identify the contended territory and precisely who is trying to take it over. Once this has been accomplished he can decide whether he wants to hold on to it or relinquish it to the aggressor. Obviously if the person does want to hold on to it, he has to prepare an effective defense and not simply enter into a blind struggle, such as was exemplified by the couple after the husband's late arrival home. However, if he recognizes a territory as the legitimate property of someone else, he may save himself considerable headache by readily conceding it to the other, for the defense of it is usually ineffective and always a source of discomfort.

"I DO IT FOR YOUR OWN GOOD"

We have already given some attention to this weapon in the discussion of criticism, but will deal with it in greater detail here because of its importance. The technique of "I do it for your own good" serves several purposes. It convinces the aggressor of the fact that he has a right to the territory he is taking. In that it is a "moral right"—for it is commonly accepted that a man who comes with love and good intentions should be welcomed with warm hospitality—it gives the user of this technique a sense of righteousness and provides him with the self-assuredness which comes with knowing that he is on home ground, a fact that contributes to the effectiveness of this weapon. Simultaneously, it takes the wind out of the sails of the defender. It betrays bad manners, after all, to rebuff an individual who comes to help. This combination of factors often succeeds in throwing the victim in a state of confusion. Even if the confusion does not last long, it gives the aggressor the advantage.

Since this technique causes considerable confusion about choice of response, we will analyze such situations further. First one must realize that the person who engages in action under the cover of "I am doing this for your own good," assumes the position that he is the ultimate judge of what is good for the other. He acknowledges that a person might object to what he does, but tells him that he shouldn't because "I know best." Thus the aggressor has assumed something that might be called "overall guardianship" of the other's territory, implying that the other is to defer to him in final judgment. Of course it is quite conceivable that the victim would agree that the aggressor's judgment is better and perhaps would even welcome his guardianship. He might willingly go along with the actions the aggressor advises and enjoy a sense of relief, knowing that he can take a vacation while his affairs are in good hands. But very possibly the victim does not agree that the other person has judgment which is ultimately superior to his own. Maybe he would prefer to hold on to his own territory, even though he respects the other's judgment and even if it means making his own mistakes. He just might find the quality of the other's judgment rather irrelevant, for it seems primarily intent on taking away territory, rather than assisting in defending it.

An old lady at the venerable age of 84 lives by herself in a small house. Her strength is not what it used to be and at times she is a little forgetful. She doesn't keep the rooms as tidy as ten or twenty years before and her appearance shows lack of concern about her own grooming. Her relatives have been rather worried about her, and her two daughters have frequently discussed how much better it would be to put her in a nursing home. She would be taken care of and would not run the risk of getting ill with no one else around to help out. At long last they decide to go ahead and find a nice nursing home. Then comes the difficult moment of telling mother about the impending move. Mother is at first surprised. She is rather happy in her place, and even though it is a little big for her, it is filled with the many memories of the past which seem to occupy most of her time now; somehow it is her own place, it is home. Her daughters argue, and their reasoning makes good sense—that she is getting too feeble to take care of herself. They try to convince her that she would be so much happier in the nursing home they have found for her.

At first mother firmly resists, but after several weeks of repeated discussions, she has to admit that it is, indeed, for her own good and that an 84-year-old woman "should" be in a place where she can be taken care of. A week later she is moved into a nice, clean, modern nursing home. Her daughters drive her there. The couple running the home seems friendly and the room is really quite comfortable. But in the weeks that follow the daughters find their mother increasingly confused and withdrawn. Sometimes she is quite lucid, but on other occasions she seems to have no idea of where she is, and she even fails to recognize her own daughters. She is less and less capable of taking care of herself, a fact which before long makes her maintenance in the nursing home impossible. When repeated consultations with the psychiatrist yield no improvement, she has to be transferred to a special unit which takes care of completely senile and helpless individuals.

This course of events is not an unusual one. In her own home, where everything had a long history and where her own identity was written in the objects that surrounded her, there the old woman maintained a semblance of a personal life in spite of the gradual restrictions that had come with old age. It was obviously true that she could manage less and less territory and did so less and less well. It was also true that she could have come to an unfortunate, albeit hardly premature, end of her life. She could have fallen down the stairs with no one around to help her, or she might have become ill because of lack of attention to her own diet. The fact remains, however, that the relatives, *with genuinely good intentions,* managed to take away the territory of this old woman when she no longer had the vitality to defend it with vigor. Some years earlier she would have said, "I won't go." Now she gave in under the pressure. Perhaps if she had recognized that the statement "It is for your own good" covered the fact that she was robbed of her territory, she might still have found the strength to resist and maintain her own place until her death.

Occasionally the statement "It is for your own good" serves to hide a deliberate attempt at taking something away from a person, but more often it represents a genuine wish to do right by the other. One needs to keep clearly in mind, however, that even this genuine concern is irrelevant to the fact that the person under consideration loses his territory. The doctor who commits a patient to a hospital because he has been harmful to himself, or who injects a medication which is not wanted, takes the patient's autonomy away. If—as is sometimes the case—it is truly unavoidable that a person take over for someone else, the take-over can still be made more palatable by stating the facts as they are. If a patient has become a menace to society or threatens to take his own life and the psychiatrist takes control, it would be easier for the patient to deal with his loss of autonomy if he were told, "I do this to protect society from you," or "I do this because I could not live with myself if I stood idly by while you are destroying yourself"—rather than, "It is for your own good."

The tactic of "I'm doing it for your own good" has many equivalents which are easily recognized once one is alerted to them.[2] Other sentences which should ring the alert are: "This hurts me more than it hurts you . . ."; "Someday you will understand and appreciate what I'm doing"; or, "I have to do this because I care so much about you."

Of course, many occasions exist when an individual who feels temporarily incapable of managing his own territory welcomes, and even solicits, another person's help. On other occasions, a person may feel desperately in need of such help, and yet either fears the state of dependency which would force him to trust his well-being to the hands of others, or is afraid to ask for such help because he does not wish to be a burden. At such times, it may come as a relief if the other ignores the objections and simply takes over. The complicated way in which man seeks to justify all of his actions may lead to the paradoxical situation wherein one person intentionally stands idly by while another is being destroyed. This situation is the rather perverse extreme of "I'm doing it for your own good": The onlooker refrains from action because he does not want to reduce the other's freedom by interfering. This calls up the image of a person who

---

[2]Eric Berne, in *Games People Play* (1964, p. 143) describes the game of the mental health profession in "I'm Only Trying to Help You."

watches a blind man walk towards a precipice and who keeps silent "out of respect for the other's sense of independence," in other words, for his own good. Indeed, man's ingenuity in justifying whatever action he engages in is unsurpassed. It takes careful analysis of the territorial situation, with openness and sensitivity toward one's own feelings as well as those of the opponent, to decide which action is appropriate for his objectives on a given occasion. In case of doubt, however, there is probably considerable merit in restraining a tendency to take over for someone else "for his own good"—if one seeks to respect the other's integrity.

GIFTS AND CHARITY

Gifts are commonly used as a means of invading territory. When a person is presented with an unusually valuable gift, he is likely to experience a vague discomfort and some hesitation about accepting it, for an often not unfounded premonition rings the alert that he may incur an obligation which will give the donor a degree of control over the recipient's territory. If an individual cares to maintain his independence, he may take notice of the Trojans who failed to examine the oversized horse left to them by the Greeks. The admonition of "not to look a gift horse in the mouth" clearly applies only when the donation is too small to harbor a force of conquerors.

An interesting example of the conquest of territory by means of gifts which create obligation is given in *The Godfather* (Puzo, 1969). The God-father, a don of the Cosa Nostra, has acquired his whole power base by means of doing favors. All of the people who are in his debt together form the basis on which he has built his criminal empire: a judge whom he has supported in his election campaign; a policeman he helped when he was in trouble with the law; a shopkeeper to whom he gave a loan to start his store; and so on, multiplied a hundred times. These gifts were presents in the formal sense of the word, but they were not gratuitous tokens of friendship. Rather, they were the price by which territory was purchased, which the owner didn't even know he had for sale.

If parents surprise their newlywed children with living-room furniture, they gain some control over the home in which the couple will live, for they will have determined what it will look like inside. If the couple, as is usually the case, do not wish to hurt the parents' feelings by disposing of the furniture even if they would like to, the couple's loss of territory is substantial.

The many shoulds and should nots of social custom and the various religious notions of what "good" people do or don't do serve as a noise in the system which makes it ever so much more difficult to discern what is going on and to take a confident stand. A woman, some time after her divorce, recalled the paralysis and the confusion which mystified her and kept her from decisive action when after a two-week stay in the hospital she arrived home and found that her husband—as a surprise—had completely redone the living room, including paint, curtains, rugs, and furniture. How to respond at such a moment? The other has gone out of his way and made great sacrifice to provide such a magnificent gift; but why the inner discomfort, the incomprehensible surge of anger when gratitude *should* reign? "I must be a bad person" is all too often the inner reaction to the irritation sensed, and the next step is a phony, contrived display of happiness over so wonderful a gift. Such was exactly the reaction that our divorcée recalled making; but now, after all the conflicts that eventually destroyed the marriage, she wished that she had listened more carefully to her own signals (the anger and irritation), that she had kept away the power of the "shoulds," and had recognized the true state of affairs: This magnificent gift robbed her of the last area over which she maintained some control, the actual physical space of her home.

If parents regularly send a sum of money to their son in college, they maintain some degree of control over his life. Insofar as it gives him a feeling of obligation, it reduces his independence. The recipient of such otherwise welcome donations has a choice between two possibilities. If the money creates a sense of obligation which he cannot seem to eliminate, he is better off returning the gift if he cherishes his independence. However, he may value the gift more than his independence, in which case he can accept it as a good bargain but it is important to recognize that this will leave him with little justification for complaints about his loss of autonomy. In other situations the receiver may resolve that he will not alter his judgment in any way or reduce his independence by one iota when accepting the gift. If he succeeds in getting away with this attitude, he obviously can accept it safely and have the best of two possible worlds. An interesting variation of this giving-obligation problem has to do with the postal system. Until recently the recipient of unsolicited merchandise was obligated to pay if such merchandise was not returned within a certain time period. Now the rules state that all unsolicited merchandise may be kept by the recipient with absolutely no obligation to either return it or pay for it. In other words, unsolicited merchandise is seen as a genuine gift—no strings attached—from the sender to the receiver.

Giving takes on a special form when it occurs under circumstances which all but force the recipient to accept a gift. For instance, a bread-winner who has lost his job and has no other resources to provide for his family will have to accept help whether it comes from an individual or an agency. Ordinarily the person who extends the charity does not create the duress, but it is nevertheless the latter circumstance which forces a person to accept it. It is a previous loss of territory by the recipient that forces him to accept charity, and it makes little difference whether the loss was caused by poverty, chronic illness, or some other quirk of fate. The situation is complicated by the easily overlooked fact that the benefactor often derives substantial benefit from his charitable acts. They may give him a feeling of righteousness, for instance, which, as the term itself indicates, means that it engenders a sense of having certain rights because of having gratuitously contributed to the welfare of other individuals. The contributor to organizations supporting racial equality may gain the feeling that he now has the right to be treated as a person who is not bigoted. The person who extends charity directly to another individual easily gets the notion that his generosity gives him the right to advise the other on how to manage his affairs. Welfare workers who dole out the money of the state, rather than their own, may at times be subject to such an idea, even though such benefits are not actual charity but rights granted to individuals who live within a certain social system.

Whether any of this is good or bad is beside the point. It is, of course, most fortunate for a person in need to receive assistance from someone else. On an international plane, for instance, it appears fortuitous that richer nations provide assistance to countries that are underdeveloped. It also seems logical that the United States, when it pumps large sums of money into such countries, feels inclined to "suggest" certain steps to improve the economic situation. The fact remains, however, that the recipient of charity loses autonomy, a commodity of which he already had so preciously little, and is therefore unlikely to respond to charity with abundant, genuine joy. There may be initial pleasure and gratitude because the painful need has been remedied temporarily, but at the same time there remains resentment over the fact that autonomy has been reduced. Whoever extends charity should be prepared for a mixed response. To be surprised about the lack of gratitude displayed by have-nots betrays ignorance of the fact that those who have little or nothing can hardly afford any further loss of territory.

If one truly wants to assist another individual and at the same time wants to avoid reducing the other's territory and becoming the object of his resentment, one has to provide him with an opportunity for expansion, rather than giving charity. Does all of this mean that a person can never give anything to someone else? Certainly not, but it does imply that unless one seeks to conquer the other's territory, he had better be extremely careful in giving to a person who will never be able to respond in kind. *It is easy to give to those who have plenty. It is hard to receive for those who have nothing.* On a broader social scale this means that assistance given by the government is most constructive if it has two qualities: That it leads to expansion of the recipient's territory and that it is provided as a right which is automatically extended to all citizens.

HELPLESSNESS

Man is a social animal. This becomes strikingly apparent when one observes his spontaneous response to distress signals from his fellow mortals. Recent concern about bystander apathy notwithstanding, a scream of agony or a call for help will send people running to the scene and perhaps cause many individuals to intervene at the risk of their own lives before taking time to think it over. A display of helplessness brings out an impulse to assist which is so strong that it takes a deliberate effort to refrain from doing so, and if on occasion a person decides to ignore a call for help, he is likely to be plagued by pangs of shame for having failed in his responsibility.

So strong and so immediate a response to a relatively simple signal provides a perfect weapon which can be used to many different ends. The child uses it spontaneously and naturally, as it is his only means of muscling his way into the community of man. Some, however, continue the use of it later in life, a circumstance which gives rise to many complications. It is interesting to observe that this trick, which seems so understandably human, has already been introduced far down the ladder of evolution. Ants respond to a begging type of gesture of the young by regurgitating a drop of nourishment. Larvae of a species of beetles have cleverly tuned in to this characteristic of the ants by adopting the same gesture, an evolutional innovation which allows them to lead a life of leisure and profit from the food gathered by the ants (Hölldobler, 1971). Their imitation of the hungry ant larvae's begging gesture robs the mature ant of his food. This process is quite similar to what occurs on occasion in human circles, except that the latter has often far-reaching consequences.

Many a young woman has learned that a man's behavior can more readily be controlled by playing the role of a naive, innocent, helpless member of the "weaker" sex than through a direct assertive encounter. This interaction of the helpless female and the rescuer-protector male has peculiar consequences, including both loss and gain for each of the parties. The balance of this loss-gain exchange is of crucial importance for the relationship. The helpless woman gains considerable control over the strong man. She can make him do things for her, such as manage and defend her territory, but her loss, too, is substantial. She has little autonomy, no direct access to new territory (except via the man, making her dependent on vicarious living) and, as a consequence, little sense of identity or security. Her life depends on him, which leaves her with that nagging sense of nonbeing that comes with the absence of having real territory of her own. The protector, on the other hand, has a different balance of profit and loss. He expands his control over the life of his partner, which means that he gains territory but he pays the price of having to manage it, a time- and effort-consuming endeavor. He may derive a sense of pride and identity from his activity, but the dependent person soon becomes a millstone around his neck. This is the burden which the so-called helpless place on the strong. If this type of relationship takes on large dimensions, the woman becoming increasingly helpless and the man proportionately weighed down, the situation may end up unbearable for both. The woman, having lost all sense of autonomy, will seek to control the man through whom she lives vicariously, and the man will desperately try to shake the lifeless weight that pulls him down. As both partners are losing territory and no assertive response is open to them, a destructive hostility is unleashed.

The hostility of the dependent is well illustrated in one of the famous stories of Sinbad the Sailor. During one of his voyages, Sinbad, lost in a strange country, happens upon a crippled old man sitting by the side of a stream. The poor old fellow looks like he is in pitiful shape and Sinbad cannot refuse when he begs to be carried across the river, because his poor paralyzed legs cannot move him. Sinbad does what he is asked and takes the old man on his shoulders, but no sooner has he done so than the old man applies a vise-like grip with both legs around his neck. Sinbad suddenly remembers the stories which he has heard many years before of an old man who would hold on to his victims in this manner, eat all their food before they could get it into their mouths, and drive the poor individuals until they died of exhaustion. We will leave Sinbad in his predicament, which illustrates how the helpless can, in unexpected ways, become tyrants.

Helplessness is a weapon of considerable power, especially if it is used to obtain momentary results. However, the exclusive or predominant use of it in interpersonal relations is a two-edged sword which, if wielded too often, will make victims of both. The crucial decision for the person responding to helplessness is whether he is dealing with a genuine call for help, relating to a specific, limited situation or to an overall, nonspecific, and unlimited plea to take over because the other has defined himself as helpless.

This distinction is especially crucial for those professionals who make their living by helping other people, for being helpful to those who have defined themselves as helpless, but without a strategy which will change this pattern, will only succeed in confirming the definition, not in resolving it.

ILLNESS

Although much can be said about illness as a weapon in territorial conflict, as has already been indicated in the foregoing section on helplessness and earlier in the discussion of the obsequious ways in which territory can be taken away, there are some special aspects of this mode of interaction which deserve attention in the present context. We will focus on two interesting areas. The first one is illness as a special means of defining the other, and the second is illness as an excuse.

Jack comes home late, and to make things worse, he has forgotten to take care of an important errand that his wife Jane had asked him to handle when he left home in the morning. Just before his arrival he realizes his neglect. He is in a poor defensive position because of his sense of guilt. Immediately after he enters the door Jane asks in an irritated voice, "Why are you so late?" and after his lame excuse, she continues, "Did you take care of that matter I asked you about this morning?"

"Oh, I forgot!"

Now the wife is truly angry and berates him, "But it was essential that it be taken care of! How could you forget?" It so happens that Jane has been rather upset lately and has gone to a physician who prescribed tranquilizers for her. Jack, being in a defenseless position now, battles back with a newly gained weapon.

"What's the matter with you? Didn't you take your tranquilizers this morning?" This is truly heavy artillery. Jane stands speechless for a while. How does one find a defense against this? What the husband is saying with this small sentence is, "I cannot accept your angry behavior as justified by my failings. I rather see it as an irrational response stemming from your illness, for which you should be taking your pills." In other words, "I cannot take your comments seriously—you're sick," a nasty trick indeed, devastating but very effective.

There are many variants on this theme: "What's the matter, didn't you sleep well last night?" "Why are you so critical, are you having your period?" "Do you have a headache again?" "Are you getting too tired?" In this manner one simply ignores the relevance of the other's actions by defining him in such a way that his behavior is attributed to an illness and is stripped of all its pertinence. The person who is the object of such an attack feels strangely helpless. He feels as if all power has been taken away from him. By no longer being held responsible for his actions he has lost all impact. A comparable situation, but on a more drastic level, happens when a person is committed to a mental hospital or is placed under guardianship.

Occasionally an individual is not held responsible for breaking the law because his behavior supposedly did not result from his own intentions, but rather, from an uncontrollable impulse or a psychiatric disease. The defendant is usually most willing to play this game and understandably so, for it gets him off the hook. He is willing to pay the price in terms of a temporary loss of autonomy for the profit of not having to be punished. In cases of murder where the stakes are high, this defense enjoys considerable popularity. With this example we have shifted from not taking someone seriously "because he is sick" to the opposite case, in which sickness is used to disclaim responsibility for certain actions. "I can't help it, I get these sudden uncontrollable urges," or, "I'm sorry, it must be my period." And in court, "You cannot hold me responsible, I am sick," or, as presented by the attorney for the defense, "My client had a lapse of awareness when he killed the victim."

A recent newspaper report of a murder trial described the circumstances under which a killing took place. The defendant had been waiting in a parking lot for a cab driver to come out of a building. When the expected person appeared, the defendant pulled a loaded pistol out of his briefcase and killed him. The motive for this murder was revenge, as the defendant was the father of a child who had been killed in an accident in which the cab driver had been negligent. The jury decided that the father was not guilty of first-degree murder because he had been temporarily insane and did not know what he was doing.

When a person uses sickness to excuse his behavior, he usually maintains the right to determine which of his actions are caused by illness and which are not. He uses this method to deny others the right of counterattack by saying, "It wasn't really me who did it, it was some unknown force or some illness that controlled my actions." Here it is the "sick individual" who chooses when to use his sickness as a weapon and when not, whereas in the earlier case it is the opponent who uses the individual's sickness when it suits him so that his actions don't have to be taken seriously. Once illness has been brought into the picture, however, each party involved is likely to end up using the illness alternatively as a weapon or to find that the same weapon is turned around and used against him. Clearly it is a weapon which is highly effective when used, but which, once introduced, always makes the individual vulnerable to having it used against himself at some unexpected moment.

SEDUCTION

Seduction is a rather common way of making off with someone else's territory without his realizing what has happened. A coy daughter or wife may wind the father or husband around her little finger and succeed in making him do anything she wants, before it dawns on him that he has been had. The essential ingredients of seduction are flattery (which will be discussed below), the provision of some desirable gratification, or the creation of an expectation of some greater good to come. Of all the factors mentioned, the provision of gratification is perhaps the most effective. It may be wise to remember the general rule that a person should be alert to the possibility of losing some important part of his territory whenever an unusual amount of gratification is offered by someone else. A mother can induce her children to remain in the home even after they have grown up by giving them such good care (no one cooks better than mother) and such security that they will not risk the loss of either for the uncertainties of the world outside.

In some sense everyone is seduced by the promise of the future. "Someday my Prince will come" is a near-universal fantasy of ultimate reward for good behavior, which seduces a great many to give up much of their present life in pursuit of an empty promise—a fantasy territory. Many a person has plunged into deep depression at the moment of truth when he can no longer avoid the realization that the long-awaited reward will never come and that he has sacrificed a substantial part of his life following the piper. The hero of Proust's famous novel *Un Amour de Swann* (1929, p. 252), says at the end of his affair, "To think that I have wasted years of my life, that I have wanted to die, that I had my greatest love for a woman who did not please me, who was not my type!"*

Hope keeps man alive; it is the fountain from which he drinks the energy and the courage to face the new day. Seduction uses this human need for hope in order to control behavior. Seduction gives false, unjustified hope, not for the purpose of gratification, but rather to conquer the freedom of its victim. Those who despair of the future are most vulnerable to such techniques.

Some years ago an amazing incident occurred in which a group of seemingly average middle-class citizens waited in a back yard in the middle of the night for a spaceship to land and take them to a better world. Their prophet had foretold the imminent destruction of the earth, but promised them a better life on another planet if they put their trust in her. They did, and gave all their earthly belongings away except for a few travel items which they clutched in their hands as they waited for the ship to come (Jones and Gerard, 1967). Despair and hope make man vulnerable to seduction, and many a "prophet" has successfully utilized this method. It is of secondary importance only whether the seduction was accomplished in good faith, with honorable intentions for the ultimate salvation of the disciples, or a ruthless scheme to gain money or power. The results for the victim are pretty much the same: a loss.

FLATTERY

Flattery is an interesting weapon which, as was mentioned above, often plays an important role in seduction. In fact, in the age-old art of sexual seduction, *flattery is likely to be more potent than sexual desirability by itself.* The man who feels uncertain of his attractiveness or his masculine

---

* Authors' translation.

prowess may be easy prey for the woman who includes flattery in her arsenal. A wife who is neglected by her husband may take a lover, not primarily to alleviate her sexual frustration, but rather because her paramour makes her feel like a desirable person.

Flattery is like bragging in reverse. The boaster proclaims loudly his ownership of a territory which he either does not possess or cannot manage. Flattery, on the other hand, allocates a territory to a person even though the recipient has no claim on it and does not have the capability to manage it. If a parent looks at a child's unsuccessful attempt at producing a painting and claims that it is a beautiful piece of work, certainly indicative of a phenomenal talent, he allocates to that child an area of artistic productivity that the young person cannot possess for the simple reason that he has neither the skill nor the talent to manage it. The person who is prone to bragging is also sensitive to flattery; or, to put it more broadly, the person who is dissatisfied with the size of his territory or the way he manages it, easily falls victim to flattery.

What is the objective of flattery and how does it work? The basic design is very simple. One allocates some territory to the other, carefully choosing it in such a way that it does not entail a loss to oneself; at the same time, and while the other is preoccupied with the territory he just gained, the flatterer takes away some area over which the victim previously had control. While keeping the other happily diverted through flattery, one can borrow his money or have an affair with his wife.

A rather subtle form of flattery that may escape even the very alert assumes the disguise of *asking for advice or instruction.* Many times such requests are genuine, which makes it all the more difficult to discern whether they stand in the service of flattery. Several features may help alert one to the hidden agenda. A request for advice or instruction about an area in which one does not have real expertise is suspect. Of course it takes considerable honesty to detect such flattery, for it seems a shame to have to become suspicious on the possibly not too frequent occasions that one feels appreciated. As always, it is necessary to keep a sharp eye on oneself: If one *feels* flattered by the request, chances are that he really is, a consideration which can put him on guard against the territorial aggression that is likely to follow.

This discussion may have a tinge of paranoia, and so to add a more hopeful note it should be said that such a suspicious attitude is certainly not always warranted. There is, for instance, the enjoyable game of mutual flattery that can be played with humor and is appreciated by all. In such a situation the participants know that it is only play, with no serious or important issues at stake. It provides the enjoyment of jousting, trying out one's weapons with nothing to lose. It is closely related to the frequent form of entertainment called flirting—an as-if seduction in which both partners know if they play it correctly, that there will be no consequences: The play itself is the objective, not the conquest of the other's territory.

SEX

Sexuality, which can be an aspect of man's most trusting relationship of sharing, is often used as a potent weapon in the territorial skirmishes between individuals. Several of the ways in which sex is used have been analyzed in the previous discussions of various types of weaponry. It can be an important instrument in the process of seduction and flattery. It is used in the process of definition, assigning stereotypes of behavior to males and females alike. Conversely, definition is employed as an effective weapon in taking control over an individual's sexuality. It is fascinating to observe how a person can be duped equally well by the moral standards of certain religions which demand a special brand of perfection in sexual behavior, as by the popular clichés reflecting the sexual standards of a subgroup of society which, for some reason or another, appears glamorous to the victim. As an example of the latter, one comes across men who feel that they are failures as human beings unless they are regularly on the prowl to seduce women, bringing to their friends tales of their amorous successes, not too different from the way the headhunters of New Guinea might have brought home their grisly trophies. Different as his behavior may be when compared with the moralist, such a person is nevertheless being duped by a definition which he has accepted and through which he loses his freedom to the same extent as a man who labors a lifetime to remove all sinful thoughts from his mind.

In contacts between men and women, there often ensues a peculiar struggle about who controls whose sexual performance—this sexual performance being the action territory which is disputed with all weapons available. The man who can convince a woman that she *should* freely engage in sexual relations because she is emancipated has made a big step in the direction of his intended conquest. Many a young man will try this type of weaponry as he attempts to conquer a young woman by showing utter disbelief in her resistance to his advances and by telling her that only the very naive and unsophisticated would hold to such archaic standards of sexual practice. Obviously our territorial discussion cannot decide what is right and what is wrong. Each person will have to decide for himself in what style he wants to lead his sexual life. However, the method described above, of which there exist a thousand variations, represents *a weapon in the conquest of someone else's body and not, as one might like to pretend, a true sharing by both parties.*

Even today, in spite of the impressive progress toward equal status for men and women, there remains the peculiar notion that sexual relations are a commodity highly desired by the man and provided by the woman when she so chooses. This belief has given the woman a powerful bargaining tool. Many a man has been robbed of a good amount of his territory on a promise of what he might receive. Many a husband pays a price for sexual relations with his wife, quite in excess of that charged by the prostitute. The price of sexual inequality is high. As women have been allocated far less territory than men, one can hardly be surprised that they take it back in other places when the opportunity presents itself.

One of the reasons that an individual's sexual behavior can be used as a particularly vicious weapon is that his sense of self is deeply affected by it. Impotence and frigidity are responses in sexual contact which induce a profound feeling of inadequacy and powerlessness. A woman who exposes her husband's impotence, or his lack of sexual expertise, and a man who publicly discusses his wife's frigidity wield weapons so lethal that they cannot be used in any form of aggressive pursuit of new territory. This action must be recognized for what it is, a hostile attack designed to destroy. There are many such destructive ways of wielding a weapon, but sexuality, being so close to the very sense of who one is, offers unusual opportunities. Therefore sexuality can be most comfortably enjoyed with a person whom one trusts and with whom one shares large segments of territory.

OVER THE BARREL

As every experienced fighter knows, his own effectiveness is greatly enhanced if he knows how to get the other over a barrel. Imagine a couple living in an apartment building and suppose that the husband finds it very important to appear proper, being very sensitive to the opinions others hold of him. One day he and his wife get into an argument. As the quarrel becomes more intense, she suddenly raises her voice to such a high number of decibels that she undoubtedly can be heard in the adjoining apartments. The husband immediately responds by trying to quiet her down and saying that the neighbors will hear them if she doesn't lower her voice. It so happens that the wife is not particularly sensitive to the opinions of others and now has her husband over a barrel. All she has to do is raise her voice a little more and yell, "I don't care about the neighbors!" and the husband will be putty in her hands, willing to concede any amount of territory just so his reputation will not be undermined. From now on, the wife will be able to take anything from her husband that she chooses, provided that he values it less than his reputation. Obviously this is a case of blackmail. It's a "dirty" way of fighting by most standards, but very effective and commonly used. All one has to do is to find out something that is extremely important to his opponent and one can render him defenseless, that is, until such time that the other catches on and finds a countermeasure.

Several effective ways exist for coping with being put over a barrel. First, and most simply, a person can try to hide his weak spots. The husband in the above example could have pretended that he didn't care about his wife's yelling, and he even could have invited her to scream as loud as she could. Sometimes such bluffs work; more often the partner knows better. A more effective and foolproof way is to reduce the vulnerability by recognizing that even though it is uncomfortable when the neighbors know that there is a quarrel, such knowledge is preferable to being over a barrel. What is really more important?—that the territorial struggle at home is resolved constructively or that the neighbors think that everything is O.K.? And what if the neighbors know that there are conflicts? Are there any families in which there are none? Furthermore, so what if they think that we are bad people? Is their opinion really that important? If, through this process, one can desensitize his vulnerabilities, the balance between the partners is reestablished. Such desensitization is far more effective than a counterattack which seeks out the other's vulnerable spot, for that method can only lead to an escalation. No person is without weaknesses, and as the conflict progresses, it becomes increasingly likely that increasingly vital areas will be attacked.

Earlier we discussed the father-son relationship portrayed in the movie "I Never Sang for My Father." The father was able to take the son's territory away for such a long period of time because the son was over a barrel. He was over the kind of barrel which is common to many people—he wanted life to be right. He did not want to have a final break with his father; for even though he knew better, he kept hoping that some day a truly good relationship would evolve. Many a destructive interaction is maintained for this very same reason: One simply cannot accept the fact that it has been a failure.

In a similar way, many individuals are over a barrel by virtue of their perfectionism. If a person has to be perfect, if life has to be without flaws, if he cannot accept failure, he can never acquire a true sense of directing his own life. He always remains a slave to an ideal.

RAPID TAKE-OVER AND GRADUAL INFILTRATION

Rapid take-over is a style of aggression which can be extremely effective and which many victims find difficult to deal with. An example from international affairs may paint the picture. Some years ago, when a development which was viewed as unfavorable by the United States Government took place in Lebanon, President Eisenhower gave orders for an aggressive step. With extreme speed, without prior negotiations or threats, the American Marines took over Lebanon, landed in all the strategic places, and took complete control before anybody could get ready for a counterattack or an effective defense. In spite of protests by other countries, including Russia, no concerted efforts were made by the opposition, and the American troops remained until the situation was settled in a manner consistent with American interests, as interpreted by John Foster Dulles. The advantage of such a rapid take-over is that one occupies the territory before anybody can respond. By the time the other regroups, one is firmly dug in and cannot be dislodged without a major counterattack.

This technique is used with equal effectiveness on an interpersonal level. When a PTA committee gets together for the first time, a person employing this strategy may say: "It is obvious that the major problem confronting the schools is the X problem. This year we have to focus all of our interest and attention on this issue. In order to get on with the solution, I have brought with me a number of articles which each member of this committee ought to read so that we can take informed action." Frequently, such rapid take-over works. The reason that it works becomes more apparent after a look at its counterpart, the all-out defense. Most people are willing to expend all necessary energy to defend a territory when it is very dear to them. However, they may hesitate to present an all-out defense when relatively unimportant areas are involved and when the cost of the defense is potentially very high. Again, an example from the international scene.

When, during President Kennedy's period in office, accumulated evidence showed that the Russians were in the process of building missile sites in Cuba, a decision had to be made as to the proper response. After considerable deliberation in the Security Council, President Kennedy chose to respond with an all-out defense. He informed Khrushchev that if the missiles were not withdrawn immediately, the United States would proceed to destroy them. The risk of such all-out defense was high. It might trigger off a new war with fantastic losses to the whole world. The gain, on the other hand, was relatively small, for it would not involve a truly major shift in the balance of power. America still had its superiority in submarine-based Polaris missiles, and Cuba itself was not important to the United States. On the other hand, if it were a first step in an ongoing process, it could lead eventually to a fatal power imbalance. Kennedy chose the all-out defense with the result that the balance of power was maintained as before without any substantial cost to the United States.

On a smaller scale, the all-out defense requires a willingness to accept all consequences regardless of the cost. As such it is a counterpole to being over a barrel. The husband who, tired of his wife's nagging, pulls the car to the side of the road and refuses to drive an inch further unless she stops her running commentary, exemplifies an all-out defense. Both the rapid take-over and the all-out defense risk a sharp and perhaps violent confrontation. To be able to employ these weapons one has to be ready to stand up to such confrontation and settle the differences in direct and specific negotiations.

More often territory is not taken in one massive action, but piecemeal. If a couple, because of circumstances, feels obliged to take in the husband's mother, a territorial battle is almost certain to ensue. This is not surprising, for the mother-in-law, who moves in with no ground at all, will need to carve out a niche for herself. She does so in a stepwise fashion. First, she takes over the dishwashing, next the laundry, then part of the cooking, and so on until she, if not stopped, ends up controlling the total household. If this gradual take-over happens, a major disaster is in the offing, for the wife undoubtedly will not tolerate such a state of affairs for long and an all-out war may result with the risk of breaking up the marriage in the process. In retrospect, the younger woman may wonder why she didn't stop the mother-in-law during the very early phases of the take-over. She will probably recall that she didn't interfere because the items involved seemed minor and not worth the scenes and the potential troubles that would follow.

THE SMOKE SCREEN

Some individuals use the simple expedient of confusing their opponents by means of a smoke screen, just like the octopus when it perceives a danger. The primary objective is to confuse the other to such an extent that he is no longer sure where to attack or what to defend. One can, for example, engage in a verbal discussion which *almost* makes sense, but not quite. At times such exchanges are comparable to guerrilla warfare: Each time one makes an attack one finds the enemy gone, for he has withdrawn to an entirely different area from which he may make new forays.

An example from a mental hospital is the following: A patient had been admitted during a psychotic episode. Almost immediately he became calm and extremely cooperative. When questioned whether the patient could be discharged, the doctor answered, "No, he is still quite ill, he just seems to be improved."

"Would you let him out if he demanded to be let go?"

"No, such a demand would confirm that he is still psychotic."

This type of dialogue is not too different from the haggling exhortation, "I demand that you act like an independent person." Such a statement is most ingenious, for the other loses regardless of whether he tries to follow the command or goes against it. Mental health workers, by virtue of their training, are particularly adept at this type of attack. It may occur in the psychoanalyst's office in the following manner. The patient is in trouble and seeks help. Perhaps he has first consulted his family physician, who recommends a psychoanalyst of excellent reputation. The patient makes an appointment and eventually arrives at the proper time in the impressive-looking office. After the fee has been settled, an equally impressive $40 an hour, the analyst settles back into silence. As the weeks pass by the patient becomes increasingly insistent in his requests for advice or some help from the analyst. Eventually the analyst breaks his silence briefly to point out that a transference neurosis has evolved and that the patient is acting as if he, the analyst, could help him.

Many psychiatric interactions are of this variety. It is a clever trick, indeed, to set oneself up as an expert, to be paid as a super-expert, but to blame it on transference when the patient demands expert help. These techniques lead to a degree of confusion which affords the psychiatrist great control and power over the patient. It takes an unusually sharp and well-prepared individual to hold out against such techniques.

Still another example is drawn from observations in a convent. Here young novices, intent on becoming nuns, are introduced to the life of the order. An extraordinary device is used which very effectively influences the young girls. They are required to practice complete obedience. For every activity, including going to the bathroom, they must ask the permission of the supervising nun. At the same time, however, they are told that obedience is a difficult aspect of their initiation and that only the very strong are able to accept and complete this phase of the training. Such a method is extremely effective; it succeeds in assuming complete control over the novices' territory without any awareness on their part of what is taking place. Even the irritation which results from the loss of autonomy is readily explained as part of the hardship. One needs to overcome irritation, therefore, as part of the heroic struggle toward complete obedience; that is, one must be strong to be weak, just as the best doormats always say "Welcome." It boggles the mind to observe the weird and complicated traps people set for each other or, for that matter, for themselves. However this may be, the smoke screen method is effective. Whether or not it is right to use it is a matter of opinion rather than of fact.

RIDICULE

Anyone who has found himself the object of ridicule and lacked an appropriate retort, knows the anger, humiliation, and helplessness induced by such an attack. Such responses are hardly surprising, for ridicule is a "big gun" and is an especially effective weapon for taking psychological space from a rival. Psychological space, the influence which an individual exerts over the feelings and thoughts of others, depends on his being taken seriously as well as being able to command attention. Ridicule effectively undermines these foundations of psychological space because the unwary person who has been made the target of the first barb of ridicule—regardless of whether the focus is on his habits, background, manners, clothing, or ideas—undergoes changes in his body language which are incompatible with personal influence and actually confirm the insinuation. In other words, he starts to act "ridiculous." He may stammer, blush, lower his eyes, look away, fidget, or, equally ineffectively, fly into an ill-directed or uncontrolled rage. This observation provides a clue to the most effective defense against ridicule: The first and most essential step is to prevent the body language changes mentioned above. The individual under attack must preserve his composure, maintaining a relaxed body posture and a steady gaze, perhaps accompanied by a patient smile. A verbal response is most effective if expressed in a deliberate, well-articulated manner.

Skills relevant to the capturing of psychological space are a primary asset of every successful politician. English statesmen have been especially famous for their practice of the art of ridicule and masterful retort. Disraeli was particularly renowned for his sharpness of wit. One anecdote about him reveals the enormous power of eloquent ridicule in the hands of a master. The story has it that Gladstone, Disraeli's bitter political enemy, attacked the latter with the admonition that he, Disraeli, would either die on the gallows or of syphilis. Disraeli replied dryly, "That, my dear Gladstone, will depend on whether I embrace your politics or your mistress."

Another example of the use of ridicule as a means of countering ridicule is contained in the following story told to us by an Italian aristocrat concerning a friend of his who was a member of the British upper class. This particular gentleman, Sir J., had partaken considerably of the good life with the result that he carried a rather impressive abdomen. One evening, while he was passing a quiet time at his club, he was approached by another club member who, being solidly fortified with Scotch, loudly teased him about the size of his belly, inquiring as to the expected date of birth and the probable name of the offspring. Sir J. looked at him solemnly, and without a moment's hesitation answered in careful, measured words, "If, by the grace of God, Sir, it is a son, I will name it after my father, heaven rest his soul, for he was good to me; and if, perchance, it would be a girl, though I scarcely hold this possible, I will name her after the great Queen Victoria. But if, and this I hold to be the most probable, on emptying my belly I find the content to be what I suspect it to be, Sir, I will name it after you!"

The use of ridicule is, of course, not limited to famous personalities nor is it always witty or clever. Ridicule, whether it be subtle or crude, is wielded with equal effectiveness by school children and adults, by men as well as women. One needs only recall the diverse occasions when one has been the involuntary and uneasy party to a scene in which a person is being ridiculed, whether that person is a child being taunted by classmates because his skin is not an accepted color, or a husband being publicly berated by his wife because of his lack of social graces.

Psychological space is an essential commodity in the classroom. A teacher must be able to hold the attention of his students if he is to carry out his teaching objectives. Any teacher, therefore, who lacks an adequate defense against ridicule is soon rendered useless in his job. Ordinarily a new teacher is put to the test by his students early in his career. A slight mistake, an unusual posture, or a slip of the tongue may evoke teasing from one of his students. If the teacher loses his composure and fails to make an adequate retort, he automatically loses psychological space—a fact which results in an immediate increase of the noise level in the classroom. It is essential, therefore, that every teacher be prepared for such occasions, and that he have a well-rehearsed response available. His response must include the maintenance of his own composure, as well as a preferably humorous rejoinder if he is to be successful in regaining the contested psychological space.

Ridicule is disruptive of rewarding interpersonal relations, for it casually takes away the victim's right to be taken seriously. In this respect it is very similar to the weapon of illness described earlier, which allows for not having to take a person seriously because his behavior is "caused by illness" and not the result of personal decision. When individuals in a marriage resort to ridicule as their primary means of fighting—painfully exemplified in Edward Albee's play "Who's Afraid of Virginia Woolf?" —total destruction of the partnership is bound to follow.

Ridicule can be distinguished from humor in that ridicule has a victim and humor does not. Ridicule is a weapon used to usurp psychological space, whereas humor is a peace-maker used to bring perspective into a tense situation and ease conflict. Ridicule polarizes a group; humor allows opposing parties to deescalate the battle and negotiate without losing face. The ability to interject humor is an extremely important skill to possess, for a humorous remark can point up the absurdity of an incident, preventing fruitless confrontation and facilitating an atmosphere of cooperation.

COMPETENCE

In addition to expanding and defending one's territory, one needs to pay attention to its management. If a person would like to control all the financial decision-making for the family, he will have to manage this area with sufficient competence. He will have to keep books, pay the bills on time, plan the budget sufficiently in advance in order not to run into trouble at any time of the year, provide for emergencies, set priorities on purchases, and take care of the taxes. Unfortunately, many management details are chores that few people enjoy. Such jobs take time and energy which keep a person from doing other things that he might find more enjoyable.

This fact, however, provides an opening wedge for those in search of new territory. The aggressor makes use of this wedge by taking on the chores of someone else. He simply starts helping out. By doing the job with competence, he gradually expands the scope of the responsibilities he accepts. The recipient of such unusual zeal and competence is naturally greatly pleased and much relieved at not having to do the work and being able to spend the newly gained time on his own hobbies. As is the case with all skills which are left unused, it does not take long before the unwary victim's own competence in managing the original area begins to decrease. Besides, he spends his time now on other activities and, for that matter, couldn't get back to the original arrangement of doing his own work even if he wanted to. The person who only came to help out has become indispensable and his power over the domain is rapidly consolidated. A beautiful example of this way of operating is given in the Indian folk tale of "The Strong Boy."

This story is about a young Indian lad who escapes the cave where he and his mother are kept captive by a ferocious bear. Being young and weak, the boy resolves to go out into the world and gain enough strength to return and save his mother. One day as he is walking along he meets a man portaging a large canoe and asks if he might help carry it. The man agrees, and so the boy takes one end of the boat on his shoulders. At first he can only assume a small share of the load but he persists, and as he grows stronger he takes more and more weight upon himself until he is carrying the canoe alone. The man, in the meantime, carries less and less and so becomes weaker and weaker.

The boy meets others on his journey and helps them also. The more he carries the stronger he becomes; the less they carry the weaker they get. After a time, his companions, perceiving the Strong Boy's great strength and their own lack of it, come to fear him and plot his destruction. The plot is revealed to the Strong Boy by a friendly spirit and he escapes their trap and chases them away. Finding himself ready to challenge the bear, he returns to the cave, defeats his enemy, and rescues his mother.

In the more pedestrian setting of daily life the same method may be employed by a mother who lives with her married daughter and makes herself indispensable to her. If the latter is not willing to work hard, she soon will find that her area at home is gradually reduced in size. Once she recognizes this unexpected result of what seemed such a fine arrangement, it might be too late to regain control over the area gracefully. Frequently such a situation ends in a struggle fought by devious means, destroying much of the positive feelings that the people involved may have had toward each other.

Competence and willingness to do chores are not necessarily used in roundabout ways only. It is possible to utilize this method in a calculated manner in order to take over a specific area, but such careful foresight and planning is too rare to play a major role in human affairs. Most of the time people do what comes naturally and leave another job undone because it seems like an unrewarding chore. Next, someone else takes care of it because he likes that kind of work, has a sense of responsibility, or has nothing else to do. It makes very little difference for the ultimate outcome whether the actions were motivated by the wish to help out or by careful planning. Of course, once the former owner catches on, the usurper will react variously, depending on his motivation. The schemer may respond with a shrug of the shoulders and acknowledge, "I guess he caught on"; whereas the person who only wished to help out is more likely to talk of ingratitude and feel the pangs of righteous indignation.

In the working world, competence is a factor in a well-structured process of territorial division. Here it is the acknowledged currency with which rank, status, and influence are obtained in a company. When a proprietor's business has expanded to the point where he cannot manage all the details of the job by himself, he hires an individual with sufficient competence to do some of them for him. As time passes and the business grows, additional parts of the job of running the company are farmed out to new people, and gradually a hierarchy of employees evolves. Surely the boss himself is on top and the whole territory carved out by his mushrooming enterprise is actually his. The fact that he cannot manage it by himself, however, puts him in the peculiar position of gradually having less control over the total territory as the business expands and the number of employees grows. He can claim only a few areas of policy-making as his direct action territory; the rest is effectively controlled by ever so many other people. As a consequence, he may have less of a sense of ownership than in those days when he worked by himself, or with just a few employees. He still has the ultimate power and could fire any of the employees if he wanted to, but this power is counterbalanced by the level of competence of his employees. Insofar as his business is based on their exclusive competence, he will find himself increasingly powerless. It may happen, if his leadership skills are unequal to the task, that a vice-president who holds all the vital information central to the total organization in his mind, has, in effect—although not in name—greater control over the territory than the president of the company himself.

Benjamin Franklin, in his autobiography, describes how he effectively used competence to acquire his station in life (Franklin, 1941, p. 84). In his younger years he worked in a printing shop for a man named Keimer. At one time he was fired from his job following an argument with the boss: ". . . and so I remained idle a few days when Keimer, on a prospect of being employed to print some paper money in New Jersey, which would require cuts and various types that I only could supply, and apprehending Bradford (the other printing house in the city) might engage me and get the job from him, sent me a very civil message that old friends should not part for a few words, the effect of sudden passion, and wishing me to return." Franklin's story shows that Keimer had lost control over his territory when he became dependent on the skills of his employee. *The man who has made himself indispensable through competence, has taken possession of the territory relevant to that competence.*

If an individual wants to hold on to a territory, he had better think twice before he delegates the chores to someone else. If, as in a large business, it is impossible to do all chores by himself, he should never forget to dilute the importance of any one person by maintaining a back-up system and by doing the most important chores himself. On the other hand, if he wants to gain territory, competence is a straightforward and effective way of accomplishing this goal.

PACIFISM

In the realm of fighting, human versatility is probably demonstrated nowhere in a more impressive way than in the paradoxical use of no weapons at all in the service of overpowering an opponent. We are, of course, not referring to the genuine pacifist who truly abstains from fighting, but rather to those individuals who employ the technique of refusing to fight as a specific *means* of fighting. Aside from other confusing features of this method, it is usually enhanced in its effectiveness by a subtle process of guilt induction. It is difficult, indeed, not to feel guilty when one is confronted with a seemingly harmless individual who puts up no apparent defense and who seems to maintain a high moral position in spite of one's own spontaneous inclination to attack. This type of pacifist acts like a mass of jelly, giving very little resistance, but molding itself around every object. The person who employs this technique avoids all actual engagements, in this manner frustrating his opponent who seeks in vain to win a decisive battle. The victim is likely to come out of the struggle without having made contact with the opponent, feeling guilty for his unreasonable desire to fight with one who radiates such peace and beatitude.

Although on first sight it may seem peculiar, it is clear from our experience that many a marriage has gone on the rocks because one of the partners had successfully maintained this pacifist stance. The way in which this type of a struggle may manifest itself can be exemplified well by a couple who sought professional help some time ago. The wife was in deep despair, a mood which, although present for the twenty years of the marriage, recently had reached new lows. The major source of her distress became apparent during the first joint interview. She accused her husband bitterly of many things, ranging from the fact that he had never given her status equal to that of his mother, to his distressing problem with premature ejaculation. When, at that point in the interview, we turned to the spouse and asked him for his opinion about this set of accusations, he looked up with wide, innocent eyes, frowned, and then broke into a very slow smile. Next he looked down, then up again, and finally said in a soft, hesitant voice, "I'm not sure."

Now his wife, with irritated impatience, broke in with, "You see? He doesn't fight! He *never* does. He drives me crazy. He never really responds."

We turned once more to her spouse, "Do you think that your wife's observation is correct?"

Again there was a pause, a new smile, and a mild look around, "That is probably . . . true . . . I think . . . she is . . . probably right."

"But why *don't* you fight back?" we asked.

Once again there was a pause with slow, innocent gaze from an overly friendly face, "I don't know . . . I don't like . . . fighting . . . I guess . . . I'm not a fighter." His voice remained gentle, unperturbed, and in sharp contrast to his wife's, whose exasperation gave a strident quality to her speech. Occasionally during the interview he got a pained look in his eyes when his wife lashed out at him, but his patient, benevolent countenance was never seriously interrupted. Then the wife brought out another accusation.

"When we first got married he agreed that the kids would be sent to public school. When the time came I registered the oldest, but, you know, on the first day of school he and his mother suddenly appeared in front of the building and took the child away to transfer him to a parochial school."

"What did you do then?"

"I yelled, I cried, I screamed at him, but he reacted then just as he did now. He just becomes quiet and refuses to fight and ignores what I say and what I feel."

The effectiveness of this "no fight" weaponry was extremely apparent in our work with this couple. By not responding to any accusation, he ignored his wife's position completely and simply continued to do what he wanted to. The wife, on the other hand, especially in the early years of their marriage, felt guilty over her own hostile feelings and impulses, which seemed in such sharp contrast to the saintly demeanor of her partner. Yet, this attitude of his only deepened her hate. The devastation of this pacifist stance in their interaction was enormous, and clearly resulted in her spending a number of years in psychiatric hospitals. This method of fighting reveals, perhaps better than any of the other techniques, the price which both partners pay when conflicts are settled by using devious tactics.

The husband, by using his pacifist style, did gain territory, but lost a wife, or at least the opportunity of truly sharing his life with another human being and experiencing the joy of real communication. The destruction which it brought to his wife was already mentioned. There is no better example than the battles fought by a pacifist to show the fallacy of judging the essence of an interaction between individuals by its superficial appearance, and nowhere does it become more clear that what may appear as a display of love may, in fact, create grief and destruction. This brings us back to a paradox which we have presented in different forms and in various contexts. The greatest promise for the maintenance of human dignity and the most effective promotion of communication and sharing derives from an interaction which is assertive, direct, and ready to face sharp confrontation, but which confines the struggle to the disputed territory. Such struggles must ultimately be settled through negotiation and by means of compromise. The person who has been alerted to the various types of devious fighting and their deleterious aftereffects may decide to eliminate such weaponry and replace it by more direct and assertive methods if he is to pursue the goal of living in friendship and enjoying communication with his fellow man.

In this chapter we have described a few of the more popular weapons wielded by Western man in his daily territorial competition. A thorough knowledge of such weaponry, combined with the practical ability to recognize the behaviors involved for what they are, will help the opponents arrive at a situation in which neither side can obtain a decisive advantage by further maneuvers.

Only after the contending parties are stalemated will they be ready for a constructive attempt at settling their conflicting interests through serious negotiation. This negotiation process itself involves several necessary steps. To begin with, the parties must identify the territory under dispute and evolve procedures for bargaining in good faith. Subsequent negotiations will follow one of two courses: territorial subdivision or territorial barter.

Territorial subdivision means that the territory under question is broken down into its component parts and divided between the contesting individuals. Peggy and Joe are at dagger points over the control of the family car. Joe claims that as head of the household and breadwinner he should have ultimate control. After all, he has to go to work every day. If Peggy wants the car she can ask him for it and he will try to make arrangements to ride to work with a friend, or, if necessary, to take a bus, even though it means leaving a half hour earlier and walking eight blocks to the bus stop. Peggy counters with the fact that since the children are engaged in many activities, she has to have control over the car. She points out that Johnny has Boy Scouts on Tuesday afternoon after school, and Jill has Girl Scouts on Wednesday and ballet lessons on Thursday, and George has scuba diving lessons on Monday and orthodontist appointments, and she has Women's League on Friday morning every other week. In addition she has to shop and run errands, and if she has to walk to the bus on rainy days her hairdo is ruined. Joe inquires sarcastically why it is all right for him to walk to the bus stop and get soaked through and through while his fifteen-year-old son is driven to the swimming pool which is only one block farther away than the bus stop. Peggy protests that George can't possible carry all of his diving equipment to the pool and back, and anyway, he has orthodontist appointments also, and so the fight goes on.

A way out of such an impasse can be opened up by *subdividing the territory* under dispute. For instance, the control over the use of the car can be split up by introducing a time factor. "I want ultimate control over the car" can become "I want control over the car half of the time." Joe will say that on Tuesday he must have the car for business purposes because he has to drive to a neighboring city to pick up supplies, and on Friday he delivers orders to his major customers in person. Once every two weeks he will have to have the car for miscellaneous business affairs, but he could negotiate that on an individual basis. Peggy says she can get a ride for Johnny to the Boy Scout meeting on Tuesday with Mrs. Grey, and in return she will take Lisa Grey to Girl Scouts with her on Wednesdays. Friday will be more difficult, but she will try to get a ride to League meetings if it is raining. If the weather is good she will take a bus. When the weather is bad she will take a taxi if she cannot find other transportation. Joe and Peggy also agree to keep notes on costs of bus, taxi, wasted time, points of conflict, and inconveniences in order to ascertain whether it would be better to get a second car. They also agree to discuss the car issue again one month from the date of the first negotiated contract.

The time limitation is particularly important because it reduces the overall importance of the decision and makes an agreement easier to reach. Setting a specific time for reviewing and perhaps renegotiating the contract also prevents the partners from making decisions in a state of crisis only. By allowing a specific contract period, both parties have an opportunity to "try on" the agreement for comfort and to gather data regarding its efficacy. By setting a definite date to reconsider any commitment, much of the pressure and discomfort inherent in any change of territory can be eliminated. The knowledge that renegotiation is possible, and in fact planned for and expected, places the interpersonal relationship on an orderly and rational basis.

Territorial barter means that one territory is traded for another of equal importance. If, for instance, Joe felt that giving up control of the car meant giving up his masculinity, then Peggy would be better off to let him keep it and instead negotiate for another territory in exchange for the one she gave up. She might say, "Well, I will let you have control over the car if you will take me to the theater once a week." In other words, "I will get five hours of your time to spend in the way I like and you will get the car." Bargaining that can lead to a relatively stable peace ultimately depends on the balance of aggressive and defensive skills of all parties. A keen awareness of devious and subtle fighting techniques is an important asset for the creation of such a balance.

CHAPTER 12

COMMUNICATION

> He said to his friend, "If the British march
> By land or sea from the town tonight,
> Hang a lantern aloft in the belfry arch
> Of the North Church tower as a signal light,—
> One, if by land, and two, if by sea;
> And I on the opposite shore will be,
> Ready to ride and spread the alarm
> Through every Middlesex village and farm,
> For the country folk to be up and to arm.
>
> *"Paul Revere's Ride" by*
> *Henry Wadsworth Longfellow**

If each territorial conflict had to be settled by means of an actual battle between the opponents, our species would never have reached the predominant status it now enjoys on our crowded globe. In spite of misanthropic denouncements of man as the only fratricidal species, our present population density inescapably shows that such impulses, if present, have by and large been kept successfully in check. Physical fighting to the point of destroying the other is relatively rare, the massive excesses of modern warfare notwithstanding.

Observe a fierce fight between two dogs; they bite and tear, growl and snarl, pitching their strength and fighting skill against each other. Eventually one gains the upper hand. The loser rolls over on his back and bares his throat. The victor, rather than using this opportunity to finish his enemy off, accepts this sign of submission and shows no further interest in his victim.

Human warfare has much in common with the fighting of animals, as exemplified in the dog fight, at least as long as it takes place between individuals. Matters change considerably when large groups do battle with each other, and get severely out of control when the opponents can no longer see one another as a result of long-distance weaponry.

---

*From *The Works of Henry Wadsworth Longfellow, Poems Volume IV*. The Fireside Edition, Boston & New York: Houghton Mifflin Co., 1901, pp. 25-26.

Erich Maria Remarque, in his World War I classic, *All Quiet On The Western Front* (1966, pp. 131-132, 136), focuses on the disjointed experience of methodically fighting an impersonal enemy from afar and the agonizing feeling of killing another human being in hand-to-hand combat. The narrator recounts at one point how, after a raid across No-Man's-Land, he becomes lost on the way back to his own lines. He is forced to take refuge in a shell-hole until he can find a way to rescue himself. The battle continues unabated and he is in terror that the enemy, who has launched a counterattack, will find him.

> . . . I have but this one shattering thought: What will you do if someone jumps into your shell hole?—Swiftly I pull out my little dagger, grasp it fast and bury it in my hand once again under the mud. If anyone jumps in here I will go for him; it hammers in my forehead; at once, stab him clean through the throat, so that he cannot call out; that's the only way; he will be just as frightened as I am, when in terror we fall upon one another, then I must be first.
>
> Now our batteries are firing. A shell lands near me. That makes me savage with fury, all it needs now is to be killed by our own shells; I curse and grind my teeth in the mud; it is a raving frenzy; in the end all I can do is groan and pray.
>
> The crash of the shells bursts in my ears. If our fellows make a counter-raid I will be saved. I press my head against the earth and listen to the muffled thunder, like the explosions of quarrying—and raise it again to listen for the sounds on top.
>
> The machine-guns rattle. I know our barbed-wire entanglements are strong and almost undamaged;—parts of them are charged with a powerful electric current. The rifle-fire increases. They have not broken through; they have to retreat.
>
> I sink down again, huddled, strained to the uttermost. The banging, the creeping, the clanging becomes audible. One single cry yelling amongst it all. They are raked with fire, the attack is repulsed.
>
> Already it has become somewhat lighter. Steps hasten over me. The first. Gone. Again, another. The rattle of machine-guns becomes an unbroken chain. Just as I am about to turn round a little, something heavy stumbles, and with a crash a body falls over me into the shell-hole, slips down, and lies across me—
>
> I do not think at all, I make no decision—I strike madly home, and feel only how the body suddenly convulses, then becomes limp, and collapses. When I recover myself, my hand is sticky and wet.

For a day and a night the soldier huddles in the shell hole, witnessing the death struggle of the enemy. He seeks to help him, dresses the three stab wounds which he caused and gives him water. This is the first person he has killed with his own hands and from an impersonal enemy he becomes a suffering fellow man. Finally the wounded man dies and the soldier is left alone, haunted by his own disturbing thoughts.

> My state is getting worse, I can no longer control my thoughts. What would his wife look like? Like the little brunette on the other side of the canal? Does she belong to me now? Perhaps by this act she becomes mine. I wish Kantorek were sitting here beside me. If my mother could see me—The dead man might have had thirty more years of life if only I had impressed the way back to our trench more sharply on my memory. If only he had run two yards farther to the left, he might now be sitting in the trench over there and writing a fresh letter to his wife.
>
> But I will get no further that way; for that is the fate of all of us: if Kemmerich's legs had been six inches to the right; if Haie Westhus had bent his back three inches further forward—
>
> The silence spreads. I talk and must talk. So I speak to him and say to him: "Comrade, I did not want to kill you. If you jumped in here again, I would not do it, if you would be sensible too. But you were only an idea to me before, an abstraction that lived in my mind and called forth its appropriate response. It was that abstraction I stabbed. But now, for the first time, I see you are a man like me. . . ." (Excerpt from *All Quiet On The Western Front* by Erich Maria Remarque. "Im Westen Nechts Neues," copyright 1928 by Ullstein, A. G.; copyright renewed 1956 by Erich Maria Remarque; "All Quiet On The Western Front," copyright 1929, 1930 by Little, Brown and Company; copyright renewed 1957, 1958 by Erich Maria Remarque. All Rights Reserved.)

It appears that the devices which have been built into the species in the course of its evolution, and which serve so well in the prevention of frequent fatal conflict between individuals, fail not because of man's innate evil, but rather, because of man's rapid progress in social organization and technical ability. Apparently when large groups of people have been forged into a hierarchical organization for the purpose of warfare, the ordinary signals fall on deadened senses. In fact, the mark of good military organization is its ability to eliminate the personal response to flee or give up when it is apparent that for that individual it is going to be a losing affair. However this may be, in small-scale interpersonal conflicts the sending and receiving of signals is still of crucial importance.

The ultimate consequences of dissension are usually prevented in the human situation by a series of signals which effectively communicate how the individual views the situation and what his intentions are. Human communication is a vast and complicated topic. In the present context, therefore, we will focus our attention only on those signals, mostly nonverbal, which reveal the state of affairs concerning human territory. By means of such signals individuals succeed in maintaining order and structure in the human organization, a vitally important accomplishment, especially under conditions of overcrowding. The signals referred to disclose the person's relative status in the group and provide others with a clue as to how he will respond to attack or friendly approach. They reveal how close he will let the other come and where the invisible borders are which surround his privacy. A slight change in facial expression when another touches on a subject that is better left alone communicates just as effectively the warning to proceed no further as the sign painted on a fence: NO TRESPASSING.

Scientists who systematically study the meaning of body language in human communication are well aware of the enormous complexity of the task.[1] Although much progress has been made in this line of research, as yet there is no comprehensive listing of even a grammar of the meanings of such nonverbal behaviors. The difficulty encountered in trying to create a master encyclopedia of the social significance of specific human behaviors lies in the fact that each behavior has its meaning modified by any other gesture which accompanies it. In addition, verbal as well as nonverbal behavior together form a complex language in which neither component stands unaffected by the other. Furthermore, the meaning of behavior can only be understood in the context of a specific social interaction, which in turn is grounded in the cultural traditions and heritage of the individual in question.

On a practical, day-to-day level, however, a person does not have to have an encyclopedia to refer to in order to interpret the behavior of another. Each individual lives in one specific culture, is related to certain tradition, and ultimately finds himself in an ongoing series of unique social situations. Within this very personal context he sends and receives signals which are understood by all participants in the situation on the basis of their common background. This understanding guides the behavior of each individual relative to others, and it determines the expectations they have of each other which form the basis of their mutual responses. Indeed, a person knows immediately how others interpret his

---

[1]Perhaps the most consistent and exhaustive studies in the area of body-motion communication have been done by Ray L. Birdwhistell in his *Introduction to Kinesics* (1952) and *Kinesics and Context* (1972). Other important contributions, especially to the study of communication and schizophrenia, have been made by Gregory Bateson in *Steps to an Ecology of the Mind* (1972).

behavior by their own response to him. If, for instance, they show deference, they have clearly judged his behavior differently than if they ignore his presence. The relevant question which the individual must ask, if he is concerned about his impact on others is: Does my behavior obtain the results I was aiming for? If the answer is no, he might consider experimenting with new and different behavioral patterns which perhaps will give him the desired interpersonal results.

THE ORIGIN OF NONVERBAL SIGNALS

The origin of the nonverbal signals used in communication derives basically from the relevance of the behavior itself. Behavior, after all, is affected by the territorial situation. Consequently, it cannot help but reveal the situation to the careful observer. This point is well exemplified by Arthur Colman's description of the impressive changes in behavior which took place in an individual when he was visited in his own home as compared to when he was seen in the hospital. The man, a musician, remained silent while in the hospital even when spoken to. The staff saw him as a disturbed, irrational, schizophrenic individual. Later when Dr. Colman made a home visit, he had quite a different experience: "Mr. Pond greeted me in a warm, gracious manner and asked me to call him by his first name .... The next hour was spent in conversation controlled by Mr. Pond. The Ponds were at ease and calm in contrast to my own anxiousness in the unfamiliar and provocative surroundings .... At no time during the visit was Mr. Pond's relaxed and confident tone lost." (Colman, 1968, pp. 464-468).

The comfort a person feels on his home ground becomes apparent in his erect posture, his relaxed muscles, his steady gaze and strong voice, as well as in his attentiveness to the environment. The moment he loses this sense of security, his voice tightens up ever so slightly, but the higher pitch does not go unnoticed, nor does the fact that his eyes look around nervously as in search for new information, while the muscles of his neck and shoulders contract. These behavioral changes may be small, but as all individuals within a given society have been extensively trained to respond to such minimal cues, they have become potent signals.

Shoulder position, openness of arms, erectness, and eye contact are influenced not only by the feelings which individuals have toward each other, but also, and most importantly, by the relative status of the communicators.[2] By the same token this relationship itself is influenced by the particular gestures and stances employed, especially important in the quick sizing-up process which occurs when two people meet each other for the first time. Each person makes a rapid, intuitive appraisal of the other's territorial powers and his dominance status. Much of the immediate like or dislike that people experience for each other is a function of this assessment. If an individual enjoys relationships of equality, he will respond negatively to a person whom he estimates has a much higher or much lower rating on the scale of relative strength. If he seeks a relationship of dependence, he will feel an immediate affinity for a person who exudes territorial power.

Other relevant signals are more direct physiological concomitants of the body's preparation for aggressive action or flight. When a person perceives that his territory is being invaded, his anger is provoked and his body automatically takes the necessary steps to be prepared for a fight. Adrenalin pours into the blood stream, the digestive functions are geared down, while glucose is mobilized and made available to the large muscles. The blood flow is increased and redirected appropriately in order to most effectively keep up the functions relevant to physical combat. Many of these physiological changes are visible on the outside. The skin may become flushed or pale, the person's mouth becomes dry, which in turn changes his voice, and his breathing becomes rapid. Desmond Morris, in his book *The Naked Ape* (1969), has drawn attention to the fact that man's lack of hair covering allows all skin changes to be extremely obvious. Such changes immediately signal alterations in disposition. Blanching of the skin combined with one posture means imminent attack. The same paleness occurring with a different set of postures signals fear or panic. If the skin reddens after a paling phase ambivalence about attack is indicated.

It is not our intention to discuss these physical changes in further detail. It is clear, however, from the above that they are relevant to the individual's response to the situation and that they reveal this response to the careful observer; in other words, they function as *signals*.

[2]Albert Mehrabian (1969) has done a thorough review of the experimental literature on body posture and communication. Although many aspects have not been adequately studied as yet, it is clear from the available research reports that the relative status of the communicators influences a wide variety of postures and gestures.

THE INFLUENCE OF SOCIAL LEARNING

The meanings of all of these signals are many and varied, as is always the case when one deals with human beings. They are, furthermore, vastly complicated by the profound influence of social learning. The style and detail of communicative behavior vary between cultures, as well as between families and individuals. Some of these behavior characteristics reveal the relative status of the individual. When the director of a company walks into a board meeting, he does this in a manner which sets him apart from the other people present. When a messenger enters the room he stands by the door, looks around hesitatingly, and waits for an opportune moment to deliver the note he carries. If he had come in like the director, everyone would have immediately perceived his behavior to be totally inappropriate. But in fact, the messenger does not make such mistakes, for he automatically behaves in tune with the situation as he perceives it. The physical position a person takes in a group in turn influences the characteristics others attribute to him. Sitting at the head of a table makes others regard him as endowed with leadership qualities, persuasiveness, and intelligence, even if the individual is unknown to the observers (Davenport et al., 1971). This perception takes place regardless of other behavioral or physical attributes of the person. Thus an individual's position in a group depends on the place he takes, which in turn influences the expectations for leadership—expectations which tend to bring about the very behavior that sustains the position of leadership.

Even at a very young age a child shows an ability to interpret social signals. In a classroom a definite relationship structure evolves among the children. The status in this structure is reflected in the behavioral patterns of each child. Some of the children stay on the periphery. They take very little psychological space and not much action territory, but depend primarily on the privacy of their personal domain. Their behavior may be shy and unassuming, and its nonintrusiveness does not evoke negative responses from the more dominant individuals. Other children are constantly the focal point of trouble as they make frequent forays into the psychological space of the class. They do so, however, in an unconvincing manner, which invariably results in their being rebuffed by the group leaders. Still others accept a totally submissive role, receiving in this fashion some psychological space, but always at the price of placing themselves at the mercy of the more aggressive individuals. Their sub-missive gestures include frequent smiling, continuous attention to the dominant members of the group, and, in case of emergency, crying. It is interesting that these dependency signals—and especially crying—which indicate "I'm harmless and helpless, please protect me," make it almost impossible to attack the individual. As a person approaches adulthood, he increasingly displays the tendency to spontaneously come to the rescue of those who plead for help.

A particularly interesting situation arises when, because of a variety of possible causes, a person does not learn to send out the appropriate signals. This inadequacy may simply be the result of a physical handicap: A face severely distorted by heavy scarring, or a monotonous voice resulting from surgery on the vocal cords can create such problems. Both the congenitally deaf and the blind are seriously handicapped in this respect. The eyes play a most important role in the signaling function of the face. Their absence or unresponsiveness renders the afflicted in-dividual's physiognomy difficult to understand. This situation is further aggravated by the fact that for the blind, seeing, and for the deaf, hearing, are not available as avenues for receiving the signals of others. Even if a congenitally deaf person learns how to talk, he will still not acquire the ability to modulate his voice so that it will signal his feelings or his intent. In order to receive signals, the blind individual concentrates on the subtle qualities of the other person's voice. This makes up, at least in part, for his visual deficit. The deaf can do the same with sight. For both of them, however, it is their sending capacity which remains the most seriously restricted and which creates as great an obstacle for them in playing a social role as does the actual sensory deficit itself.

The cause of others' serious signaling deficiencies may be less apparent. For some of these individuals, the deficiency is the result of confusing or inadequate modeling in the family, which results in a lack of opportunity to learn socially functional communication patterns. For others this deficit is perhaps congenital, either on a genetic basis or because of brain damage. A major characteristic of the most severe psychiatric disorders (primarily schizophrenia and infantile autism) is a lack of ability to send out understandable social signals. This issue has been debated extensively in the psychiatric literature for several decades. A Dutch psychiatrist coined the term *praecox feeling* to indicate the sense of strangeness which one experiences when he attempts to communicate with a severely disturbed schizophrenic person (Rümke, 1943). The problems are compounded by the patient's inability to read signals.

> The newcomer, or the patient who has become less organized, most likely fails to "read" the actions of the other patients accurately, upsetting the social balance. Of one of our patients, Ms, who sustained a broken nose for walking unwittingly into Pk's territory, the top-ranked patient Ro said: "He should have known better than coming close to Pk in *that* room." Society does not usually tolerate people "who should have known better," and many are hospitalized for inappropriate behaviour. In turn, schizophrenic patients often complain that their actions are misinterpreted or not understood by others. They are aware that something is wrong . . . [Esser, 1970, p. 46].

The absence of clearly readable signals—whatever the reason may be—creates a disturbing sense of discomfort in the person who tries to interact socially with such a noncommunicator. This discomfort is largely the result of the other's unpredictability. A person shapes his role relative to someone else on the basis of his own intentions, as well as his anticipations of the other's responses. If the other does not send out understandable signals, he cannot form such anticipations. Without them he is forced to act blindly, a situation which is experienced as anxiety-provoking. Under such circumstances one can observe two possible responses: (a) *The nonsignaller is left alone.* If this happens most of the time, he is gradually ostracized from the community, a pattern which not only leads to the ever-greater isolation of the individual, but also further reduces his chance for learning adequate patterns of communication. (b) *An attempt is made to evoke a more readable response.* The latter is an important basis for *teasing behavior.*

Schizophrenic individuals commonly have a history of having been subjected to continuous teasing by their peers during their early school years. Our observations lead us to hypothesize that such teasing is, in large part, caused by their inability to send out readable signals. Teasing is a playful jousting, of aggressing and pulling back, for the purpose of finding out how the other might respond to more serious social interactions. By means of teasing one finds out whether the other will defend his territory and how effectively he will do it, whether he will launch an assertive or hostile counterattack, and what his style of fighting is. As a result of such teasing and other skirmishing, each child obtains a definite place in the social hierarchy of peers. As long as this hierarchy or, more specifically, the territorial division is stable, there is comfort for all involved.[3] Each person knows his place. This social stability is maintained by the continuous exchange of nonverbal signals. If one individual fails as a sender, he automatically provokes a response from the others to find out where he stands. Unfortunately, if a person has a basic lack of signaling ability, an unresolvable situation is created and, as a consequence, a continuous state of teasing, jousting, and skirmishing surrounds the victim. The schizophrenic individual, or, more broadly, a person who does not signal appropriately and has no obvious anatomical reason for his lack, is particularly vulnerable. As children mature they begin to realize the reasons for the strangeness of the blind or the deaf, and the simultaneous growth of their helping response usually makes the teasing come to an end in the junior high school years. However, the person who does not have such an obvious anatomical basis for his handicap does not become the beneficiary of the helping response until much later, and even then he is more likely to be avoided than helped.

Our observations lead to the conclusion that the child who, early in his school years, can be recognized as a deficient signaler needs *special remedial training* to obtain the necessary nonverbal communication skills. He needs to partake in a special program through which he can learn what different kinds of signals there are, what they mean, and how he can use them. He needs to rehearse this new behavior and try out interaction with other children and grownups under skillful guidance. In order to assist such a child early in his development, it is most important that children who are repeatedly and consistently the object of teasing by their peers be carefully observed for their signaling ability. If the problem of the child is recognized in this manner, it may be possible to retrain him early, rather than twenty years later when additional problems have accumulated, owing to the years of social isolation.

As was already briefly mentioned, in the social context a dynamic balance exists between the territories of each individual. This balance can shift at any moment, but insofar as it remains stable and predictable, it provides a sense of comfort and security for all of the participants. The

---

[3]Observations on various groups of rhesus monkeys have shown that the major determinant of fighting behavior among that species is the degree to which the internal social structure is settled. "When social strangers were introduced into the group antagonistic interaction increased four to ten fold. Attack initiative was led by the sex and age group corresponding to the newcomers" (Southwick, 1969). This last observation is particularly interesting, for it shows that conflicts are most likely to occur between individuals who will occupy and control the same territories in the group.

signals we have discussed serve the purpose of maintaining this balance and keeping the interactions predictable. Thus actual fighting is minimized and also potential damage to all concerned.

In daily life each individual comes across a great many nonverbal messages to which he responds. Some of these we have already mentioned in the context of the above discussion. Others one deduces from complex bits of behavior. For example, one decides that a person is defensive and vulnerable when he consistently overreacts to each minor invasion of his territory. Some signals are misleading because they are deployed in an unusual fashion. Certain nonverbal behaviors, for instance, are ordinarily used as sexual signals. When this same behavior is used in the process of a territorial conquest, a circumstance is created which may cause trouble for the person who misreads the message. In her behavior a woman may accentuate various sexual signals because she has learned in the course of her life that such signals yield a great measure of attention. When a man misreads this signal and responds to the sexual aspect of it rather than to the territorial intent to get psychological space, he will be surprised when the woman responds to his seemingly appropriate behavior with an indignant, "The only thing that men are interested in is sex!"

A whole different set of nonverbal communications, which we briefly alluded to in the chapter on sharing, are part of the process of self-disclosure in establishing friendship and intimacy. In this context the individual may signal, "I'll leave myself open and I will not harm you." If one of the partners moves too fast, however, the signal may change to "Slow down, you're coming too close, too fast." When one person seeks to establish contact with another who is vulnerable and finds it difficult to develop a sense of trust, it is especially crucial to remain aware of these signals. As many a person who has worked in psychiatric clinics can report from experience, when he fails to recognize that he is coming too close to a patient, he can be subject to a vicious counterattack, a last-ditch defense by a cornered individual.

People have a remarkable capability of communicating with each other by nonverbal means, even without clearly realizing either what they are sending or receiving. On the other hand, it has become known in recent years that even fairly primitive animals have well-differentiated techniques of signaling their territorial intent to each other. A series of fascinating studies of the catfish have demonstrated that these fish are able to signal to each other, by means of chemicals which have been called pheromenes, who is dominant, aggressive, submissive, or nonterritorial.

For instance, water taken from the aquarium of a dominant catfish and added to an aquarium where other catfish are housed will cause the latter to flee to a far corner, cowering as if afraid of an attack (Todd, 1971). The recognition of such capability in the catfish will perhaps leave one less surprised by the accomplishments of man, with his incomparably more sophisticated brain.

This same brain has given man the ability to deceive; recognizing his own behavior and its consequences leads to the possibility of imitating signals which do not reflect the actual way in which he experiences the situation. Even in this respect man is not unique. Many examples of deception are perpetrated by other species by means of the process of evolution. An example is a type of fly which has acquired the same yellow-and-black striping as the yellow jacket, with the result that it is carefully avoided by many potential enemies in spite of the fact that it is unarmed.

Man does not have to rely on the slow process of evolution to create such fake signals. He is ingenious enough to learn many of them in the course of his life. One can, for instance, assume the kind of behavioral attributes which ordinarily come naturally when one is on home ground, such as poise, a relaxed position, a firm handshake, a steady voice, and a direct gaze. By means of such acting a person may succeed, if he does well, in convincing others that he is on his own territory. An individual who can effectively pull this off may discourse with great authority about the merits of a nonexistent Spanish painter of the seventeenth century, convincing his audience not only of the merits of the artist who never lived, but also of his own erudition and his excellence as an art critic. Successful confidence men make extensive use of these kinds of false nonverbal signals to convince their victims of the fact that they can be trusted.

LEARNING NEW SIGNALS

To produce these signals convincingly is not as easy as it seems. A person may assume the posture of self-assuredness, but he will find it difficult to control a slight quaver in his voice, the hesitancy in his gait, not to mention the excessive functioning of his sweat glands. Subtle physical changes are prone to give him away, even if he has mastered the gross motor behavior with great efficacy. If a person wishes to acquire mastery over a new set of signals, therefore, imitation is not enough. Instead, he needs a tandem operation. The first step is to rehearse the desired behavior pattern. While doing so, it is essential that he induce the feeling in himself of the desired state, for example, self-assuredness, by use of the imagination. If he succeeds in feeling self-assured, then the finer details of the signals will fall in line automatically. Even if he accomplishes all of this, the behavior will remain artificial. Becoming an excellent actor of self-assuredness does not eliminate the knowledge that such behavior is phony. To make the new behavior genuine, a second step is needed. This step consists of the use of the new behavior in actual life situations, engaging in actions consistent with the signals. Through a process of rehearsing the new behavior, followed by trying it out, one eventually arrives at the point where the newly gained self-confidence is genuine.

A young medical student, dressed in a white coat, his stethoscope hanging casually out of his pocket, enters a patient's room to do a physical examination. It is the first time that his preceptor has sent him in by himself. In this case the patient happens to be a young woman. The physician-to-be desperately collects all his "cool" in order to act matter-of-factly and ask with a self-assured voice that the patient take off the necessary clothing so that he can proceed with the examination. The nurse, who has seen a great many students come and go, recognizes the slight breaking of his voice and takes over, helping the patient get ready for the physical. The student proceeds with shaking hands but developing confidence as he goes on.

The student, in this example, is playing the role of a doctor, feeling inside like an imposter. Hardly a year later he will have attained the self-confidence which goes with a new identity. No longer does he play the role of a doctor, he *is* one; he has acquired a new territory, including "the right" to examine the patients.

The process of acquiring the behavioral habits that communicate relative status and signal territorial intent depends, to a large extent, on what is often called excess learning. When a child learns arithmetic in school, he simultaneously acquires a number of additional notions. He finds out, for instance, that he is good at mathematics, that studying can be fun, and that he is smarter than the majority of his schoolmates. If a person defends his territory well, he learns that he is a capable defender who can hold his own in most any circumstances. This learning is the source of his self-confidence. Each time, however, that he avoids a struggle he learns that he is weak and defenseless. As a result, a vicious circle is set in motion (Wender, 1968). The individual who has learned that he is defenseless sends out signals consistent with his learning, which in turn evoke complementary behavior in others, which again intensifies his feeling of defenselessness.

Another observation from the previously mentioned catfish study is of interest in this respect. When a dominant catfish has been beaten in a fight, it sends out new signals which in essence say, "I'm beaten, don't be afraid of me." The other catfish respond immediately by no longer paying any attention to him at all. The experience of having won or lost a battle for dominance determines the signals which the catfish sends out. Although man uses an entirely different signaling system, the same holds true in his situation. To break out of the circle he will have to begin with consciously changing his signaling behavior in the manner described above. The whole process is further intensified by the fact that what we called excess learning is not limited to the subject himself, but also takes place in the people he interacts with. If a person holds his own in conflict with others, he will be remembered as a forceful person. In this manner he develops, over time, a reputation which reinforces the immediate signals that he sends out. In fact, in the human community a reputation may eventually be more powerful than the impact of the apparent behavior. "He looks gentle, but he's real tough," or "His bark is worse than his bite," characterize such situations.

COMMUNICATION WITH ONESELF

Thus far we have primarily focused on the importance of various signals for communication between individuals. Equally important, however, is the communication which the individual has with himself. Internal feelings, such as a general discomfort, a sense of guilt, or the exhilarating experience of triumph, serve as signals to oneself which frequently have territorial implications. An individual can also differentiate between many other feelings, such as anxiety, irritation, hope, joy, anger, hate, or despair, all of which tell him something about his present state of affairs, provided he attends to them and recognizes their implications. When he notices a sense of triumph he must ask, "What did I conquer? Did I displace someone? Or did I expand into a new, free area?" Being irritated means that he feels that someone is encroaching on his property, and therefore he needs to find out whether the encroachment has actually taken place and who the culprit is, or whether he had assumed that he owned a certain territory that in actuality he did not. When an individual becomes aware of a feeling of righteous indignation, the question he must ask himself is whether he has lost something or if he is perhaps in reality preparing an attack of his own, using a small loss to justify the struggle for a greater gain. If the latter is the case, it might well be that his claim is correct, but at the same time he could far better anticipate the consequences of such aggressive action if he did not try to fool himself about his motives. Dishonesty may pay off, perhaps, but not self-deception.

One of the problems inherent in recognizing the meaning of internal signals is that they are frequently unreliably labeled. Each person learns to give names to a wide variety of subjective experiences in the course of growing up. Family members are especially important in this learning, for they continuously assist in recognizing and labeling such feelings. When a small child burns his finger for the first time, his mother will console him, but she will also tell him that he is suffering pain. In similar fashion he will learn the experiences that go with the words happiness, anger, or fear. The situation is complicated by the fact that society places a definite value judgment on the presence of such feelings. Anger, hatred, resentment, jealously, and envy are judged to be bad, whereas love, compassion, friendship, and concern are rated as good. As a consequence, people have a strong tendency to label bad feelings with terms that have a more neutral connotation. A person often prefers to say that he is depressed or anxious, rather than recognize his real feelings of hatred or anger. This force toward avoiding disapproved labels is especially strong if a person seeks to maintain a particular myth about himself, such as that he is a very loving person. Man's general tendency toward internal cognitive consistency provides the force which brings about such a shift in the labeling of experiences.

A keen and precise awareness of one's own internal signals provides a substantial advantage in assessing territorial situations. These feelings are the signals through which the individual knows what a given situation means to him. If he ignores or distorts them, he has no appropriate basis for action. When in a crowded subway someone stands on his toe, he is informed of this situation by a quick and unequivocal message: pain! Having read the signal he responds immediately, withdrawing his foot or pushing the occupant of his toe aside. Imagine for a moment that he would have responded here in a manner similar to that often employed in reacting to territorial signals. He might spend time deciding whether a person like himself *should* experience pain. If he found pain inconsistent with his self-image, his father's wishes, or his religious tenets, he may decide against the above action, much to the detriment of his toe. The example is ridiculous, but it does put in sharp focus what commonly happens with the inner signals under discussion here. When an individual experiences envy—a signal indicating that he would like to have what others have—he might ignore the message because "good people should not be envious."

From a territorial perspective, and in order to enhance effective social interaction, it is of primary importance to acquire the habit of paying attention to one's own feelings. To concentrate on these feelings, to let them appear as they are, and to label them, regardless of the positive or negative connotation, is the first and most crucial step toward autonomous action. If afterwards a person wishes to judge the merit of his feelings, he can certainly do so, but when he fails to read the signals as they are, he submits to a handicap which will drastically curtail his social effectiveness.

CHAPTER 13

TERRITORIALITY IN THE FAMILY

If I quit hoping he'll show up with flowers
And he quits hoping I'll squeeze him an orange
And I quit shaving my legs with his razor
And he quits wiping his feet with my face towel
And we avoid discussions like, Is he really smarter
Than I am or simply more glib?
Maybe we'll make it.

Judith Viorst*

The word *family* covers a multitude of styles, ranging from the avant-garde chrome-and-glass career couple with child, to the conglomerate company of many generations of blood-related individuals who live together under ancient and unchanging rules of authority and order. (By *family* we specifically refer to two or more generations currently living together. *Marriage* refers to the contractual relationship between a man and a woman.) As diverse as these two extremes of family may seem to the observer, they both have as their *raison d'être* one of the most fundamental of biological imperatives, reproduction, and both styles are socially evolved attempts at providing the best possible environment in which a new generation can develop the knowledge and tools necessary to meet the challenges unique to the culture in which it grows. Each parent in each family has a personal history of growth and experience out of which he must try to project the needs of his offspring. The primitive person who came of age and was initiated at thirteen will have a different social and educational timetable to follow in bringing up a child than the nuclear physicist who finished an elaborate schooling at 26 and whose success potential must be reached between ages 30 and 40. The primitive parents

---

*"Maybe We'll Make It," in *It's Hard To Be Hip Over Thirty And Other Tragedies of Married Life*. New York: The World Publishing Company, 1968, p. 19.

living in a changeless environment will have little room for innovation in the education of their child, but will have the comfort of knowing that what they do is right and proper, whereas modern parents caught up in the rapid fluctuations of a fluid social system will be free to experiment but stay forever in doubt as to their own wisdom and ability to do the job adequately.

Family style, then, is a social adaptation evolved to meet the needs of a biological necessity. As cultures change, old methods of child-rearing are put aside in favor of new ones. Only a hundred years ago the middle-class family was a bastion of authority and security. Everyone knew his place and recognized his duty. Sin and virtue were easily identifiable, and fathers and mothers could transfer knowledge and skills to their offspring with confidence and a feeling of moral rectitude. Divorce was rare, not because married bliss was common, but because duty was more important than happiness. Children "belonged" to the family, and it was the parents' task to train them to be mannerly, respectful, courageous, and the like. Marriages were contracted for social, political, or monetary reasons, and individuals were spoken of as being "well bred," a reference which included ancestry as well as training. The well-bred person had the advantage of knowing who he was, and territorially speaking, of knowing what belonged to him. He had little guilt about his own good fortune and would defend his ground with righteousness. Critics of the Victorian era point out its rigidity and deplore its moral pretenses. The fact remains, however, that despite the layers of linen and lace, the stays and corsets, and the ban on carnal knowledge, the Victorian family somehow managed to increase and multiply and teach its children what they had to know to carry on.

The modern liberated family is charged with the same responsibility: The orderly transfer of knowledge and skills from one generation to another. The new emphasis is on personal freedom and happiness, instead of duty and security. Simultaneously, absolutes are rapidly disappearing. Few modern men know of a categorical imperative, and those who do can rarely agree on its form or implementation. The structure of the family, therefore, will have to change to accommodate the enormous cultural pressures inherent in such social changes. While society still formally clings to its traditional patterns of family organization, experimentation with unorthodox alternatives, whether they prove useful or not, may well be instrumental in the eventual establishment of a new structure suitable for modern life in the Western Hemisphere. In the meantime, we will look at the present family structure in the light of a territorial model and see if any practical guidelines can be found to ease some of the tensions and doubts which result from the lack of traditional controls in marriage and child-rearing.

GETTING MARRIED

The young man and woman who decide to get married have usually established only a bare semblance of autonomy over a territory of their own when they decide on a merger. The motives for getting married are many, and even though the one that has the most to do with the social function of marriage, that is, to provide a haven in which a new generation can develop, is likely to have the lowest ranking, there appears to be no other reason that each society and culture protects marriage as a sacred institution. It certainly makes little sense to look at marriage as the place where love can exclusively grow, or the only possible sanctuary (although it certainly can provide much security), or even as the great legitimizer of sexual pleasure. Whatever the reason that two people get married, whether they have fallen in love, enjoy the comfort of each other's presence, seek sexual release, or are simply driven to do what "every normal person in our society is supposed to do," a difficult, though unavoidable, task awaits them.

Marriage is, first and foremost, a contract between two individuals and secondly, a contract with the rest of society. This contract between the two partners means a major shift in the territories which each of them occupies and therefore requires a new type of sharing. Perhaps the first lesson that a married couple has to learn to say is "we" rather than "I," "ours" rather than "mine." The thorny job ahead of the newlyweds consists of reaching an understanding concerning those areas which each of them will maintain under exclusive control, and dividing the labor involved in the management of what they share. The former is complicated by the fact that in a marriage the privileges and special interests of the one always affect the other. The latter creates problems in that most individuals are rather prone to shirk the management job but are loathe to give up control over an area. During the first few months, and perhaps years, of their union, the new partners will have to find a *modus vivendi* which allows both of them to function as a unit, while leaving enough room to each person to develop and maintain his own identity.

John is a likeable young man, a good athlete, and very popular with peers. He is 20 years old, but thus far he has had little opportunity to assume major responsibilities in life. This situation is about to change, however, for he has met Alice, a lovely young woman two years younger than himself, and they are planning to get married. Alice has been particularly attracted to John because of his comfortable, self-assured manner, his refusal to fret about the future, and the friendly, fatherly way in which he brushes off her apprehensions. Alice feels safe with him. She is sure that John is capable of handling all new situations, and will serve as her protector. John feels very tender toward Alice when he holds her small hand in his. He senses her admiration when he takes her to a restaurant and suavely orders dinner for two. He feels strong and mature, willing to tackle the adult world with Alice by his side. Both have found the courtship a wonderful experience; they know that they are just right for each other. Both sets of parents agree and, therefore, a marriage date has been set in the near future.

If one could revisit this couple and secretly observe their interaction a year after the ceremony, one would be surprised at the change that has taken place. It is hard to believe that this is the same young couple that so sincerely exchanged vows only one year earlier, for the marriage has not gone well. John is still going to school, but has failing grades, and he will probably flunk out at the end of the quarter. His behavior has become increasingly irresponsible. He comes home late or not at all, and seems to get his main enjoyment out of being with the boys. Although there are still occasional moments of tenderness, much of the time John is inconsiderate and even very critical of Alice, something which would have hardly seemed possible during their courtship. Alice, too, has changed. Her voice has acquired a somewhat strident quality, and even though there are occasional times when she is "the old Alice" who likes to cuddle up in John's protective arms, most of the time she is rather tough and bossy. John detests her nagging and her constant complaining about his behavior, his parents, her parents, the house, and everything else. It is beginning to dawn on John and Alice, and also on the parents, that the marriage was a mistake; perhaps they were too young, or maybe they weren't suited for each other after all. In any case, they soon decide to divorce before children arrive on the scene.

Couples like John and Alice are not uncommon, and they raise the regretful question: Was this hassle necessary? Why do two people who seemed just right for each other, and who were so obviously in love, change in the course of only one year to almost opposites of themselves, thus destroying their relationship? Several observations may clarify the process. In discussing the process of matching partners for marriage, one is easily seduced into thinking that the best match is obtained when each individual has personality characteristics which *fit* those of his spouse-to-be. Alice and John seemed to fit this way: The calm, strong, fatherly type matched so well to the admiring, rather dependent, daughterly type. This static notion which sees the contact between people rather as the connecting of two pieces of a jigsaw puzzle is very compatible with human thought processes, but stands in direct contrast to the reality of human interaction. Professionals who have worked intensively with families have discovered: It is the process, the interaction system, that determines what personality type each family member develops, and not the other way around (Lederer and Jackson, 1968). That process pushed John in the direction of irresponsibility and Alice toward becoming a bitchy complainer. This perception gives new credibility to the observation that when one gets married it is not so much a matter of *making the right decision,* but rather of *making the decision right.* The mechanism which is set in motion when two parties decide to make a marital contract is, to a substantial degree, a process of negotiating a satisfactory territorial compromise.

Prior to the marriage, Alice, a young person ready to leave the nest and undertake the frightening task of establishing a territory of her own, welcomed the security of being under John's protection, while at the same time enjoying the excitement of traveling in new directions. In this manner, however, she relinquished her autonomy to John. John greatly enjoyed this. He was rapidly expanding the territory under his control, and Alice's admiring eyes and small hands intensified his sense of power. He was acting like a real grown-up who had his own place in the world firmly established. He felt like a young prince who unexpectedly has succeeded to the throne and who, after the coronation ceremony, stands on the balcony of his palace listening to the cheers of the populace, "Long live the King, for he's going to protect us." Like a king, however, he soon found out that it's very difficult to protect the people and make them happy. And like the king who suddenly realizes that running the affairs of state is a business far beyond his training and capability, so the young husband found that managing all of the territory that had been so generously allocated to him became a burden he would just as soon dispose of. In fact, he would prefer to maintain the control over the territory but leave the management of it to Alice.

The consequence of such rapid expansion of territory without simultaneous acceptance of and training for its management easily leads to actions which are branded as irresponsible, for the person's behavior will be inconsistent with the responsibilities implied in the role that comes with the expansion.

Alice's situation was quite the opposite. At first she enjoyed the safety provided by her fatherly husband, but soon she rather painfully sensed her own lack of autonomy. The loss of action territory was probably largely offset in the courtship days by the gain in psychological space. John was so unbelievably attentive to all her needs; he appeared absorbed by her whole being. After the marriage ceremony and the honeymoon weeks, his attention gradually turned back to other parts of his life. At this point the unavoidable process of carving out some territory of her own was set in motion. Soon it became intensified by the fact that her husband's neglect of his duties left her the responsibility of doing the necessary work in his place. Since John was careless in handling the finances, she had to watch the budget or else they would have been out of a home by the end of the month. As John continued to spend more than they could afford, she had to take a job. And as John didn't get up in the morning to make it in time for his classes, he would not graduate and she would have to continue to work, rather than stay home and have children.

Through the process of taking over the management, Alice unavoidably took over the territory itself. The wonderful feeling of being in John's protection disappeared. At the same time, John lost the sense of being king. Instead, he experienced a vague feeling of anger against the woman who seemed to have taken all of his power away. She not only absorbed his territory, but also nagged and complained all the time—the result of the overextension of her territory. To compensate for the loss, John formed a new life with his friends and avoided his home as much as possible.

The marriage of John and Alice went wrong because *marriages which start with basic inequalities run unusually high risks of failure.*[1] John had most of the territory as well as the responsibility to manage it. Alice owned very little ground and hardly any autonomy. If things had gone well, there would have been a gradual shift, so as to divide the territory and the responsibilities for the management equally. But things were not likely to

---

[1]This observation holds true for modern Western society, where the marriage contract is ideally one of equality. If the contract is unequal, there is no reason to expect problems if this inequality is *consistent with each partner's reference group* and if the partners are willing and able to handle the particular territories and the specific chores which the contract assigns to them.

go well if the one partner married because he enjoyed the feeling of being master over the life of his spouse as well as himself, but lacked the capability of management, while the other was motivated by the sense of security without realizing that security was gained at the expense of her personal freedom. In John and Alice's first year of marriage the situation evolved into a transitional process whereby John still claimed controlling authority while Alice took care of the actual management chores.

Such a state of affairs is highly unstable unless specific arrangements (such as payment for a job done) compensate for the inequity. As a general rule, the stability of a relationship is enhanced *if the territory and its management rest with the same individual.* If the territory is shared, all partners share in the management. Marital bliss is not usually enhanced if the husband claims the right to decide what meals will be served, while the obligation to produce those meals remains with the wife. Neither does harmony usually remain when the wife decides exactly how the house should be remodeled, but the husband is expected to implement her decisions in his spare time.

To reemphasize: A relationship of inequality is hazardous to the marriage unless this inequality is an accepted part of the existing culture. It is advisable, therefore, that young couples, prior to getting married, first determine whether they are going into it as equals or whether, as in the case of John and Alice, this balance is seriously upset.

Today's young lovers have an extremely hard task before them precisely because they are expected to enter marriage in a relationship *of relative equality.* One could make a good case for the thesis that it is a far more difficult problem than that which confronted their forebears fifty or one hundred years ago, when there still existed some rather precise hierarchical standards for the division of territory between man and wife. At that time, each partner was left with specific areas with little overlap. To be sure, the woman's rank and sphere were not only lower but were also more completely delineated than those of the man, for the latter had almost unlimited possibilities outside the home. From today's perspective, the wife was kept in a matrimonial cell. Much of the management fell to her, whereas the ultimate control remained in the hands of the husband; but each partner knew where he stood. The wife was mostly confined to the realm of the household, child-rearing, the company of some female friends and relatives, and some pastimes ranging from embroidery to music and literature. Whatever judgment one wishes to place on such past arrangements, from a perspective of the present it can hardly be denied that the precision of territorial definition made the job of finding one's place relative to the other infinitely more simple than it is today.

With the rejection of a hierarchical division as a way of keeping marital order, a strict adherence to territorial rights becomes imperative. Robert Sommer (1969, p. 13) draws an interesting parallel to the animal studies which "show that both territoriality and dominance behavior are ways of maintaining a social order, and when one system cannot function, the other takes over. With pairs incompatible in dominance, such as two highly dominant individuals, no stable order can be found, so aggression is limited by strict adherence to territorial rights." In other words, as the strictly defined hierarchical relationship has disappeared, it has become essential to create a structure in the marriage for working out a precise, detailed territorial division.

The social upheaval of the last century has raised women's awareness of the inequality of their status in marriage, but the continual mixing of cultures and philosophies and the gradual erosion of class and racial distinctions and barriers have been among the major factors contributing to a general uncertainty about territorial rights and allocations. Within the family structure this uncertainty has created enormous stresses and strains which, as the rising figures of family dissolution and the growing tendency toward family experimentation indicate, still have not reached a peak. This intrafamilial turmoil has now come to the point that the guidelines for the territorial division on which the newlyweds can anchor their future interactions are almost nonexistent. Their personal notions often vary greatly, owing to differences in their backgrounds. In the United States the role of the parents in the wife's family is frequently at variance with that in the husband's, with the result that the two young people start with a totally different set of expectations, and a near unresolvable confusion about where it should all end up. A further complication arises out of the tendency of many families to cover their own interactional system with a moral mantle which fosters the belief that their behavioral patterns are "right" or "better." Thus statements like "The woman's place is in the home," or "It's the man's place to fix the wiring," instead of being taken simply as matters of opinion, become ethical precepts (values) that are nonnegotiable.

In this chaos it is vital that the partners gradually clarify their own unique division of territory in their own specific marriage. To accomplish this, they will have to assert themselves, fight fairly for what they want, but at the same time maintain an overriding willingness to make compromises which are acceptable to both and which are in the interest of their union. This statement is not intended as a moral judgment proclaiming the ethical superiority of individuals who are willing to compromise. On the contrary, it is a simple pragmatic expedient of the "if A . . . then B . . ." variety. If a stable marriage is desired which would provide the couple with comfort as well as room to live, then each partner needs to be able to fight effectively and remain willing to compromise, for although both parties must take part in the struggle, neither one may win or lose. The greatest danger to the relationship occurs when one of the partners either wins a decisive victory or suffers a final defeat. Paradoxically enough, *both* partners lose in either case, for unless the settlement allows for a fair share for each, the marriage itself will be defeated. The ideal status is like a stalemate between the major powers in the world today: No one may win. Even the country that would deal the first blow and destroy the other completely would subsequently be destroyed by the automatic retaliation and the fall-out.

If the above observations are correct, then one cannot avoid the conclusion that the chances of a successful marriage depend on the relatively equal ability of both partners to hold their own, as well as their willingness to accept a fair settlement. Neither one of them may fight with a technique so superior that the balance of power would be fundamentally disturbed.

The most important prerequisite for a successful, stable marriage, then, is not the matching of certain personality types, similarity of background, sharing of interests, or even sexual attraction and depth of devotion, but rather, an equal ability to fight and negotiate. This ability includes a willingness to assert personal demands, to fight when necessary (but only then), to listen to the other's side and try to understand the position taken, to keep clear perspective on overriding goals so as not to get bogged down in minor skirmishes, and finally, to be able to accept a compromise which does not violate either partner's most vital claims. To enhance the success probability of a new marriage, it is probably much more useful, prior to marriage, to train both partners in the process of negotiation and effective fair fighting than to spend time pointing out their respective responsibilities, the nature of love, or the vicissitudes of sexuality. Each partner has to realize that the autonomy of the other has to be protected at all costs and that fighting over territory by fair means and bargaining for maximum concessions are both necessary and desirable. Destruction of the other's integrity, however, leads inescapably to the destruction of the partnership.

The modern marriage is a mixed blessing. It presents the partners with a task which at times seems nearly impossible. At the same time it *is* an exciting contract, for it leaves both parties the freedom to follow a creative process in which they work out a unique solution that suits them personally. To emphasize fighting and negotiating skills as the stuff that makes for a good marriage may well perturb the reader, although those who were turned off by the Machiavellian flavor of this book in all probability have long since put it down. The relationship between man and wife has been colored in romantic pastels ever since the Cathars spread their peculiar type of love across the Western world through the songs of the troubadours.[2] It is likely, therefore, that many individuals will object to the idea that the most important support of the marriage is derived from fair fighting for a reasonable territorial division, rather than from love, trust, and the happiness which both partners derive from their sharing and their intimacy. There is no doubt in our minds that the happiness, the security, and the many rewarding experiences that one derives from a truly close relationship form the backbone of the marriage, as these gratifications reinforce the partners' desire to make the marriage succeed. However, these facts should not obscure the observation that such rewarding experiences are only possible when an equitable arrangement between the partners is maintained. Without it even the greatest love will be short-lived, as in the example of John and Alice. *Love and trust do not endure when a person is robbed of his autonomy.*

THE FIRST CHILD ARRIVES

> Last year I studied flamenco
> And had my ears pierced
> And served an authentic fondue
> On the Belgian marble table
> Of our discerningly eclectic dining area
> But this year we have a nice baby
> And Spock on the second shelf of our Chinese chest
> And instead of finding myself

[2]Their extreme taboo on sexuality and physical contact between man and woman (for example, a man would not sit on a chair previously occupied by a woman) is thought to be the source of courtly love and the start of romantic literature, which still continues to influence the Western world (de Rougemont, 1956).

I'm doing my best to find a sitter
  For the nice baby banging the Belgian marble
With his cup while I heat the oven up
  For the TV dinners.

Judith Viorst*

It seems particularly fortuitous that nature, by means of a nine-month period of gestation, provides couples with a relatively long respite before the first child arrives. And since it takes a longer time to work out the terms of the modern marital contract, it is even more fortunate that readily available means of birth control can offer the couple additional time; for one thing is certain—the major turf disputes had best be settled before the first child is born and upsets the applecart once more. The child who arrives on the scene while the territorial struggle of his parents is still in the stage of out-and-out warfare has a most unfortunate start in life. The parents themselves might labor under the illusion that everything would be O.K. if they only had a child. The fact is that one rarely solves a problem by making it more complicated. For the child it is difficult enough to arrive empty-handed in a strange new world even if peace reigns; to find himself on a battlefield is hardly encouraging.

Even under the best circumstances a new territorial arrangement needs to evolve in the family after the child's arrival. The newborn child alters the parents' roles and creates completely new responsibilities for each of them. They will have to decide who will assume the various new chores, which areas they will share, and which will be exclusively the domain of the one or the other. With the new roles each partner acquires a new identity, and consequently there is a shift in the marriage relationship. Perhaps the wife, in assuming most of the new responsibilities for the child's physical care, decides to drop a part of the action territory which she handled before. For example, the husband may now have to get up earlier to make his own breakfast. Perhaps the wife will no longer have time at night to listen to a three-hour account of his day at work. Although we do not need to belabor the point, it is clear that an accommodation to the new situation has to be made. In this new adjustment it is most interesting to see what happens to the child himself. He arrives completely helpless, without any degree of autonomy and without any territory. He lacks all management skills as well as the ability to defend himself; and yet

*From "Nice Baby," *It's Hard To Be Hip Over Thirty And Other Tragedies of Married Life.* New York: The World Publishing Company, 1968, p. 21.

when he has reached adulthood, he will have to have his own autonomous territory and all the skills that are needed to handle and expand it.

Parents have an unusual relationship to their children; they neither own them nor compete with them. On the contrary, their primary intent is to allow the child to grow up and gain an independent domain of his own. This parental stance is the prototype of all brotherly love: To guard the welfare of the other and take pleasure in his growth. This does not mean that parents never get into competition with their children or always live in territorial harmony. Our later discussion will show that conflict on a day-to-day basis is not only unavoidable, but even necessary and desirable. However, the parents, in spite of the fact that they may lose track of the primary intent of parenthood in the heat of conflict, will ordinarily seek the child's growth and not his subjugation.

DIVERSITY IN CHILD-REARING PRACTICES

One can gain a perspective on child-rearing by defining the goals to be reached. Presumably, the process of guiding the child from infancy to adulthood pursues a goal and visualizes an end product, but how explicit are these? And who sets the goals anyway? And are the child-rearing practices in vogue today consistent with such objectives? These questions are not commonly asked, let alone answered. In the not too far distant past, parents did not need to ask such questions, for they knew exactly how to raise their children and what was to become of them. If the outcome did not fit the expectations, if the child went astray, it was more likely to be attributed to the cunning of the devil than to the faulty child-rearing practices of the parents.

This blissful state is now a thing of the past, sent on the road to oblivion by the rapid transitions in the social structure and the theories of psychiatrists. The latter have added their share to the burden of the already bewildered parents by convincing them of the many deleterious effects which their own behavior, motivated by their "unconscious," may have on their offspring. The parental sense of mastery has not been greatly aided by this revelation, as it has implied that they are capable of doing great damage to their child without being at all aware of it. If someone had the devilish intention to design a special theory to undermine parental confidence, he would find it difficult, indeed, to upstage Freud.

The depth of the bewilderment of earnest young parents was brought home to us over a decade ago when we lived in a housing project near one of America's major universities. Most of our neighbors were graduate students with one or more small children. One Sunday morning we were up at an unusually early hour, six in the morning. The area was quiet, neighbors still asleep, and we had just begun to prepare our breakfast when the head of a young neighbor woman appeared in the open kitchen window. She held a women's magazine in her hand and with the obvious pressure of concern she introduced the new day by saying, "This doctor here says that it is very harmful to spank children; is it?" The plight of the parents who seek to do well by their children and who will judge themselves severely in retrospect by what has become of them, but who have no standard child-rearing practices to rely on, can be exemplified by a few diverse situations.

A young woman got a frantic call from her parents. They were at their wit's end and did not know what to do. Would she please come home immediately and talk with her 15-year-old sister who had just presented them with an ultimatum: Either they could allow the girl's boy friend to stay overnight every Saturday so that she could sleep with him, or else she would run off and get married.

During a visit to a progressive private kindergarten we observed a wide range of behavior among the young pupils. Some of the children were busy finger-painting, while others spent their time drawing on large sheets of paper. One little boy ran noisily around the room, continuously interrupting the teacher, who responded to him with unlimited patience and friendliness, or at least a somewhat strained show of it. In the middle of the room on the floor sat a little girl, preoccupied with the rhythmic rubbing of her genitalia. The school had the explicit goal of assisting in the production of creative human beings.

Some friends had gathered in a private home and, sitting around the fireplace, were engaged in an animated discussion. The nine-year-old son of the family strolled in, turned on the television set, and sat down to watch the program. The room was fairly small and the television volume was turned on rather high. The participants in the discussion became distracted and uncomfortable. The host turned to his son in a somewhat apologetic manner and said, "John, would you please turn the television set down a bit?" There was no response from John. Five minutes later the father repeated his plea with the same result. John continued to watch his program, interrupting his vigil from time to time to come over to the circle of adults and load up on the various delicacies displayed on the coffee table. Around 11 o'clock he got up, turned off the television, and sauntered away to some other part of the house.

Child-rearing techniques vary greatly from culture to culture, but in the modern Western communities glaring differences exist even between families, although they may belong to the same social class and live in the same area. Aside from the specific ways in which each family raises its offspring, there may also be considerable differences in the ultimate results they seek to obtain with these methods.

THE GOALS OF SOCIETY, PARENTS, AND THE CHILD

Although parents have a difficult time defining exactly how they wish their children to grow up, three sets of goals can presumably guide the endeavor of child-rearing, namely, society's, the parents', and those of the child itself.

Society—being itself an abstraction rather than an entity with a clear purpose of its own—can influence the process through which the prospective citizens grow up. If one considers the welfare of society as an essential prerequisite for the well-being of its citizens, then it follows that the community has a number of global goals for the child as it grows into an adult. Such a good citizen would be expected to abide by society's rules, contribute to its orderly development, produce approximately as much as he consumes, and participate in the defense of the common ground when needed. Within such broad confines the possibilities are nearly unlimited.

The objectives of the parents are usually not at variance with these broad societal goals, but they tend to focus more on the personal characteristics which the child will develop and the career he will choose in life. On a number of occasions, the authors have asked groups of parents to describe their hopes for their children. The lists of goals obtained show remarkable similarity. The characteristics agreed upon by the parents included such items as: independence, sensitivity to the feelings of others, creativity, optimism, ability to hold his own, ability to enjoy pleasures with an eye for beauty, ability to be self-supporting, a good sense of humor, resiliency, decisiveness, ability to form close relationships, a good dose of common sense, ability to be comfortable in being alone, and ability to love.

It is interesting to note that these characteristics are very similar to the ones which Abraham Maslow (1954) listed as typical for what he has named the "self-actualized person." Maslow studied a number of individuals whom he considered unusually successful, who had realized their potential and their effectiveness of living in outstanding fashion. His observation is of particular interest in the present context because the attributes which he singled out as most remarkable about the self-actualized person could just as well serve as a description of a territorially effective individual. Thus there is good reason to believe that the goals which many parents have for their children, but which are rarely reached, coincide with Maslow's self-actualized person and are most likely to be attained if the individual is effective in respect to his territoriality.

One can broaden the perspective of parents' goals for their children by bringing in some additional hopes which are usually present regardless of whether they are made explicit or not. The characteristics mentioned above are primarily skills of living; by themselves they have no content. As a rule, however, parents also have ideas about what they would like the child to do with these skills. Such wishes may be narrowly defined: "I hope my son will become a doctor," or, more broadly conceived, the parent may hope that his son will become an "upstanding citizen" and not a "bum" or a "hippy." Hidden behind such broad statements may be a good many specifics relative to dress, habits, social company, and earnings.

In our discussion of territoriality we are concerned with human skills and not with the purpose to which the individual puts them. The parents, however, usually have a number of strong ideas about what constitutes a right or a wrong goal and hope that their offspring will avoid the latter.

It seems peculiar that although neither society nor parents seek to raise their children to be failures, each new generation, nevertheless, contains a number of people who are just that. This inescapable occurrence often gives rise to the assumption that the derailment is primarily a consequence of the propensities of the child himself. Although this proposition is logically correct—for it is obviously quite possible that the child was born lacking the type of properties of brain, enzymes, or whatever that are needed for acquisition of skills and information— such a hypothesis must nevertheless be kept as a last resort only, for most of the time it is used as a convenient escape hatch for teachers, parents, and society in general. For instance, when a child fails in school it is far more productive to ask what there was about the teaching method that failed to bring about the desired results than to conclude that the youngster lacked the necessary brain power.

From a territorial perspective, one can discern several reasons that the educational efforts of the parents end up with results which were desired by no one: (a) The child is not provided with circumstances which allow him to learn and practice techniques for effective dealing with life situations. (b) The child develops coping mechanisms which have some degree of utility under early life circumstances but which will be a liability at a later point in life. (c) The circumstances under which the child grows up may be so unconventional that unusual techniques are resorted to for the maintenance of some semblance of autonomy. In such cases the child-now-adult will be totally unaware of certain of his atypical behavior or signaling patterns which to others seem obviously inappropriate or antisocial and therefore inevitably lead to conflict.

Before we continue, a brief clarification is in order concerning the way in which children learn. Whenever parents are confronted with the fact that some of the behaviors they detest in their child, and for which they have sought professional help, represent a learned pattern, they reject out of hand that this behavior was learned in their home. They did not teach the child to have temper tantrums or to wet the bed; the very idea horrifies them. Of course they are right—they did not teach their child to behave in such a manner. Children, however, learn far more than that which is expressly taught them. When a child is taught arithmetic in school, he may learn to add, subtract, and multiply, but he also learns that the teacher likes him best if he works quietly, that his parents become bored when he talks about math, and so on. When the child throws a temper tantrum and mother gets angry, he may learn that mother dislikes that type of behavior, but he may also find out that she will stay with him as long as she expects another outburst. It is the child's enormous ability to learn many things at the same time which makes child-rearing such a difficult task and which can result in undesired consequences despite the best intentions. Simultaneously, however, it is this enormous ability to learn which makes it possible to alter the child's behavior by changing its consequences.

ACQUISITION OF TERRITORIAL SKILLS

The child has to learn a tremendous amount if he is to grow up within a reasonable period of time into an effective adult. We will limit our discussion to the skills the child needs to acquire if he is to hold his own successfully in the territorial competition of the adult world. To simplify our discussion we will make the assumption that it is the objective of the parents as well as society that the young person reach adulthood having gained a sufficient amount of territory (including each of the four major types: private, personal, action, and psychological) over which he has control, which he can both defend and share when he wishes, which he can manage effectively, and from which he dares to seek expansion when he desires new challenges. We do not propose this goal for adulthood as an absolute ideal, but rather, as an example of a concrete target that can guide a person's aim even if his goal is not identical with it. If a parent would prefer to emphasize managerial over defense skills, or to accent the child's ability to acquire psychological space, or to guide any other such specific disposition, he can modify the approach described here to suit his purpose.

Starting from the assumption mentioned above, an optimum child-rearing situation is one that initially provides the child with a safely protected area where he can acquire and try out his first management skills, that provides graduated learning situations, and that offers opportunities to conquer territory of his own as his skills improve. The parents can give the child territory only on a temporary basis. If he is to grow up into an adult, able to conquer the territory he desires, to manage it effectively, defend it when necessary, and share it as desired, *then it is not essential to provide the child with a permanent territory, but rather, to have him gain excellence in territorial skills.*

The child, born helpless, and with few capabilities outside the sucking reflex, needs to be protected and cared for by the parents until he has learned all he needs to know to lead an autonomous life. The acquisition of skills is a gradual process, proceeding from one step to the next in an orderly fashion. Sequentially, the child learns to focus his eyes, coordinate what he sees with what he feels, organize bodily sensations and movements until he masters such complex processes as crawling and eventually walking. With his hands and his eyes, with all his senses and his whole physical being, the child explores the world in which he lives, and gradually learns to anticipate the consequences of each event. He becomes aware of what is pleasant, what is dangerous and what is unpredictable, and bit by bit he becomes a master in his little world, ready to venture beyond his borders. *This gradual process of growing up requires a careful coordination between the child's increasing skills and the amount of territory in which he is allowed to operate.*

When he first begins to crawl, the infant has no knowledge of the wider world in which he lives, and he has ample room within the safety of the playpen. He can thoroughly explore this small area, fondle objects, coordinate their appearance with their feel and the sounds he can make with them. He can stack blocks and learn to push them over, and he can throw objects out of the playpen, watching where they go and at the same time increasing his skill in estimating distances. To reason that the playpen is too confining to the child because it seems that way to the adult scarcely makes sense. It is not advisable for either the adult or the child to expand his territory before he is able to manage what he currently has. It is the parents' task to open up new areas to the explorations of the child whenever they observe that adequate mastery has been gained over the previous one. The balance between the gradual acquisition of skills and the stepwise expansion of the territory is the crucial dimension around which we will look at the child-rearing process. This process as it evolves between parents and child must be seen in the broader context of society. Each subculture takes for granted certain notions about the rate at which the child's skills can increase and his territory should be allowed to expand. In the United States all children are supposed to be ready for school when they are six, and advance from year to year at roughly the same rate. Some children, however, acquire skills at a faster pace than others, which means that their territory could be allowed to grow at a faster rate, whereas others will have to remain longer at each stage. Problems are frequently created when a child's territory is expanded before he has skills to cope with a previously more restricted area, and vice versa.

Kevin, a six-year-old, is brought to a psychiatric clinic because of school phobia. After the first few days in class, he became extremely frightened and resisted to the utmost of his ability, including a horrendous howling and wailing, any further efforts to take him to school. His parents obviously felt equally uncomfortable about the child's leaving home, and would have readily agreed to have him stay home if it weren't for the tremendous social pressure which demands that Kevin go to school just like the other children. Talking with the parents and the child and receiving some impressions from his schoolteacher show that Kevin is rather immature. He does not dress himself as yet and has acquired little skill, especially in the area of dealing with other children. When playing with his peers he demands a great amount of attention, but is unable to join consistently in play or abide somewhat reasonably by the rules of a game. When Kevin enters a schoolroom he finds himself confronted with a monumental task. He has to apply skills of which he doesn't even have the rudiments as yet. Consequently, he experiences a nearly unbearable anxiety. He is faced with a situation in which he has to act, but for which he lacks the necessary mastery. It is not surprising that the parents who sense their child's inability to manage the situation share his fear.

One can, of course, say that the parents are trying to keep the child an infant, that they are maintaining a symbiotic relationship with him and do not allow him to grow up and increase his independence. Indeed, there are probably many reasons that the child did not acquire the expected amount of skills in the appropriate time. The reason, however, that the child became anxious in the class was not that he longed for his parents, but rather, that he lacked the skills to handle the expanded territory. If he wanted to flee to the safety of mother's and father's protection, it was as a result of his inability to cope.

The case of Kevin exemplifies a basic rule which has broad application throughout the course of human development. Substantial expansion of domain without adequate mastery over previously held territory will result in serious difficulties. The counterpart of this rule is equally important for the process of growing up: There is a limit to the skills one can learn in a given situation. Once this limit is approached, new territory is needed to stimulate further learning. Again it is the balance between skill acquisition and territorial expansion that dominates the process of maturation.

Two types of imbalance are possible between the child's development of skills and the expansion of his territory. In the first the territorial expansion does not keep up with the skill acquisition (constriction); in the second, the speed of the expansion is greater than skill acquisition (dilation).

CONSTRICTIVE CHILD-REARING

Constrictive child-rearing is the practice of keeping the child from expanding into new areas in spite of the fact that he has a sufficient level of skill to do so. The constriction of the child's territory can be global or it may pertain specifically to selected areas. For instance, if a child is reared in a remote rural area and both parents are illiterate and lack interest in formal learning, it is conceivable that he may be raised without having access to schools. In other respects, the child may not be constricted at all. This type of child-raising shows a specific constriction, and as a result is impoverished in respect to the area of formal education. Many children grow up in environments which are impoverished in one way or another. In some families book learning is very important, but the parents may provide no access whatever to the world of manual skills. No child receives equal introduction to all known territories which are potentially accessible, but certainly some live in a richer environment than others. Although a truly impoverished environment will lead to less than optimal exploration of the world and less than desirable acquisition of skills and information, it does not prevent the child from attaining a balanced growth in the areas which he is allowed to explore, nor does it preclude gaining an adequate mastery of the three major territorial skills.

Totally different is the fate of the child who is constricted in a global fashion. Most extreme examples of this kind of constriction are the unfortunate individuals who are completely neglected by their parents, perhaps isolated in their room without communication with the outside world, or raised as animals. Although these are rare phenomena, milder forms of parental delinquency, combined with hostile, destructive punishment whenever the child bothers the parents, are far from uncommon, as can be observed from the neglected children and the youngsters suffering from the "battered child syndrome" (Zalba, 1971) who have come to the attention of physicians. In a rather ironic fashion, the constriction of the child's world can result from both an overconcern on the part of the parent, as well as from a callous refusal to be bothered by him. Parents may leave a child in a playpen for the first three years of life because he creates no trouble that way, or because they think he will be safer there. As we have emphasized before, the motivation is of limited importance for the territorial consequences. *Whether one constricts the child out of love or callousness, in territorial terms the results are very similar.*[3] In either case, the child ends up considerably behind his peers in skills to acquire, manage, and defend territory independently.

If one compares the child with a specific territorial constriction with one who has been globally suppressed, one sees that the former is much better off because he has not been hampered in the development of basic strategies for acquisition, defense, and management. If, later in life, new areas open up to him, he can apply these same abilities. This conclusion is consistent with observations on children who have grown up in deprived areas. The Head Start Programs provided an enrichment of the deprived

[3]This is not to say that these two different conditions will not have a differential impact in other respects. It is quite likely that the overindulged child will, for instance, acquire better communication skills than the neglected one. On the other hand, it is possible that the overindulgent basis for territorial constriction is harder on the child because it makes it more difficult to fight the parents when they act out of love rather than out of a desire to harm.

child's environment early in his life, which resulted in an acceleration of his development as compared with other children from the same background who did not have such a benefit. However, a finding which was disturbing to those who were enthusiastic about the early results showed that the non-Head Start children caught up around the fifth or sixth grade and thereafter did not show any particular deficit when compared with the Head Start group. This observation supports the notion that the basic skills were equally present in both groups of deprived children, and that all of them extended their development when new opportunities were offered. The only difference was that the Head Start group received the opportunities earlier than the control group.

The problems confronting the globally restricted child are far more serious. As he grows up, he seeks to increase his territory, but as all avenues are consistently closed off, he will either have to give up or find new, devious ways to expand. Presumably he will give up if he cannot perceive any path leading to success, thus arriving at an extreme slowdown or arrest of behavioral growth. Much more likely, for human ingenuity seems to be well-nigh without limits, he will design new ways of fighting attuned to his anomalous situation.

In the process of acquiring new skills and expanding his territory, the child is bound to learn some major facts of life. He learns to anticipate the results of different types of territorial expansion, as well as the strategies and specific methods which are most likely to provide him with the desired results. In order to live most effectively as an adult in Western society, the child needs to learn that if he shows ability and skill, demonstrates a growing sense of responsibility, and pushes hard and aggressively, he will gradually acquire some of the territory he desires. He will have to receive practice in how to fight with vigor, and he needs to acquire the conviction that he has at least a fair chance of winning. It would be most unfortunate, on the other hand, if the child learned that the acquisition of territory is not related to his own ability to manage it, or to his skill and sense of responsibility, but rather, that gains depend on the unpredictable whims of his parents or other authorities. If one accepts the simple tenet of learning theory that behavior is reinforced by its consequences, then one must anticipate that the child in the latter example would have little motivation for the acquisition of new skills, for skills never brought him results. He has learned, instead, that his parents can be manipulated in other ways (by crying, pouting, being cute, clowning) which are consistently effective in yielding the desired results.

The unfortunate consequence of the latter type of learning is that it fails to train the child for aggressive and assertive interaction with adults later in life. After he grows up, he may find that he was well trained for dealing with his parents, but ill prepared for effective interaction with others. As we have emphasized earlier, man's freedom depends on his ability to gain new territory, manage it, and defend it. To the degree, therefore, that the child has not learned these skills in childhood, he has been cheated out of his freedom, and he will have much catching up to do if he desires to be an autonomous person.

In the early years of the child's development the decisions concerning the gradual expansion of his territory lie entirely in the hands of the parents. If they are controlling individuals, who are reluctant to yield anything to another person, they might eventually find themselves deadlocked in a struggle with the child. In the adolescent years this frequently results in a bitter conflict with gradual escalation of hostilities on both sides. The situation is particularly prone to develop if the parents have taken the position that they are weak individuals unless they maintain complete and total control over their child. Then, parents do not simply get into a conflict with their child over the amount of territory the latter can have, but rather, will dispute the ultimate autonomy of the young person in respect to everything. The child is expected to defer to the parents' opinions in all respects, and therefore doesn't have any territory at all that truly feels like his own. The child, however, is a growing, separate individual whose feelings, wishes, and opinions cannot be controlled for long. The parents who cannot tolerate this waxing independence, and who lose their self-esteem unless they maintain total control, make it impossible for the child to reach adulthood without a termination of the relationship. In other words, either the child breaks forcefully away from the parents and continues to expand his territory on his own, or he resigns himself (usually resentfully) to his fate and remains a vassal of his parents, without the feeling of having a right to his own opinions and decisions. To avoid such destructive deadlocks it is essential for both sides to see each conflict as a difference of opinion concerning a certain specific area and to engage in a process of negotiation about that area. An individual who has grown up in this manner will continue to use what he has learned well beyond the years of childhood.

As was implied earlier, constriction based on overindulgence has essentially the same effect as authoritarian constriction. In the case of overindulgence, however, the constriction of the child's territory is offset by all sorts of gratifications, ranging from hugs and kisses to candy, toys, and other attentions. As the child becomes bored with his restricted territory, he is likely to venture out in new directions and seek new challenges. The parents see this independence as a threat, however, and consequently obstruct expansion and reward adherence to the status quo. As no action territory is left open to the child, he often seeks to expand his psychological space. Such a child is usually labeled spoiled. People often express surprise over the difficult behavior of the child who has temper tantrums, he seems to receive much more gratification than other children. One forgets, however, that if the parents close off the possibility of exploration, the child depends entirely on the immediate interpersonal situation for new and interesting stimuli and that his obstreperous behavior is one sure way he can keep others involved with him. It follows that the spoiled child can be helped by (a) providing gradually expanding possibilities for the acquisition of new skills through the exploration of new territories, and (b) teaching him at the same time that he will be allowed *no more than a fair share of the psychological space.* The latter can be done by using principles of operant conditioning—not giving him the reward of attention as a consequence of the undesired behavior.

Whether the constrictive approach to child-rearing stems from too much parental concern or too little, the child who is confronted with it is forced to come up with innovative ways of beating the parents' game. To expand his territory he will try many types of subterfuge, be it seduction, flattery, running away, or any of the many other possibilities. As a result, he is bound to become very skilled at such types of fighting; and as an individual usually does a lot of what he is good at, it is likely that he will continue to use these methods, perhaps for a lifetime. The specific techniques acquired vary from one child to the other. Constrictions are imposed in many different ways, and besides, other factors, such as imitation of parental and sibling behavior, influence the development of the child's territorial style. However, the concept of constriction has utility when one takes a practical look at a particular family situation in order to determine whether the pace at which the child is allowed to expand is in accord with the rate at which he acquires his skills. After having scrutinized the situation, the parent or guardian can speed up or slow down the child's territorial expansion and provide improved learning opportunities where possible.

DILATED CHILD-REARING

Dilated child rearing is the practice of allowing the child to enter new territories when he wants to, regardless of the level of skill he has attained. An example is the six-month-old baby who is let out of the playpen because he cries and the parents feel that they should not keep him in. Very early such a child is allowed to roam freely around the house and perhaps into the yard. The tendency to provide him with a dilated territory comes close to what is usually called permissiveness. When it is time to go to bed at night, the six-year-old may decide that he wants to stay up longer. The permissive parents will allow him to do so. In essence, they turn over to the child the responsibility for deciding what is an appropriate bedtime, regardless of whether he has matured sufficiently to manage this area with a judgment adequate to maintain his health by taking enough rest. The permissive parents may have a variety of reasons for putting so few restrictions on the child. They may harbor the idea that the creativity and the initiative and the freedom of the child should be respected or that restraints placed upon him would bruise his spontaneity. Perhaps the parents simply don't want to argue because they believe that this in itself would be damaging to the child. It is also possible that the dilated environment results from a total lack of concern on the part of the parents. Whatever the motivation, the outcome is likely to be similar in many respects.

The child who is the victim of dilated child-rearing practices will learn behavior patterns which are very different from those acquired under constrictive circumstances. However, the consequences of the former are as detrimental as those of the latter. Some of the deficits in learning which result from dilation are the following: (a) The child, having no resistance to his expansion, fails to acquire skills which allow him to conquer new areas later in life when such conquest requires fighting hard and long for results. One would anticipate, therefore, an inclination to seek many new areas but give up as soon as a major effort is required. (b) Having roamed over wide areas in all directions, the child is likely to acquire a smattering of management skills but none with sufficient thoroughness to provide a real sense of competence; he becomes a jack-of-all-trades, master-of-none. (c) Having experienced little opposition to expansion, the child may fail to learn that other individuals have definite territories and are willing and able to defend them. As a consequence, once the child ventures outside the home he will continually trespass across others' boundaries and find himself *persona non grata.* (d) Having no restrictions on his territory, not having to fight for what he gets, and experiencing a general lack of mastery, the child will be impaired in the development of a personal identity. One of the most important aspects of growing up is exactly this development of a firm sense of identity. In Chapter 2 we described how a specific, limited territory over which a person has firm control, which he defends well, and which he has gained with much effort, is the backbone of his identity. The child raised in a permissive setting is cheated out of the opportunity to establish an identity. We have characterized this behavior on the part of the parents as a "Russian Retreat." When, in 1812, Napoleon entered Russia, he encountered no resistance. Before long he found himself spread so thin over the immense area that he was unable to manage it with his limited troops and long supply lines. Eventually this spreading out resulted in the total destruction of his army. The child of the parents in "Russian Retreat" fares no better. He, too, is eventually spread so thin over so much territory, with such limited skills, that his identity becomes increasingly diffuse and he fails to develop a sense of self.

The future of the permissively raised child is obviously poorly served by the lack of development of the skills needed for the maintenance of freedom and independence in adult life. The welfare of the parents is served no better by this style of parent-child interaction. When one observes the relationship between the permissive parent and the child, one cannot fail to notice the repeated incursions by the child into the parents' domain. If the child is allowed to go to bed when he pleases, the parents will find their time alone together reduced to a few moments late at night. If the parents cannot tell the child to be quiet, as in the example given at the beginning of this chapter, they will find their control over their own home drastically reduced. If the parents have their favorite chairs by the fireplace, but cannot tell the child to stay out of them, they will soon have lost that part of their territory also. In other words, the permissive parent will progressively lose territory to the child. One should anticipate, therefore, that they will strike back and, as they have failed to be assertive, *there is a considerable risk that their retaliation will be hostile.*

Neither the parents nor the child stand to gain anything in a dilated child-rearing situation. If such a condition were changed in the direction of an assertive defense by the parents of their own territory and a gradual expansion of the child's, based on skill acquisition rather than demands, it would result in better training and a greater sense of self for the child and a more constructive interaction among all concerned.

One should not lose sight of the fact that the home in which the child is born is not his territory, but rather that of the parents. The latter may provide it to the child as a laboratory in which he can learn the skills needed to conquer his own. The parents who simply relinquish their territory to the child are a menace to him. The child who is given the false notion of control over his parents' territory because they have given him free reign will leave the nest truly empty-handed, for his parents' domain will remain theirs when he goes. He has been given the privileges of territory without learning how to acquire, manage, and defend it, and he will be a man without a country, and therefore without identity, when he leaves his parents' door.

BALANCED TERRITORIAL EXPANSION

Avoiding the extremes of constriction and dilation may perhaps be fairly easy, but how is one to judge that fine balance between the child's skills and his ever-growing territory? How can the parents decide whether he is ready for new responsibilities and new privileges? Is there a definite rate of expansion which is identical for all children? Is the rate of expansion the same in all cultures and at all times?

Since not every child acquires skills and mastery at the same rate and not every culture offers the same opportunities, growing up is an ongoing bargaining process between the child and his environment. The child is always knocking at the gate, asking for more room, while the rest of the world wonders whether it's time to let him out. In other words, there are no definite time schedules and neither is there a valid rule book which can guide the bewildered parents, intent on doing the right thing by their children. Their only reliable tool is careful observation of the child in order to arrive at an answer to two questions: (a) Which aspect of the child's current territory does he master so well that it no longer provides a significant challenge to his skills? and (b) In which direction can the child's territory be expanded so as to provide new, stimulating learning opportunities?

Looking at it from this perspective it must become even more apparent that growing up is an interaction process between parents and child. The child's natural curiosity, linked with the parents' ability to open up new, stimulating areas, is progressively balanced with the former's ability to gain mastery and the latter's cautious resistance against overexpansion.

The speed of growth in the child's management skills depends on physiological factors such as maturation of the nervous system, endocrine evolvement, and physical growth, as well as on the effectiveness of the learning process. Obviously, the availability of challenging stimuli, combined with teaching and modeling by those more advanced than the child, are bound to speed up the process, whereas the impoverished, constricted setting will retard it. However, in their eagerness to aid the child's growth, the parents may easily allow for too rapid an expansion and in doing so not only confuse the child, but perhaps also restrict his development of skills for territorial acquisition. Accordingly it would seem most fortuitous if the child could become aware of the desirability of new areas first and then gradually gain access to them against a measured resistance by the parents or, for that matter, by the environment in general. The goals that have been desired for a long time and obtained after much effort are the most sweet and precious. The child will value that territory most for which he had to put up a persistent struggle.

In the end, the answer to the question "When is the child ready for territorial expansion?" remains ambiguous, not primarily because of lack of knowledge—although we admit to plenty of that—but rather, because child-rearing by its very nature is an experiment unique to each family, with objectives which, although rarely spelled out precisely, vary from one family member to the next. Thus we come back to the question which parents need to ask themselves: How do we want this child to grow up? The parents can judge the child's responses from this perspective. As in all trial-and-error situations—and child-rearing certainly belongs to this class—the parents will know that they will need to provide modifications in the child's situation if the results are not in the direction of their basic objectives. Ultimately, no theory of child-rearing is of any value in an individual situation if the results are not the desired ones.

THE ADOLESCENT IN THE FAMILY

Adolescent turmoil is a term frequently used to characterize the upheaval which takes place in the life of many young persons on the brink of entering adulthood. Few individuals doubt that adolescence is a period of unusual stress to all who have to deal with it. Parents generally agree that their contact with their teen-agers presents the greatest challenge to them. The same is true for those who run the schools, the law-enforcement agencies, the correctional institutions, and a wide variety of mental health organizations. That this time is as difficult for the child as for the society in which he lives is apparent from the frequency at which psychotic episodes occur in this phase of life.

Such a degree of turmoil has not been the mark of adolescence at all times (Van den Berg, 1961), nor is it part of all cultures. There is no indication that this time of life was experienced as one of unusual challenge in Western society prior to the seventeenth century. In Western society today a sharp contrast exists between the world of the adult and that of the child. The adult finds himself in a network of numerous and complicated responsibilities, but he has, at the same time, an unprecedented array of possibilities and a freedom of choice that is almost paralyzing. The child, on the other hand, is completely sheltered, protected from illness, want, and hardship, and deprived of nearly all personal responsibilities. The contrast between the situation of the child and the adult is not by itself of significance. The crucial cause of adolescent turmoil is the transition between the two. In our culture this takes place in a few short years and with a minimum of structure and guidance.

In contrast, the process of growing up for a child in the sixteenth century in Western Europe was gradual and continuous. Little by little he was given an increasing amount of territory, simultaneously learning the skills to deal with it and assuming the responsibility for it. To the adult of that time the child appeared primarily as "a little adult." He was dressed, therefore, in clothes that were the same as those of the adult except that they were smaller. The child had a great opportunity to learn the necessary skills to cope with his ever-expanding realm, for he could observe his parents in action. It is difficult to imitate the behavior and therefore learn the skills from a father who disappears after breakfast and is not seen again until dinnertime, as is the case for most American families today. In contrast, the young boy of several centuries ago did not only see what his father was doing, but was expected to participate to the extent of his abilities. In this manner he gradually acquired both the skills and an independent territory.

Up until very recently the opportunities were better for the girl because the modeling of mother was still largely present in the home. As the woman's role is rapidly changing, one may anticipate a parallel increase in adolescent turmoil among girls.

A rather different way of dealing with the transition from child to adult is presented by some tribes which use initiation rites to mark the passing from one phase to the other. What seems to happen under such customs is that the child is carefully taught all the skills he needs to have to be a successful adult: hunting, farming, tribal customs, and so on. However, he is not given adult privileges and responsibilities. This adult territory is his only if he passes a final examination of prowess, skill, and endurance: The initiation rite. The advantages of this system are that it provides the child with a specific repertoire of skills he has to master before becoming an adult and that the adult territory acquired through effort and pain will be truly experienced as rightfully owned and therefore probably well defended. Whatever the case, observations in the field clearly indicate that adolescent turmoil does not occur under these circumstances.

A special physiological challenge to the young adolescent is the sudden spurt of growth combined with rapid sexual maturation. Even in centuries past an adolescent had to adjust to these changes, but access to this new area was simplified by the fact that the child had already gained mastery over most of the territory needed to lead an adult life, and the road from sexual maturity to marriage was standardized by the traditions of the community. In today's society, the young person is still basically a child without responsibilities when he begins to blossom into sexual maturity, and the very contact with the opposite sex lacks a clear structure. In fact it is obscured by peculiar contradictions between the various expectations and demands of the parents, the peer group, and society in general. Teen-agers are expected to act out, drive irresponsibly, disregard their parents' and teachers' admonitions, get involved in drugs, sex, and so on. They are at the same time confronted from all sides with strict rules of conduct which they are supposed, but not expected, to adhere to. Thus a contrasting ethic of society and peer group evolves which throws the adult-to-be in continuous conflict with the one group or the other.

With the increased complexity of society and the decreased presence of the parents, the schools have acquired a more important position in mediating relevant skills and facilitating territorial expansion for the new generation. Recognizing the importance of the schools, not just for the transfer of information, but also for the total process through which the child reaches maturity, one must ask whether they indeed provide an opportunity for a gradual expansion of territory which keeps pace with the acquisition of skills. Frequently this seems open to serious question. Many schools are more intent on opening up new territories for the child than on imparting the skills to manage them, whereas others eliminate all challenge and stimulation from their curriculum, as if they sought to halt the growth of their more gifted pupils. A blatant example of the former is the method of teaching foreign languages in high schools and in most colleges. The students are encouraged to learn French, German, or perhaps Spanish. The teaching in these languages is usually such that the young person who has completed the curriculum can report, "I took two (or three, or four, or five years) of French," but he cannot say, "I know French; I can speak and read it." No sense of mastery is obtained, and as a consequence the area is lost as soon as he leaves school.

In the present era, the amount of information to be transferred to the new generation has assumed fantastic proportions. It therefore appears totally irrational to continue a practice which seduces the child to dabble in a vast number of areas, teaching him mastery over none. There is little enough merit in the notion that all children should know a foreign language, but there is even less defense for a situation wherein the majority of students take it and only a negligible minority learn to master it. The lack of challenge, especially for the most capable children in school, results from the untenable idea that all children must learn at about the same pace, a remnant of the confusion between equality and equal opportunity, and the lack of recognition for the high level of competence and creativity required of a teacher who leads the new generation to maximum levels of competence. If the capabilities of emerging adults are recognized as society's most important assets, then unavoidably the teacher who guides the child effectively towards maximal development deserves high social recognition.[4]

Schools across the United States have tried in various ways to be responsive to some of the problems mentioned above. One notion which has been of considerable importance for the development of today's education is that the child should learn to think properly, to get a good grasp of basic principles rather than a vast collection of facts; that he should learn an approach by means of which he can solve problems, rather than detailed knowledge of problems already solved.

Although it is hard to quarrel with these basic principles which undoubtedly have turned into profit for many students, the approach has had

---

[4]This is not a plea for higher salaries for all teachers, but rather a suggestion to reward outstanding teachers who have proven results on a level equal to college professors, in order to stimulate competent individuals to assume this important responsibility, especially in junior and senior high schools.

unintended, but nevertheless undesirable side effects. By no longer being required to have a high level of factual information *in addition* to competence in the application of principles, the student runs the risk of remaining an amateur, a person who knows bits and pieces about a field but has no sense of adequacy; the area never becomes his autonomous domain. This is especially likely for students who work better with concrete facts than abstract principles. The classical education in many European schools and in a number of private schools in the United States has a great advantage in this respect. These schools, with their high regard for expertise, tend to create such a formidable image of each area of learning that its accessibility is substantially reduced. If one would overstate the comparison and therewith intentionally distort it, one could say that the European method creates experts with a great sense of mastery over small areas, who are not inclined to venture beyond their borders, whereas the American system creates individuals who have no hesitation to move in any direction, who are not hampered by undue respect for expertise, but who fail to attain that sense of mastery which makes a territory truly their own.

All school systems, those in the United States as well as in Europe, are currently in flux. Inclusion of principles of territoriality in the considerations for optimal teaching methods are likely to bear fruit in having the public school become of greater assistance in the transition of childhood to adulthood and thus reduce the present turmoil that accompanies it.

It is not our intention to give an exhaustive discussion of adolescence, but it may be of value to summarize our territorial observations in the form of a hypothesis which, although by no means proven, appears to have a certain level of plausibility: *To the extent that the territorial expansion from birth to adulthood is a gradual process which goes hand in hand with skill acquisition, to that extent one may expect adolescence to be peaceful, rather than marked by turmoil and disruption.*

THE PEER GROUP

As the child grows up and reaches the age that he has to go to school, he begins to build up a part of his world which is increasingly his own, away from the family. He finds a toehold outside the home when he establishes relationships with his teachers and his schoolmates. In the contact with his peers, he has the first real opportunity to carve out a niche which is permanently his own. It is not given to him by his parents; he himself has to conquer it, and its importance is, therefore, especially vital. This separate part of his life where he functions as an independent individual in the context of his peer relations grows in size and importance. To maintain and enlarge it he engages in a daily struggle with his schoolmates. He seeks to be noticed, accepted, admired, to be "popular," and he tests out his skills in territorial defense as well as expansion as he does so. While he establishes himself as an individual among his peers, he simultaneously becomes a member of the peer group. Together they share one territory, one common ground which they, teenagers by now, defend in unison against the world of the grown-ups—the teachers, the parents, the authorities. At this point, the teen-ager participates in two major, entirely separate co-territories, that of the peer group and that of the family.

The peer territory is exciting, but often exhausting, owing to the many challenges that require response and the constant struggle necessary to hold ground. It provides the exhilarating experience of standing together with a sense of group independence in opposition to the authority of the older generation. Nevertheless, it is with some degree of relief that the teen-ager shifts back to the family territory which, although perhaps less exciting and more restricted, provides privacy and security. In this comfort he can relax and try out new behavior, for there is an invisible protective barrier around the total family territory. Here he can come back to lick his wounds, or to be comforted when the day on the peer territory has been one of defeat. The teen-ager who, coming home from such a struggle amidst his peers, finds himself locked in angry battle with his parents is very unfortunate. He fares much better if his parents, with a gentle sense of humor, can accept his face-saving protests and his token struggles which serve the purpose of maintaining a sense of consistency with his behavior among his peers and, after such formalities, if they can allow him to enjoy the family grounds where he is respected but does not have the territorial controls.

Recognizing that the young individual participates in these two separate territories makes it readily understandable that he will shift his life to that area which provides him the best balance of comfort, security, identity, and new possibilities. The child who is not prepared for this peer struggle, who, for one reason or another, cannot maintain himself on that battleground, will increasingly withdraw to the territory of the family. Thus he runs the risk that a vicious circle is set in motion. If he avoids the peer territory, he loses the opportunities to gain greater facility in holding his own among persons of his own age. Consequently he falls further and further behind the others in social capabilities. If, for instance, an individual avoids the first steps in the contact with the opposite sex and does not participate in these clumsy efforts when he is supposed to be clumsy, he will have to learn such skills later when ineptness will appear out of place, if not weird, thus hampering his optimum choice in mate selection.

On the other hand, the teenager who lives amidst unbearable conflict at home and who does not have an opportunity to acquire a sufficient sense of autonomy in the family situation will increasingly shift his life to the peer territory. In extreme cases this territory may be the only area left to him, perhaps leading to his running away from home. Even if he continues to sleep at home, he shifts his loyalty to the peer group rejecting anything that stems from the world of his parents, which he generalizes to all of society or "the establishment." Under such circumstances the relationship with similar teen-agers leads to the formation of a subgroup that may become uncompromisingly hostile to the society in which the group members could find no place. Again, a vicious circle is initiated. As the teen-ager slips away from the control of the family, he is confronted with increasingly desperate attempts on the part of his parents, later aided by the appropriate social agencies, to control him. These efforts reduce his autonomy at home even further and drive him to more exclusive reliance on the gang for self-respect. The peer group now provides the protective function which was once given by the family. The group will defend its common territory against hostile outside forces and protect each of its members with a loyalty otherwise only found in the family relationship.

Ideally, the young person gradually shifts to an independent territory outside the family without the polarization described above. Such polarizations are destructive to the child, the family, and the society. The nature of the two vicious circles described above creates a great risk that the young victim will end up in one of the two major problem groups of society: *those who withdraw from it,* unable to hold their own and thus never acquiring a territory adequate to live an autonomous life; and *those who reject society but stay on its fringes* in the company of small groups of fellow outsiders.

FRINGE GROUPS

On the fringes of society there exists a wide variety of groups which have much in common, even though their style may vary widely and their names range from "hippies," "Black Panthers," and "Hell's Angels" to

"Jesus Freaks." The fringe group provides its members with a common territory where they can be safe in the protection of a common defense system which is handled by the group as a whole. The popularity of the communes in all likelihood derives from this family quality of the group as well as from disenchantment with society. Membership in a fringe group unavoidably leads to isolation from the rest of society, but this is a price the members are prepared to pay for their newly gained security. Similarly, the individual who remains in the protection of the family home pays a comparable price. In the fringe group, however, one has a much greater opportunity to establish a territory of his own within the context of the larger group and thus acquire the skills to handle it. As a consequence, it will be easier for group members to move away from the commune back into society than it will be for the person who has withdrawn into the family home.

The fringe group exemplifies in an extreme form the dichotomy that derives from the split we mentioned earlier, namely, between peer territory and family territory. This split evolves into the territory of the "younger generation," which today seems to have its cut-off age at about 30, and the "older generation, the establishment." There has been much talk about the so-called generation gap referring to a supposed inability for the two groups to communicate with each other. A certain amount of mythology surrounds this issue, including notions that the younger ones are more concerned, more able to share, better informed, perhaps even wiser, and certainly less conformist than their elders. It is fascinating to observe how both old and young are willing to accept these ideas which we advisedly call myths, in that they are maintained in spite of the lack of any evidence to support them and in the face of the obvious common-sense observation that the young obtain most of their information and ideas from their elders.

We will now focus on the gap between the generations, which is quite clearly present on a territorial level. It is true that the two groups have polarized by each claiming a territory of its own. One of the great advantages of this polarization is that the struggle between the generations draws each group together in close unity against an opposing group. This territorial opposition creates a sense of home, a sense of belonging, of community. Perhaps the most striking examples of the separate territory of those under 30 were the mammoth rock festivals in recent years, where thousands upon thousands of young people gathered on *their* terrain, in *their* clothes, to listen to *their* music. Here they were free, on an island within the hostile world of the establishment. They needed this establishment, however, and the police, and the harassment to truly savor the freedom within their small enclave. Smoking marihuana, listening to music, or just strolling and sitting around provided that sense of brotherhood which ironically seems to emerge only when one is surrounded by a common enemy.

If our observations are correct, and we suspect they are, then it is obvious that the generation gap cannot be closed by teaching the two groups how to communicate with each other or by encouraging the older generation to learn the new language and get with the new styles in music or clothing. The generation gap simply disappears when the young person acquires a role in the context of the establishment, earning a living on a job or raising a new generation.

THE CHILD LEAVES HOME

The child is only a temporary guest in the family. Even though the whole meaning of marriage centers around providing a home where the children can be reared, the inevitable fact is that one day the parents will suddenly find themselves alone together, after their last child has moved out. Now the existence of the married couple has to be reshuffled all over again. A drastic reorganization has to take place. The disappearance of the children means that the parents have lost part of their territory, but at the same time they now have at their disposal time and energy to move into new directions. If things have gone well in the family, the abruptness of the change is not as great as portrayed here, for gradually as the children have gained their independence and have assumed responsibility for their own lives, the parents will have reestablished their own territory separate from that of the offspring. Often, however, the transition is sudden and ill prepared in spite of the fact that it was long anticipated.

A particularly difficult situation evolves if the parents, usually without realizing it, have expanded their own territory by means of the child. This unwary expansion occurs when their total life is concentrated on what the child does and when they are deeply involved in every new piece of territory that he conquers for himself. To such a situation we can apply the following general rule: *Insofar as the territory of the parent is dependent on*

*the presence of the child, to that extent does the child's departure create a
threat to the parent.* This statement may alert one to what are often called
"symbiotic relationships" between parent and child. In such a situation
the child has been literally made into the territory of the parent. The latter
is managing this territory all the time and will staunchly reject anybody or
anything that may take it away. To the degree that the child obtains
autonomy, the parent suffers a territorial loss. Any attempt, therefore, by
outsiders to help the child gain independence is likely to be counteracted.
It is crucial in this respect that one recognize the parent's intent. He is not
motivated by the malicious design to keep the child dependent. In fact, the
parent is as much the victim of this relationship as the child, for both have
arrived at the disastrous situation because in the process of raising his
child the parent has lost all other territory. Consequently, he or she has
nothing to fall back upon and has to hang on to the child for dear life.
Outside help from mental health professionals is often sought because of
the behavior problems the child begins to develop under these conditions.
The usual conclusion is that the child has to break away from the parents
if he is to survive as an independent human being.

Looking at the situation from a territorial perspective leads to the
recognition that the break-away will be accomplished far more easily and
with less disastrous results for the parent if the latter is provided with an
opportunity for territorial expansion elsewhere. As a start, one can have
the parent maintain an intensive control over and preoccupation with one
specific area of the child's territory, while at the same time expanding the
child's autonomy elsewhere. One can combine forbidding all interference
with one area (for instance, school work) with urging intensive concern
with another one which is preferably very time-consuming but less central
to the child (for instance, taking the youngster to a wide variety of physical
education classes, music lessons, and the like). Simultaneously, efforts
should be made to have the parents expand their energies toward the
acquisition and management of new territories by encouraging them, for
instance, to work with the Boy Scouts, do volunteer work, learn a new
hobby, or join a political party. A counselor or psychotherapist may have
the natural inclination to protect the child against the overpowering
parents. In all likelihood, however, he would fare better if he would
abandon this stance and recognize that both parties are in need of an
avenue toward a new and desirable territory. The more effectively he can
assist the parents in finding a new role in life, the better chance he provides
the child to develop his own.

Although this chapter is longer than most others in this book, it has been far too short to deal exhaustively with the many aspects of family life. To do so would require a separate volume and a lengthy one at that. We completely avoided dealing with such an important aspect as retirement, which obviously has profound impact on each individual's territorial situation and which often bears significantly on the nuclear family when grandparents move in. Our intent with this chapter was not to be complete, but rather, to indicate how territorial considerations can shed light on the complexities of family life.

EPILOGUE

THE PRINCE AND THE MAGICIAN

Once upon a time there was a young prince, who believed in all things but three. He did not believe in princesses, he did not believe in islands, he did not believe in God. His father, the king, told him that such things did not exist. As there were no princesses or islands in his father's domains, and no sign of God, the young prince believed his father.

But then, one day, the prince ran away from his palace. He came to the next land. There, to his astonishment, from every coast he saw islands, and on these islands, strange and troubling creatures whom he dared not name. As he was searching for a boat, a man in full evening dress approached him along the shore.

"Are those real islands?" asked the young prince.

"Of course they are real islands," said the man in evening dress.

"And those strange and troubling creatures?"

"They are all genuine and authentic princesses."

"Then God also must exist!" cried the prince.

"I am God," replied the man in full evening dress, with a bow. The young prince returned home as quickly as he could.

"So you are back," said his father, the king.

"I have seen islands, I have seen princesses, I have seen God," said the prince reproachfully. The king was unmoved.

"Neither real islands, nor real princesses, nor a real God, exist."

"I saw them!"

"Tell me how God was dressed."

"God was in full evening dress."

"Were the sleeves of his coat rolled back?"

The prince remembered that they had been. The king smiled.

"That is the uniform of a magician. You have been deceived." At this, the prince returned to the next land, and went to the same shore, where once again he came upon the man in full evening dress.

263

"My father the king has told me who you are," said the young prince indignantly. "You deceived me last time but not again. Now I know that those are not real islands and real princesses, because you are a magician." The man on the shore smiled.

"It is you who are deceived, my boy. In your father's kingdom there are many islands and many princesses. But you are under your father's spell, so you cannot see them."

The prince returned pensively home. When he saw his father, he looked him in the eyes.

"Father, is it true that you are not a real king, but only a magician?" The king smiled, and rolled back his sleeves.

"Yes, my son, I am only a magician."

"Then the man on the shore was God."

"The man on the shore was another magician."

"I must know the real truth, the truth beyond magic."

"There is no truth beyond magic," said the king. The prince was full of sadness. He said,

"I will kill myself."

The king by magic caused death to appear. Death stood in the door and beckoned to the prince. The prince shuddered. He remembered the beautiful but unreal islands and the unreal but beautiful princesses.

"Very well," he said, "I can bear it."

"You see, my son," said the king, "you too now begin to be a magician."

*John Fowles**

If a person wants to participate in life, he has, like the young prince, but two choices: to accept the spell of someone else, be it his father or a stranger, or to become a magician himself and create his own world, marked by mistakes and full of flaws no doubt, but his own. However, a man cannot create his reality in a vacuum. Like water needs a container, the personal life which he wishes to create requires a specific structure. Without a structure he is like a person who wishes to be an actor but cannot make up his mind which role to play. The careful scrutiny and purposeful building of the territorial aspects of his existence can provide the stage as well as the role in which he can give his acting talents full reign.

The essence of freedom resides in man's opportunity to choose. To do so he needs a goal and a set of alternatives. If there is nothing to choose between there is no freedom, and if a person travels without a destination

*From *The Magus*. New York: Dell Publishing Co., Inc., 1968, pp. 499-500.

he has no choices, because every possible direction is equally desirable. Even if one has choices and has decided on a goal, there remains the final step toward the realization of his freedom: To find the specific road along which to advance. Freedom, as we have used the word here, does not represent a philosophical concept, but rather, the direct experience of being the prime mover of his own destiny, or to use Fowles' words, "of being a magician himself." To intensify this sense of freedom, it is necessary to take stock of one's life situation over and over again, to review one's goals, and to ask, "Where am I? Where do I want to go and how do I get there?" With the emphasis on "I," these questions open the door toward self-directed action.

As we forewarned in the subtitle, this book represents a series of explorations in human territoriality. There are many other directions in which we could have traveled, and we might have surveyed each area in greater detail. The road which we took in the end was mostly guided by our actual work with individuals who sought to alter their life situation. As these individuals worked together with us, we explored whatever aspects of their territorial situation emerged and could be brought into focus. It was the excitement of observing the growth of personal autonomy in the course of this process which made us decide to write this condensed report on our explorations.

GLOSSARY

In this book we have given our own definitions to a number of commonly used words. In order to minimize the confusion unavoidably resulting from such redefinition, we have added this glossary in which the reader can review the precise meaning which we have attributed to each of these terms.

Acquisition. The extension of the areas an individual presently owns either by *displacement,* which means that the newly acquired territory has been taken away from someone else, or by *expansion,* which means moving into areas not claimed by others. (See *Aggression.*)

Action territory. The area of *functioning* in which a person considers it his prerogative to act, exert control, make decisions, exercise his expertise, and take responsibility. (See *Public arena.*)

Aggression. Any *act* which results in the extension no matter how temporary of an individual's territory. The term indicates growth rather than destruction. Any behavior, therefore, that leads to the enlargement of a person's territory can be described as aggressive.

Anger. Refers to a person's emotional state. Anger is not in itself a behavior, but rather a feeling which may or may not accompany specific behaviors such as aggression or defense.

Anxiety. The experience which occurs when an individual finds himself in a situation in which he wants or needs to act, anticipates unpleasant consequences if he does not, but has insufficient experience, information, or knowledge to behave in a way that will give him control.

Assertive complaint. A type of complaint, very close to a protest, which seeks active solution of a territorial problem. It involves pursuit of this goal through a relevant third party rather than by direct confrontation of the opponent. (See *Complaint.*)

Assertiveness.   A response, direct and specific, to an aggressive act. Such a response is designed to retain or regain control over the area under dispute and let the aggressor know that he has intruded upon occupied ground and must remove himself immediately.

Centrality.   The degree to which a territory is essential in order to maintain access to various other areas that the individual claims. The loss of a central territory leads to the secondary loss of other important areas.

Child-rearing.   The process of providing the child with the information and skills necessary for adult life in the existing social environment, including the territorial skills of acquisition, management, and defense. (See *Constrictive* and *Dilated child-rearing.*)

Communication.   The means by which each individual signals to others the impact their behavior has on him in the context of a given situation. Such signals carry implicit information on how each individual interprets the particular circumstance and therefore, how he is likely to respond.

Complaint.   An expression of discontent directed toward a third party rather than a direct confrontation with the person involved in the conflict. Complaints range from *helpless* to *assertive.* (See *Assertive complaint, Helpless complaint, Protest.*)

Constrictive child-rearing.   A process in which the child is kept from expanding into new areas in spite of the fact that he has reached the skill level to do so.

Constructive criticism.   Criticism falling within the confines of a formal or informal contract in which a person *allows* himself to be criticized on specific points because he either gains or expects to gain personal advantages from such an arrangement, such as expansion of territory or increased mastery over it. (See *Criticism.*)

Co-territory.   A territory which is shared by two or more individuals, recognizable by the fact that it is necessary for each member to have the approval of the others to perform actions relative to it.

Criticism.   An attempt to influence another person to comply with the critic's preconceived notions of proper behavior. It constitutes an invasion of territory unless it is part of a contractual arrangement. (See *Constructive criticism.*)

Defense.   Actions which resist attempts by others to take over territory which an individual has claimed for himself.

Destructive envy.   Envy aimed at the destruction of an individual or his possessions. It occurs when a person sees no way to obtain that which he *thinks* he rightfully should have. Similar to *hostility.* (See *Envy, Hostility.*)

Destructive jealousy.   Destruction of personal territory by an individual to keep it from falling under another's control or ownership. Includes self-destruction. (See *Jealousy.*)

Dilated child-rearing. The practice of allowing a child to expand into new territories before he has acquired the skills to deal with the areas he has available already.

Envy. The desire to have that which currently belongs to others. As such, it is the major motivator of territorial displacement. (See *Destructive envy.*)

Fear of envy. The attempt made by a person to avoid evoking the envy of other members of his reference group. It prevents an individual from engaging in behavior which is extravagant by the standards of the reference group, thus providing a strong force towards conformity and social stability. (See *Reference group.*)

Freedom. An individual's feeling that he is engaging in actions by his own choice, on his own initiative, and in the pursuit of his own goals. A person feels free if he experiences himself as the initiator of his actions rather than the victim of them. Having a sufficient territory under control and knowing that new areas can be acquired when necessary are the most powerful contributors to a sense of freedom.

Generosity. The ease with which an individual parts with that which he owns. This ease depends on his ability to defend his territory, the ampleness of his resources, and the importance of the territory involved.

Guilt. An uncomfortable, disquieting feeling which occurs when a person claims or occupies an area which he believes to belong rightfully to someone else.

Helpless complaint. A type of complaint, close to *lament,* which avoids an active solution to a territorial problem. Instead, it serves to induce others to take over the individual's territorial chores so that he can maintain an area too large for his own territorial skills. (See *Complaint, Lament.*)

Hostility. Behavior which seeks to destroy or injure an individual or his territory. A person is likely to resort to it when he fails to rebuff territorial take-over assertively. Hostile behavior is retaliatory in nature and no longer concerns itself with the specific area under dispute.

Identity. Identity refers to a complex set of roles which characterize each individual. It is based on the sum total of his past history and his expectations for the future, combined in the process of his present social interaction. The term denotes a certain continuity and consistency in the person's behavior which makes him predictable to himself as well as to others. Identity in this sense is largely influenced by the individual's territorial conditions. A change in his territorial status, therefore, unavoidably creates a change in his identity.

Jealousy. An individual's fear that others will succeed in taking from him that which he considers rightfully his own. As such, it is a major motivator of behavior aimed at defending territory against aggressive moves by others. (See *Destructive jealousy.*)

Lament. An outcry of sorrow resulting from a serious loss. It seeks the comfort and consolation which comes with sharing one's feelings with another human being, rather than seeking an immediate solution to the problem. (See *Helpless complaint.*)

Love. The resolve to honor and safeguard the territorial integrity of another person. (See *Trust.*)

Management. The specific actions which serve to keep a territory intact, functional, and useful to the owner.

Personal space. The space immediately surrounding an individual which he seeks to keep free of other people. The distance he maintains between himself and others is contingent on his relationship with them and on the social situation. (See *Private domain.*)

Privacy retreat. A place free from the influence and attention of others, where a person can find safety and relaxation in order to replenish his energies and ready himself for the stresses of renewed interaction with other people. It includes the realm of thoughts and fantasies. (See *Private domain.*)

Private domain. The specific area which an individual stakes out in order to insure his privacy and security. There are two aspects of private domain: *privacy retreat* and *personal space*. (See *Personal space, Privacy retreat.*)

Protest. A direct expression of discontent with an existing territorial division, specifically indicating which area is felt to be incorrectly occupied by the opponent. The protest is made from actual or pretended strength and implies a willingness to enter into forceful action if necessary. (See *Complaint.*)

Psychological space. The total amount of influence which one person exerts over the thoughts and feelings of others, whether directly, as in a group discussion, or indirectly, that is, through the media. The most crucial aspect of psychological space is the attention which an individual receives from others. (See *Public arena.*)

Public arena. In contrast to *private domain,* this is the area of interaction between individuals and it is here that the vicissitudes of territoriality become most clearly visible. In the public arena two types of territory are frequently the object of competition: *psychological space* and *action territory.*

Reference group. The group of individuals a person identifies with and with whom he is in the habit of comparing himself. Within a reference group territorial rights are experienced as similar.

Regression. Behavior which results in a decrease in the size of a person's territory.

Revolt. The forceful relocation of territorial boundaries. It usually occurs when the existing territorial division is grossly out of keeping with the prevailing ideology.

Security. The sense of relative personal safety which depends on an individual's ability to respond adequately to specific social, environmental, or psychological challenges. An adequate amount of territory which is well managed and easily defended contributes in a major way to a person's security.

Self-disclosure. A stepwise process in which one individual reveals increasingly more private information concerning himself to another. It is an important aspect of the establishment of *trust,* when it is done on a mutual basis. (See *Trust.*)

Sharing. The acquisition, management, and defense of a common territory by two or more individuals. It demands that the individual subordinate some aspects of his behavior to the dictates of the group.

Territorial behavior. A set of observable behaviors which an individual consistently exhibits relative to any concrete or abstract area. Such behaviors include efforts to gain control over an area, actions to mark the area in order to proclaim ownership, and defense of the area against intruders.

Territoriality. The *inclination* toward ownership rather than the object of this tendency. Territoriality can only be inferred from observed territorial behaviors.

Territorial rights. The reasons given to justify a claim to any particular territory. Such justifications are correctly called rights only insofar as they are based on an implicit or explicit agreement binding all parties to the territorial arrangement.

Territory. Any *object* of territorial behavior. It may be a stretch of land, an idea, a function, or anything else that holds a person's fancy to such a degree that he seeks to own it.

Trust. The belief of one person that another individual will respect and, if necessary, protect his territorial integrity. (See *Love.*)

Violence. Indicates that a specific action involves the explosive use of force. As such it is only one of the many ways in which an act of aggression, hostility, or assertiveness may be carried out.

Weapon. Any method—obvious or subtle, violent or gentle—by which territory is defended or acquired.

BIBLIOGRAPHY

Ardrey, Robert. *The Territorial Imperative.* New York: Dell Publishing Co., Inc., 1966.

———. *African Genesis.* New York: Dell Publishing Co., Inc., 1967.

———.*The Social Contract.* New York: Atheneum, 1970.

Argyle, Michael, and Janet Dean. "Eye Contact and Affiliation," *Sociometry,* 1965, *28*:289-304.

Bartholomew, George A. As discussant of "Aggression as Studied in Troops of Japanese Monkeys" by Syunzo Kawamura, in *Aggression and Defense* (C. D. Clemente and D. B. Lindsley, Eds.). Berkeley and Los Angeles: University of California Press, 1967, pp. 217-218.

Bassin, Alexander. "Daytop Village," *Readings in Social Psychology Today* (J. V. McConnell, Ed.). Del Mar, California: CRM Inc., 1967, pp. 117-123.

Bateson, Gregory. *Steps to an Ecology of Mind.* New York: Ballantine Books, Inc., 1972.

Berne, Eric. *Games People Play.* New York: Grove Press Inc., 1964.

Birdwhistell, Ray L. *Introduction to Kinesics.* Louisville: University of Louisville Press, 1952.

———. *Kinesics and Context.* New York: Ballantine Books, 1972.

Bolles, Edmund Blair. "The Innate Grammar of Baby Talk," *The Saturday Review,* March 18, 1972, p. 55.

Bonaparte, Napoleon. *The Corsican, A Diary of Napoleon's Life in His Own Words* (Collected by B. M. Johnston). Boston and New York: Houghton Mifflin Co., 1910.

———. *Forty Thousand Quotations* (Compiled by Charles Noel Douglas). New York: Halcyon House, 1917, p. 732 A.

Brodie, Fawn J. *The Devil Drives.* New York: Ballantine Books, Inc., 1967.

Brown, Jerram L., and Gordon H. Orians. "Spacing Patterns in Mobile Animals," *Annual Review of Ecology and Systematics,* Vol. *1,* 1970, 239-262.

Butler, R. A. "Discrimination Learning by Rhesus Monkeys to Visual-Exploration Motivation," *Journal of Comparative Physiological Psychology,* 1953, *46*:95-98.

Caldwell, Bettye M. "The Effects of Psychosocial Deprivation on Human Development in Infancy," *Annual Progress in Child Psychiatry and Child Development* (S. Chess and A. Thomas, Eds.). New York: Brunner/Mazel, Inc., 1971, pp. 3-21.

Calhoun, John B. "Population Density and Social Pathology," *Scientific American,* February 1962, *206*:2, pp. 139-148.

Camus, Albert. *The Rebel.* New York: Vintage Books, Random House, 1965.

Capote, Truman. *In Cold Blood.* New York: Random House, 1966.

Carpenter, C. R. "Territoriality: A Review of Concepts and Problems," *Behavior and Evolution* (Anne Roe and George G. Simpson, Eds.). New Haven: Yale University Press, 1958, pp. 224-250.

Castaneda, Carlos. *A Separate Reality.* New York: Pocket Books, 1971, p. 216.

———. *Journey to Ixtlan.* New York: Simon and Schuster, 1972, p. 12.

Chance, M. R. A. "Attention Structure as the Basis of Primate Rank Orders," *Man,* December 1967, pp. 503-518.

Cohen, Elie A. *Human Behavior in the Concentration Camp.* New York: The Universal Library, Grosset & Dunlap, 1953, p. 130.

Colman, Arthur D. "Territoriality in Man, A Comparison of Behavior in Home and Hospital," *Journal of Orthopsychiatry,* 1968, *38*:464-468.

Darwin, Charles. "The Origin of Species," *The Darwin Reader* (Marston Bates and Philip S. Humphrey, Eds.). New York: Charles Scribner's Sons, 1956, p. 107.

Davenport, W. G., Gail Grooker, and Nancy Munro. "Factors in Social Perception: Seating Position," *Perceptual and Motor Skills,* 1971, *33*:747-752.

Daves, Walter F., and Patricia W. Swaffer. "Effect of Room Size on Critical Interpersonal Distance," *Perceptual and Motor Skills,* 1971, *33*:926.

de Baena, Duke. *The Dutch Puzzle.* The Hague: L. J. C. Boucher, 1967.

de Rougemont, Denis. *Love and the Western World (L'Amour et L'Occident),* Mongomery Belgion Revised & Augmented Ed. New York: Pantheon, 1956.

Dinesen, Isak. *Ehrengard.* New York: Random House, 1962, p. 41.

Dollard, John, Leonard W. Doob, Neal E. Miller, O. H. Mowrer, and Robert R. Sears. *Frustration and Aggression.* New Haven: Yale University Press, 1939.

Eaton, Joseph W., and Robert J. Weil. "The Mental Health of Hutterites," *Man Alone* (Eric Josephson and Mary Josephson, Eds.). New York: Dell Publishing Co., Inc., 1962, pp. 498-504.

Esser, A. H., A. S. Chamberlain, E. D. Chapple, and N. S. Kline. "Territoriality of

Patients on a Research Ward," *Recent Advances in Biological Psychiatry,* 1965, 7:37-44.

Esser, A. H. "Interactional Hierarchy and Power Structure on a Psychiatric Ward," *Behavior Studies in Psychiatry* (S. J. Hutt and Corinne Hutt, Eds.). New York and London: Pergamon Press, 1970, pp. 25-59.

Feldman, Sandor S. *Mannerisms of Speech and Gesture in Everyday Life.* New York: International University Press, 1959.

Feldman, Shel, Ed. *Cognitive Consistency.* New York: Academic Press, 1966.

Festinger, Leon. *A Theory of Cognitive Dissonance.* Evanston, Illinois, and White Plains, New York: Row, Peterson & Co., 1957.

Fowles, John. *The Collector.* New York: Dell Publishing Co., Inc., 1964.

———. *The Magus.* New York: Dell Publishing Co., Inc., 1968.

———. *The Aristos.* New York: A Signet Book, New American Library, Inc., 1970.

Franklin, Benjamin. *Autobiography of Benjamin Franklin* (Gordon S. Haight, Ed.). New York: Classics Club, Walter J. Black, 1941.

Goffman, Erving. *Asylums.* New York: Anchor Books, Doubleday & Co., 1961.

———. *Relations in Public.* New York: Harper & Row, 1972.

Golding, William. *Lord of the Flies.* New York: Capricorn Books, G. P. Putnam's Sons, 1959.

Green, Hannah. *I Never Promised You a Rose Garden.* New York: A Signet Book, New American Library, 1964.

Gun, Nerin E. *Eva Braun: Hitler's Mistress.* New York: Bantom Books, 1969.

Hall, Edward T. *The Hidden Dimension.* Garden City, New York: Anchor Books, Doubleday & Co., 1969.

Halverson, Charles F., and Roy E. Shore. "Self-Disclosure and Interpersonal Functioning," *Journal of Consulting and Clinical Psychology,* 1969, *33*:2, 213-217.

Handlin, Oscar. *The Uprooted.* Boston: Little, Brown & Co., 1951.

Harlow, M. F., and M. K. Harlow. "Social Deprivation in Monkeys," *Scientific American,* 1962, *207*:137-146.

Hediger, Heini P. "The Evolution of Territorial Behavior," *The Social Life of Early Man* (S. L. Washburn, Ed.). London: Methuen, 1963, pp. 34-67.

Hekmat, Hamid, and Michael Theiss. "Self-Actualization and Modification of Affective Self-Disclosure During a Social Conditioning Interview," *Journal of Counseling Psychology,* 1971, *18*:2, 101-105.

Heller, Joseph. *Catch-22.* New York: Dell Publishing Co., Inc., 1970.

Herrigel, Eugen. *Zen in the Art of Archery.* New York: Vintage Books, Random House, 1971.

Hildreth, Arthur M., Leonard R. Derogatis, and Ken McCusker. "Body Buffer

Zone and Violence: A Reassessment and Confirmation," *American Journal of Psychiatry, 1971, 127:77-81.*

Hintze, Otto. "The Nature of Feudalism," *Lordship and the Community in Medieval Europe* (Fredrick Cheyette, Ed.). New York: Holt, Rinehart & Winston, Inc., 1968, p. 27.

Hokanson, Jack E. "Psychophysiological Evaluation on the Catharsis Hypotheses," *The Dynamics of Aggression* (Edwin I. Megargee and Jack E. Hokanson, Eds.). New York: Harper & Row, 1970, pp. 74-86.

Hölldobler, Bert. "Communication Between Ants and Their Guests," *Scientific American,* March 1971, *224*:86-93.

Horowitz, Mardi J. "Spatial Behavior and Psychopathology," *The Journal of Nervous and Mental Disease,* 1968, *146*:24-35.

Hovland, Carl I., and Robert R. Sears. "Minor Studies of Aggression: Correlation of Lynchings with Economic Indices," *The Dynamics of Aggression* (Edwin I. Megargee and Jack E. Hokanson, Eds.). New York and Evanston: Harper & Row, 1970, pp. 66-74.

Huizinga, J. H. *The Waning of the Middle Ages.* Garden City, New York: Doubleday, 1954.

Jenkins, Elizabeth. *Elizabeth the Great.* New York: Berkley Medallion Books, 1958.

Jones, Edward E., and Harold B. Gerard. *Foundations of Social Psychology.* New York: J. Wiley & Sons, Inc., 1967.

Jourard, Sydney M., and M. J. Landson. "Cognition, Cathexis, and the 'Dyadic' in Man's Self-Disclosing Behavior," *Merrill-Palmer Quarterly of Behavioral Development,* 1960, *6*:178-186.

Kawamura, Syunzo. "Aggression as Studied in Troops of Japanese Monkeys," *Aggression and Defense* (Carmine D. Clemente and Donald B. Lindsley, Eds.), UCLA Forum in Medical Sciences, No. 7. Berkeley and Los Angeles: University of California Press, 1967, pp. 196-223.

Kelly, George. "Hostility," *Clinical Psychology and Personality* (Brendan Maher, Ed.). New York: John Wiley and Sons, Inc., 1969, pp. 267-280.

———. "The Threat of Aggression," *Clinical Psychology and Personality* (Brendan Maher, Ed.). New York: John Wiley and Sons, Inc., 1969, pp. 281-388.

Kinzel, A. F. "Body Buffer Zone in Violent Prisoners," *American Journal of Psychiatry,* 1970, *127*:59-64.

Krebs, Dennis L. "Altruism—An Examination of the Concept and a Review of the Literature," *Psychological Bulletin,* 1970, *73*:258-302.

Lagerkvist, Pär. *The Dwarf.* New York: Hill and Wang, 1945.

Latané, Bibb, and John Darley. "Bystander 'Apathy,'" *American Scientist,* 1969, *57*:2, pp. 244-268.

Lederer, William J., and Don D. Jackson. *The Mirages of Marriage.* New York: W. W. Norton & Company, Inc., 1968.

Lifton, Robert Jay. *Death in Life.* New York: Random House, 1967.

Little, Kenneth B. "Personal Space," *Journal of Experimental Social Psychology,* 1965, *1*:237-247.

Longfellow, Henry Wadsworth. *The Works of Henry Wadsworth Longfellow. Poems Volume IV.* The Fireside Edition. Boston & New York: Houghton Mifflin Co., 1901.

Lyman, Stanford M., and Marvin B. Scott. "Territoriality: A Neglected Sociological Dimension," *Social Problems,* 1967, *15*:236-249.

Lyons, H. A. "Depressive Illness and Aggression in Belfast," *British Medical Journal,* 1972, *1*:342-344.

Maslow, Abraham. *Motivation and Personality.* New York: Harper and Row, 1954.

———. *Toward a Psychology of Being.* New York and Cincinnati: Van Nostrand Reinhold Company, 1968.

Mehrabian, Albert. "Significance of Posture and Position in the Communication of Attitude and Status Relationships," *Psychological Bulletin,* 1969, *71*:359-372.

Milford, Nancy. *Zelda.* New York: Avon Books, 1970.

Milgram, Stanley. "Liberating Effects of Group Pressure," *Journal of Personality and Social Psychology,* 1965, *1*:2, 127-134.

Milne, A. A. "The Knight Whose Armor Didn't Squeak," *Now We Are Six.* New York: E. P. Dutton & Co., 1955.

———."Solitude," *Now We Are Six.* New York: E. P. Dutton & Co., Inc., 1955, p. 3.

Morris, Desmond. *The Naked Ape.* New York: Dell Publishing Co., 1969.

———. *The Human Zoo.* New York: Delta Books, Dell Publishing Co., Inc., 1970.

Newman, Oscar. *Defensible Space.* New York: The Macmillan Company, 1972.

Nietzsche, Friedrich. "The Birth of Tragedy," *The Philosophy of Nietzsche.* New York: The Modern Library, Random House, 1927, pp. 947-1088.

Nissen, H. W. "A Study of Exploratory Behavior in the White Rat by Means of the Obstruction Method," *Journal of Genetic Psychology,* 1930, *37*:361-376.

Nizer, Louis. *My Life In Court.* New York: Pyramid Books, 1963.

Packard, Vance. *The Status Seekers.* New York: Pocket Books, 1959.

Paluck, Robert J., and Aristide H. Esser. "Controlled Experimental Modification of Aggressive Behavior in Territories of Severely Retarded Boys," *American Journal of Mental Deficiency,* 1971, *76*:23-29.

Perls, Frederick, Ralph F. Hefferline, and Paul Goodman. *Gestalt Therapy: Excitement and Growth in the Human Personality.* New York: Julian Press, 1951.

Poe, Edgar Allen. "Hop-Frog," *Selected Writings of Edgar Allen Poe* (Edward H. Davidson, Ed.). Boston: Houghton Mifflin Co., 1956, pp. 237-246.

Proust, Marcel. *Un Amour De Swann,* Paris: Gaston Gallimard, 1919, p. 252.

Puzo, Mario. *The Godfather.* New York: Putnam, 1969.

Read, Kenneth E. *The High Valley.* New York: Charles Scribner's Sons, 1965.

Remarque, Erich Maria. *All Quiet On The Western Front.* New York: Fawcett World Library, 1966.

Riley, James Whitcomb, *The Complete Works of James Whitcomb Riley* (E. H. Eitel, Ed.). Indianapolis: Bobbs-Merrill Company, 1882, 1913, p. 244.

Rosenthal, R., and L. Jacobson. *Pygmalion in the Classroom.* New York: Holt, Rinehart & Winston, Inc., 1968.

Rümke, H. C. *Studies en Voordrachten over Psychiatrie.* Amsterdam: Scheltema & Holkema, N.V., 1943.

Sartre, Jean-Paul. *No Exit and Three Other Plays.* New York: Vintage Books, 1955.
———. *Being and Nothingness.* New York: Philosophical Library, 1956.

Savicki, Victor. "Self-Disclosure Strategy and Personal Space Proximity in Intimacy Development," Unpublished Ph.D. Dissertation, University of Massachusetts, 1970.

Sawrer-Foner, G. J. "Human Territoriality and Its Cathexis," *Diseases of the Nervous System,* November 1970, *31*:82-87.

Schlesinger, Walter. "Lord and Follower in Germanic Institutional History," *Lordship and the Community in Medieval Europe* (Fredrick Cheyette, Ed.). New York: Holt, Rinehart & Winston, Inc., 1968, p. 68.

Schoeck, Helmut. *Envy, a Theory of Social Behavior.* New York: A Helen and Kurt Wolf Book, Harcourt, Brace and World, Inc., 1969.

Solzhenitsyn, Alexander. *Cancer Ward.* New York: Bantam Books, 1969.

Sommer, Robert. *Personal Space.* Englewood Cliffs, New Jersey: Prentice-Hall, Inc., 1969.

Southwick, Charles H. "Aggressive Behaviour of Rhesus Monkeys in Natural and Captive Groups," *Aggressive Behavior* (S. Garattini and E. B. Sigg, Eds.). New York: John Wiley and Sons, Inc., 1969, pp. 32-43.

Spiro, Melford E. *Kibbutz.* New York: Schocken Books, 1963.

Strayer, Joseph. "Feudalism in Western Europe," *Lordship and the Community in Medieval Europe* (Fredrick Cheyette, Ed.). New York: Holt, Rinehart & Winston, Inc., 1968, p. 18.

Suzuki, Shinichi. *Nurtured by Love.* Jericho, New York: Exposition Press, Inc., 1969.

Todd, John H. "Chemical Languages of Fishes," *Scientific American,* May 1971, *224*:5, pp. 99-108.

Turnbull, Colin. *The Mountain People.* New York: Simon and Schuster, 1972.

Van Buren, Abigail. "Dear Abby" Column, January 20, 1971, New York: Chicago Tribune-New York News Syndicate, Inc.

van den Berg, J. H. *The Changing Nature of Man.* New York: W. W. Norton & Company, Inc., 1961.

van Lawick-Goodall, Jane. "New Discoveries Among Africa's Chimpanzees," *National Geographic,* December 1965, *128*:6, 802-831.

Verhulst, Johan. *Pokerspelgeneeskunde.* De Nederlandse Boekhandel, Antwerpen-Utrecht, pp. 177-202, 1972.

Viorst, Judith. "Maybe We'll Make It," *It's Hard To Be Hip Over Thirty And Other Tragedies of Married Life.* New York: The World Publishing Company, 1968, p. 19.

———. "Nice Baby," *It's Hard To Be Hip Over Thirty And Other Tragedies of Married Life.* New York: The World Publishing Company, 1968, p. 21.

Weisstein, Naomi. " 'Kinder, Kuche, Kirche,' as Scientific Law: Psychology Constructs the Female," *Sisterhood is Powerful* (Robin Morgan, Ed.). New York: Vintage Books, 1970, pp. 205-230.

Wender, Paul H. "Vicious and Virtuous Circles: The Role of Deviation Amplifying Feedback in the Origin and Perpetuation of Behavior," *Psychiatry,* 1968, *31*:309-24.

White, Robert. "Motivation Reconsidered: The Concept of Competence," *Psychological Review, 1959, 66*:297-333.

Zalba, Serapio. "Battered Children," *Social Science and Modern Society,* July/August 1971, *8*:58-61.

Zimbardo, Philip G. "The Psychological Power and Pathology of Imprisonment," Statement Prepared for the U.S. House of Representatives Committee on the Judiciary (Subcommittee No. 3, Robert Kastenmeier, Chairman: Hearings on Prison Reform), October 25, 1971, Federal Courtroom, Federal Building, 450 Golden Gate Avenue, San Francisco, California.

Zing Yang Kuo. "Studies on the Basic Factors in Animal Fighting: VII. Inter-Species Coexistence in Mammals," *The Journal of Genetic Psychology,* 1960, *97*:211-225.

INDEX